BARRON'S
POCKET GUIDE
THESAURUS
Second Edition

Arthur H. Bell, Ph.D.
University of San Francisco

All inquiries should be addressed to:
Barron's Educational Series, Inc.
250 Wireless Boulevard
Hauppauge, New York 11788
http://www.barronseduc.com

Library of Congress Catalog Card No. 2003043701

ISBN-13: 978-0-7641-1995-8
ISBN-10: 0-7641-1995-8
Library of Congress Cataloging-in-Publication Data

Bell, Arthur H. (Arthur Henry), 1946-
    Barron's pocket guide thesaurus / Arthur H. Bell.
        p. cm.
    At head of title: Barron's.
    ISBN 0-7641-1995-8 (alk. paper)
    1. English language–Synonyms and antonyms. I. Title: Barron's
a pocket guide thesaurus. II. Barron's Educational Series, Inc.
III. Title.

PE1591.B425 2003
423'.1–dc21   2003043701

PRINTED IN CHINA
9 8 7

Introduction to the Second Edition

This new, revised edition of the *Barron's Pocket Guide Thesaurus* adds more than 3,000 synonyms and antonyms as an enhanced resource for writers and speakers who want to find the right word quickly and efficiently. The alphabetical arrangement of key terms allows the user to turn to the approximate word in order to find the precise word.

Let's say, for example, that a writer requires a synonym (a word with a similar meaning) for the word *beautiful.* A quick flip of the *Thesaurus* pages to that word brings many useful alternatives: *lovely, attractive, pretty, gorgeous, fair,* and *handsome.* Antonyms (words with opposite meanings) are also suggested.

One note of caution: neither synonyms nor antonyms are automatic replacements or contraries for your words. Each word carries with it a unique set of associations, implications, and feelings. To test the suitability of a synonym or antonym for your use, try it out in the context of a sentence. You must judge whether a given synonym or antonym expresses your desired meaning.

One special set of words, the Most Overused Words in School and Career Writing, has been highlighted with a bullet (•) and also listed separately at the beginning of the *Thesaurus.* Although these words are perfectly appropriate in many contexts, you should exercise caution in their use simply because they have become somewhat threadbare from overuse. In other words, many writers find themselves in an unfortunate language rut by using these words over and over. You can avoid this predicament by locating an appropriate synonym or antonym to express your meaning in a fresh way. For each of the identified overused words, a full sentence example has been provided to show language alternatives in action.

Standard dictionary abbreviations are used for each entry to specify parts of speech: N., noun; V., verb; ADJ., adjective; ADV., adverb.

Special thanks go to Ms. Nikki Thomas, an MBA candidate and my graduate assistant at the University of San Francisco, for her help with this project. I am also grateful to many colleagues at Harvard University, the University of Southern California, Georgetown University, and the University of San Francisco, whose insights and suggestions have contributed to this revision. *Barron's Pocket Guide Thesaurus, Second Edition* is dedicated to my daughter, Lauren Elizabeth, a budding writer with a genuine love of words.

Arthur H. Bell, Ph.D.
Professor of Management Communication
Director of Communication Skills
School of Business and Management
University of San Francisco

January 2003

The Most Overused Words in School and Career Writing

Because they are both useful and common, the following words are often overused. This *Thesaurus* provides full-sentence examples showing synonym alternatives for these overused words, identified by a •

additionally
adequate
adjust
adopt
advisable
agreement
alienate
all right
almost
also
amazing
analyze
apparent
appearance
approximately
argument
ascertain
assertion
assess
assistance
assume
attention
attitude
authorize
available
avoid
awful
barely
basically

beautiful
begin
behavior
believe
belong
beneficial
besides
bizarre
blame
bore
brief
brilliant
build
bunch
business
busy
capable
capacity
careful
casual
cause
certainly
challenge
change
claim
clarify
combination
common
communicate

company
compete
comprehend
compute
conceive
concept
concern
condition
confuse
connect
conscious
consequence
consider
considerable
consideration
consistent
control
convenient
cooperate
creative
crisis
crucial
decide
decrease
definite
deliver
demand
depend
describe

determine	future	justify
develop	general	know
difference	generate	limit
direct	good	logic
discover	guess	luck
discuss	happy	manage
distribute	help	mankind
duty	helpful	matter
easy	helpless	maybe
economical	hesitate	meaning
educate	hinder	meaningful
efficiency	honest	mental
eliminate	honesty	minimum
emphasize	hope	misconception
employ	hopeful	mistake
enable	hostile	money
enlighten	huge	mostly
environment	idea	motivate
equal	ignorant	natural
essential	imagination	nature
establish	immediate	necessary
evident	immense	necessity
example	importance	nice
excellent	important	nonsense
exceptional	impossible	nothing
expectation	impression	objection
explain	improve	obvious
explore	inadequate	occur
express	increase	opportunity
extreme	indicate	option
fact	individual	ordinary
factor	inefficient	organize
false	influence	original
famous	influential	outstanding
favorite	initial	participate
feel	insecure	people
flexible	insist	personal
follow	interest	physical
frequent	interpretation	place
fulfill	involve	pleasing
function	irrelevant	point
fundamental	issue	point of view

popular
position
possess
possible
practical
precisely
pretend
previous
primary
probable
project
provide
purpose
qualify
quality
question
ready
reality
really
receive
recognize
regular

relative
remarkable
review
satisfactory
schedule
sensitive
several
significance
situation
society
solution
specific
standard
strengthen
substantial
suggestion
superior
suppose
technique
temporary
tendency
tension

terrific
thorough
tremendous
trivial
typical
unconscious
undeniable
understand
undesirable
unfavorable
unlimited
unnecessary
unreasonable
usually
vague
valuable
variety
weak
weird
worthless
young

A

abandon V. desert, quit, forsake, leave.
Ant. maintain, keep, pursue.

abase V. belittle, demean, degrade, humiliate.
Ant. praise, aggrandize, extol.

abashed ADJ. embarrassed, ashamed, mortified.
Ant. confident, self-assured, poised.

abate V. decrease, diminish, reduce, subside.
Ant. increase, intensify, prolong.

abbreviate V. shorten, reduce, condense, contract.
Ant. expand, lengthen, increase.

abbreviation N. truncation, summary, ellipsis.
Ant. extension, elaboration, amplification.

abdicate V. forsake, renounce, relinquish, give up.
Ant. commit, claim, assert, maintain.

abdication N. renunciation, abandonment,
resignation.
Ant. commitment, assertion.

abduct V. kidnap, seize, shanghai, capture, steal.
Ant. relinquish, give up.

aberrance N. abnormality, deviation.
Ant. regularity, normality.

aberrant ADJ. abnormal, errant.
Ant. direct.

aberration N. deviation, irregularity, insanity,
abnormality.
Ant. regulation, normality.

abeyance N. latency, inaction, suspension, reservation.
Ant. action, operation.

abhor V. despise, hate, loathe, dislike, detest.
Ant. love, enjoy, admire.

abhorrence N. hate, horror.
Ant. enjoyment, delight, admiration.

abide V. dwell, reside, live, remain.
Ant. leave, resist, depart.

ability N. capability, skill, ableness, faculty.
Ant. limitation, incompetency, ignorance.

abject ADJ. hopeless, miserable, horrible.
Ant. optimistic, cheerful, sanguine.

abjure V. retract, take back, repudiate.
Ant. put forth, inject, assert.

ablaze ADJ. blazing, fiery, burning.
Ant. extinguished, cold.

able ADJ. competent, proficient, capable, qualified.
Ant. incompetent, unable, inept.

able-bodied ADJ. strapping, sturdy, strong.
Ant. weak, frail, disabled, crippled.

abnormal ADJ. uncommon, peculiar, odd, unnatural, irregular.
Ant. regular, common, normal.

abnormality N. aberrance, anomalism, deviation.
Ant. normality, regularity.

abode N. home, dwelling, residence.
Ant. wilderness.

abolish V. erase, obliterate, undo, revoke, negate.
Ant. establish, legalize, confirm.

abolition N. negation, annulment, nullification.
Ant. establishment, institution, confirmation.

abominable ADJ. horrible, loathsome, disgusting, hateful, unspeakable.
Ant. pleasant, likable, enjoyable.

aboriginal ADJ. native, prehistoric, primeval.
Ant. foreign, borrowed, acquired.

abort V. miscarry, stop, terminate, kill, sever.
Ant. continue, institute, save.

abound V. flourish, overflow, teem.
Ant. need, want, lack.

about ADV. nearly, approximately; —PREP. relating to, concerning, involving, having to do with.
Ant. exactly, precisely; exclusive of.

abrasion N. scratch, scrape, injury, scuff.

abridge V. condense, shorten, abbreviate, cut.
Ant. lengthen, increase, expand.

abrogate v. cancel, revoke, abolish, annul, nullify.
Ant. invoke, establish, ratify.

abrupt ADJ. sudden, short, brusque, hurried, blunt.
Ant. slow, gradual, deliberate.

abscond v. flee, retreat, escape, disappear, steal away.
Ant. remain, stay, advance.

absence N. want, need, lack, defect.
Ant. presence, existence, attendance.

absent ADJ. missing, void, away, lacking.
Ant. present, attending, existing.

absentminded ADJ. inattentive, forgetful, preoccupied.
Ant. mindful, prescient.

absolute ADJ. complete, thorough, perfect, total, entire, unlimited.
Ant. partial, incomplete, limited, imperfect.

absolutely ADV. positively, doubtlessly, definitely.
Ant. doubtfully, questionably, dubitably.

absolution N. forgiveness, blessing, pardon, release.
Ant. accusation, indictment, grudge.

absolve v. pardon, forgive, exonerate, acquit.
Ant. convict, blame, censure.

absorb v. consume, engross, incorporate, digest.
Ant. expel, emit, dissipate.

absorbed ADJ. engrossed, consumed, preoccupied, rapt.
Ant. ejected, dispersed, dissipated.

absorbent ADJ. absorptive, assimilating, bibulous.
Ant. dissipating, dispersing.

absorbing ADJ. gripping, enthralling, engrossing.
Ant. boring, tedious, uninteresting.

absorption N. engrossment, preoccupation, assimilation.
Ant. distraction, disinterestedness.

abstain v. refrain, fast, forbear.
Ant. indulge, take part in.

abstemious ADJ. temperate, abstinent.
Ant. immoderate, indulgent.

abstinence N. continence, temperance, abstention, self-denial, fasting.
Ant. indulgence, greed, intemperance.

abstract ADJ. theoretical; —N. synopsis; —V. remove, detach, separate.
Ant. concrete, practical, applied; entirety; restore, join.

abstracted ADJ. engrossed, absentminded, withdrawn, oblivious, preoccupied.
Ant. focused, intent.

abstruse ADJ. profound, difficult, abstract.
Ant. obvious, plain, clear.

absurd ADJ. foolish, ridiculous, senseless.
Ant. rational, logical, sensible.

absurdity N. foolishness, insanity, ridiculousness.
Ant. certainty, wisdom.

abundance N. opulence, plenty.
Ant. scarcity, rarity, sparseness.

abundant ADJ. plentiful, opulent, lavish, profuse.
Ant. scarce, rare, sparse.

abuse V. scorn, disgrace, defame, injure, violate, malign.
Ant. praise, acclaim, esteem.

abusive ADJ. damaging, slanderous, invective.
Ant. respectful, applauding, approving.

abysmal ADJ. terrible, horrible, awful, deep, yawning.
Ant. excellent, wonderful, shallow.

abyss N. pit, hole, gulf, chasm, void.
Ant. peak, mountaintop, crest.

academic ADJ. scholastic, scholarly, learned, literary.
Ant. illiterate, ignorant, practical.

accede V. concur, agree, consent, assent.
Ant. denounce, protest, refuse.

accelerate V. hasten, quicken, facilitate, expedite, hurry.
Ant. slow, retard, hinder.

accent N. tone, emphasis.
Ant. monotony, evenness.

accentuate v. emphasize, underline, affirm, heighten.
Ant. minimize, moderate, subdue.

accept v. acknowledge, receive, agree, concur, acquire.
Ant. reject, decline, refuse.

acceptable ADJ. agreeable, pleasing, welcome, unobjectionable, average, adequate, fair.
Ant. objectionable, inadequate, disagreeable.

acceptance N. agreement, assent, acquiescence, consent, approval.
Ant. denial, refusal, rejection, disagreement.

accepted ADJ. orthodox, conventional, approved.
Ant. unconventional, unapproved, unorthodox.

access N. admission, outburst, seizure.
Ant. denial, release.

accessible ADJ. approachable, open.
Ant. closed, unapproachable.

accessory N. assistant, helper, partner, accomplice, attachment.
Ant. opponent, enemy.

accident N. misfortune, mishap, misadventure, disaster.
Ant. calculation, intent, purpose.

accidental ADJ. unintentional, inadvertent, unplanned, unexpected.
Ant. desired, planned, essential.

acclaim v. applaud, praise, honor.
Ant. dishonor, berate, revile.

acclimate v. adapt, harden, get used to.
Ant. disregard, soften.

acclivity N. ascent, incline, slope.
Ant. descent, decline, declivity.

accolade N. distinction, honor.
Ant. dishonor, punishment, shame.

accommodate v. oblige, adapt, conform, supply, adjust.
Ant. inconvenience, obstruct, hinder.

accompaniment N. associate, companion, attendant.
Ant. enemy, unknown.

accompany V. escort, join, attend.
Ant. abandon, desert, forsake.

accomplice N. coconspirator, helper, accessory, collaborator.

accomplish V. achieve, attain, perform, realize, perfect.
Ant. block, nullify, foil.

accomplished ADJ. practiced, skilled, finished, successful.
Ant. unfinished, unskilled.

accomplishment N. completion, fulfillment, attainment, achievement.
Ant. failure, frustration, defeat.

accord V. concur, agree, concede, allow, permit;
—N. treaty, agreement, unanimity, reconciliation.
Ant. disagree, refuse, dispute; refusal, disagreement, opposition.

accost V. greet, address, salute, hail.
Ant. avoid, ignore, shun.

account N. report, description, statement, explanation.

accountable ADJ. liable, responsible, amenable.
Ant. blameless, irresponsible, unreliable.

accoutrement N. outfit, dress, apparel.

accretion N. buildup, increase, accumulation, yield.
Ant. decrease, waste, dissipation.

accrue V. accumulate, collect, acquire, increase, gather.
Ant. lessen, decrease, scatter.

acculturate V. socialize, initiate, involve.
Ant. isolate.

accumulate V. collect, gather, amass, hoard, accrue.
Ant. scatter, disperse, waste.

accumulation N. concentration, collection, amassment, store.
Ant. separation, division, dissipation.

accumulative ADJ. additory, additive.
Ant. partial, part.

accuracy N. preciseness, precision, accurateness.
Ant. inaccuracy, imprecision.

accurate ADJ. precise, exact, sure, certain.
Ant. uncertain, imprecise, inaccurate.

accusal N. implication, accusation, incrimination.
Ant. exoneration.

accusation N. charge, denouncement, indictment.
Ant. exoneration.

accuse V. incriminate, implicate, charge, blame.
Ant. exonerate, hold blameless.

accuser N. incriminator, indicter, accusant.

accustom V. acclimatize, familiarize, habituate.
Ant. unfamiliarize, inhabituate, unaccustom.

ache V. desire, feel, hurt; —N. pain.
Ant. joy, pleasure.

achieve V. attain, accomplish, perform, succeed.
Ant. fail, relinquish, abandon.

achievement N. accomplishment, execution, attainment, feat.
Ant. failure, loss, defeat.

aching ADJ. painful, punishing, afflicting.
Ant. joyful.

acid ADJ. sharp, sour, bitter, tart.
Ant. sweet, bland, mild.

acknowledge V. admit, confess, declare, allow, concede.
Ant. deny, refuse, renounce, ignore.

acknowledgment N. confession, admission, recognition, acceptance.
Ant. denial, refusal, repudiation.

acme N. climax, apex, zenith.
Ant. low, base, bottom.

acquaint V. announce, present, inform, introduce.
Ant. mislead, deceive, falsify.

acquaintance N. familiarity, experience, knowledge, friend.
Ant. strangeness, unfamiliarity, ignorance.

acquainted ADJ. familiar, informed, knowledgeable.
Ant. unfamiliar, inexperienced, ignorant.

acquiesce V. assent, surrender, relinquish.
Ant. object, protest.

acquiescence N. obedience, acceptance.
Ant. objection, disobedience.

acquiescent ADJ. willing, passive.
Ant. unwilling, resistant, disobedient.

acquire V. achieve, obtain, get, secure.
Ant. forfeit, give up, lose.

acquisition N. accomplishment, purchase, asset,
possession.
Ant. loss.

acquit V. pardon, absolve, clear, prove innocent,
liberate.
Ant. condemn, convict, blame.

acrid ADJ. bitter, sour, biting.
Ant. sweet, soothing, mild.

acrimonious ADJ. resentful, bitter, malevolent.
Ant. kind, pleasant, forgiving.

acrimony N. malevolence, bitterness, anger,
resentment.
Ant. kindness, forgiveness, tenderness.

act V. simulate, perform, execute, accomplish; —N.
operation, action, performance.
Ant. halt, refrain, cease.

acting ADJ. temporary.
Ant. permanent.

action N. feat, achievement, accomplishment, activity.
Ant. inaction, inactivity, idleness.

activate V. energize, stimulate, actuate.
Ant. turn off, disinterest, slow.

active ADJ. sharp, alert, lively, energetic.
Ant. inert, idle, inactive.

activity N. business, exercise.
Ant. idleness, inactivity, laziness.

actor N. thespian, player.

actual ADJ. genuine, certain, real, sure.
Ant. unreliable, doubtful, false.

actuality N. fact, reality, existence.
Ant. unreality, falsehood, myth.

actually ADV. genuinely, really, truly, certainly.
Ant. doubtfully, improbably.

actuate V. drive, activate.
Ant. inactivate, stop.

acumen N. wisdom, insight, discernment, accuracy, intelligence.
Ant. stupidity, apathy, dullness.

acute ADJ. intense, sharp, penetrating, perceptive, precise.
Ant. dull, chronic, obtuse.

adage N. proverb, saying.

adamant ADJ. stubborn, persistent, unyielding.
Ant. flexible, reasonable.

adamantine ADJ. stubborn, resistant, unyielding.
Ant. flexible, yielding.

adapt V. conform, suit, accommodate, fit.
Ant. displace, confuse, dislocate.

adaptable ADJ. adjustable, adaptive, supple.
Ant. inflexible, unadjustable.

adaptation N. adjustment, accommodation, acclimatization, conformation.

add V. enlarge, increase, augment, amplify.
Ant. subtract, decrease, reduce.

addition N. supplement, increase, adjunct.
Ant. subtraction, loss, decrease.

additional ADJ. further, added, more.
Ant. less, subtracted, lost, deducted.

• **additionally** ADV. furthermore, still, also. *Furthermore, the hikers ignored the warning signs.*

additive ADJ. plus, additory, cumulative.
Ant. minus, detractive, diminutive.

addled ADJ. confused, disoriented.
Ant. sure, clear.

address V. approach, greet, acclaim, hail, speak to;
—N. speech, discourse, demeanor, manners.
Ant. ignore, overlook, avoid.

adept ADJ. accomplished, skillful, expert.
Ant. crude, awkward, unskilled.

adequacy N. sufficiency.
Ant. inadequacy, insufficiency.

• **adequate** ADJ. satisfactory, enough, sufficient,
adapted, suited. *Please deliver sufficient supplies for the
project.*
Ant. inadequate, unsatisfactory, inadaptable,
useless, insufficient.

adhere V. attach, fasten, unite, join, bond.
Ant. unfasten, separate, loosen.

adherence N. bond, support, agreement.
Ant. opposition, disagreement, desertion.

adhesion N. bond, traction, friction, tension.
Ant. separation, inadhesion, loss.

adieu N. parting, goodbye, farewell.
Ant. greeting, welcoming, salutation.

adjacent ADJ. bordering, beside, neighboring,
adjoining.
Ant. distant, far, separate.

adjoin V. border, juxtapose, meet, touch, neighbor.
Ant. separate, distance, split.

adjourn V. end, defer, terminate.
Ant. begin, commence, start.

adjournment N. ending, termination.
Ant. beginning, commencement.

adjudicate V. judge, decide upon.
Ant. defer, put off.

adjunct N. complement, attachment, dependency.
Ant. subtraction, disjunction, removal.

• **adjust** V. regulate, adapt, organize, get used to,
attune. *It may be difficult to adapt to new surroundings.*
Ant. confuse, disorganize, deregulate.

adjustable ADJ. adaptable, plastic, versatile.
Ant. unadaptable, inflexible.

adjustment N. adaptation, variation, alteration.
Ant. breakage, deregulation.

adjutant N. assistant, adjunct.
Ant. enemy, spy.

ad-lib N. improvisation; —V. improvise.
Ant. recite, reproduce.

administer V. govern, manage, regulate, run,
administrate.
Ant. restrain, neglect, deny.

administrate V. administer, execute, carry out.
Ant. follow, obey.

administration N. regime, government, management,
direction, application.
Ant. anarchy, rebellion, subversion.

administrator N. executive, manager, leader.
Ant. follower, worker, pawn, subservient.

admirable ADJ. praiseworthy, worthy, wonderful,
excellent.
Ant. dishonorable, scornful, abominable.

admiration N. praise, appreciation, respect, esteem.
Ant. contempt, hatred, disregard.

admire V. respect, appreciate, praise, esteem.
Ant. blame, dishonor, scorn, dislike.

admirer N. fan, devotee.
Ant. enemy.

admissible ADJ. worthy, passable, acceptable,
approved.
Ant. unsuitable, unjust, wrong.

admission N. confession, admittance, introduction,
entry.
Ant. denial, refusal, rejection.

admit V. allow, grant, receive, induct.
Ant. deny, refuse, reject.

admonish V. forewarn, warn, caution, reprimand.
Ant. praise, approve, applaud.

admonishment N. warning, advice, rebuke.
Ant. praise, applause, approval.

admonition N. warning, rebuke.
Ant. acceptance, approval.

ado N. fuss, turmoil, to-do, whirlwind.
Ant. calm, serenity.

adolescent N. teenager, juvenile, minor.

• **adopt** V. embrace, accept, approve. *The emigrants were eager to embrace their new country's customs.*
Ant. repulse, refuse, reject.

adorable ADJ. cute, precious, lovable, sweet, wonderful.
Ant. unpleasant, plain.

adoration N. reverence, devotion, love, worship.
Ant. despisal, hatred, mockery.

adore V. honor, love, praise, worship, idolize.
Ant. despise, mock, detest, abhor.

adorn V. embellish, decorate, beautify.
Ant. deface, disfigure, spoil.

adroit ADJ. skillful, proficient, clever, artful.
Ant. awkward, unskilled, maladroit.

adulate V. flatter, praise.
Ant. criticize, embarrass, dishonor.

adulation N. praise, flattery.
Ant. criticism.

adult N. mature, grownup.
Ant. juvenile, child, adolescent, immature.

adulterate V. defile, corrupt, debase.
Ant. refine, purify, improve.

adultery N. unfaithfulness, affair, fornication.
Ant. faithfulness, loyalty.

adumbrate V. prefigure, foreshadow, predict.
Ant. conceal, hide.

advance V. proceed, continue, progress, increase;
—N. increase, advancement, continuation, headway.
Ant. retreat, halt, recede; decrease, cessation.

advantage N. assistance, benefit, edge.
Ant. obstacle, hindrance, disadvantage.

advantageous ADJ. beneficial, helpful, salutary, gainful.
Ant. disadvantageous, derogatory, unhelpful, useless.

advent N. arrival, approach.
Ant. departure.

adventure N. undertaking, expedition, experiment, trip.
Ant. inaction, boredom, passiveness, avoidance.

adventurous ADJ. exciting, venturesome, enterprising.
Ant. timid, inactive, boring.

adversary N. enemy, opponent.
Ant. friend, helper, ally, compatriot.

adverse ADJ. unfavorable, opposing.
Ant. beneficial, favorable, encouraging.

adversity N. hardship, accident, misfortune, bad luck, disaster, difficulty.
Ant. fortune, encouragement, approval.

advertise V. announce, promote, publicize, proclaim.
Ant. conceal, hide, protect.

advice N. suggestion, instruction, counsel, recommendation.
Ant. deception, misinformation, betrayal.

• **advisable** ADJ. recommendable, counselable, expedient. *She found it most expedient to travel by train.*
Ant. deceptive, inexpedient, inadvisable.

advise V. recommend, inform, discuss, counsel.
Ant. betray.

adviser N. mentor, counselor, consultant.

advisory N. warning, direction, instruction, admonition.

advocate V. propose, recommend, support, promote; —N. supporter, defender.
Ant. oppose, attack.

aegis N. patronage, control, supervision.
Ant. neglect.

aerate V. air, ventilate.
Ant. suffocate, stifle.

aerial ADJ. lofty, airy, filmy.
Ant. earthbound.

aesthetic ADJ. artistic, sensitive, tasteful, literary.
Ant. crude, materialistic, distasteful.

affable ADJ. courteous, gracious, friendly.
Ant. arrogant, impolite, distainful.

affair N. business, incident, liaison.

affect V. influence, change, modify, impact.
Ant. overlook.

affectation N. pose, insincerity, pretention, falseness,
pretense.
Ant. naturalness, simplicity, naiveté.

affected ADJ. false, pretentious, artificial.
Ant. genuine, real, natural, heartfelt.

affection N. kindness, warmth, love.
Ant. dislike, animosity, aversion.

affectionate ADJ. loving, fond, doting, tender.
Ant. apathetic, unkind, uncaring, unfriendly.

affiliate V. associate, join, connect, ally.
Ant. disjoin, separate, divide.

affinity N. likeness, similarity.
Ant. difference, disliking.

affirm V. declare, state, assert, propose.
Ant. nullify, deny, refuse.

affirmative ADJ. positive, favorable.
Ant. negative, unfavorable.

affix V. attach, fix.
Ant. detach, remove, loosen.

affliction N. trouble, misfortune, curse, burden.
Ant. comfort, relief.

affluent ADJ. rich, wealthy, opulent.
Ant. poor, needy, destitute.

afford V. offer, provide, manage.
Ant. deny, revoke, fail.

affront N. provoke, insult, confront, irritate,
aggravate, offend.
Ant. satisfy, please, assuage.

afraid ADJ. fearful, terrified, cowardly.
Ant. confident, bold, brave.

afterlife N. immortality, eternity, heaven.
Ant. mortality, life.

aftermath N. consequence, result, effect.
Ant. preparation, preface, action.

afterward ADV. later, subsequently.
Ant. before, priorly.

again ADV. anew, repeatedly, also, additionally.
Ant. once, singular.

age N. period, time, era; —v. mature, grow old, ripen.
Ant. youth, vigor, unripeness; rejuvenate.

aged ADJ. old, elderly, ancient, ripe.
Ant. vigorous, young, unripe.

ageless ADJ. eternal, timeless.
Ant. mortal, limited, finite, impermanent.

agency N. means, vehicle, agent, conduit.

agent N. promoter, operator, factor, means.
Ant. originator, employer.

age-old ADJ. old, perpetual.
Ant. new, recent.

agglomeration N. accumulation, aggregate, total, mass.
Ant. scattering, dissipation, division, separation.

aggravate V. irritate, anger, annoy, intensify, worsen.
Ant. soothe, improve, relieve.

aggregate N. amount, collection, total, sum, mass.
Ant. part, individual, particular.

aggress V. attack, set upon.
Ant. regress, retire, shy.

aggression N. hostility, belligerence, aggressiveness.
Ant. bashfulness, shyness, friendliness, agreement.

aggressive ADJ. offensive, pugnacious, militant, belligerent, bold.
Ant. bashful, retiring, shy.

aggressor N. attacker, assailant.
Ant. friend, ally.

aghast ADJ. shocked, afraid.
Ant. calm, brave, relieved.

agile ADJ. graceful, nimble.
Ant. awkward, clumsy, gawky.

agility N. quickness, dexterity, nimbleness.
Ant. awkwardness, slowness, clumsiness.

agitate V. perturb, shake, provoke, stir, upset.
Ant. tranquilize, soothe, calm.

agitation N. commotion, turbulence, turmoil, disquiet.
Ant. tranquilization, calmness, soothingness.

agonize V. suffer, afflict.
Ant. enjoy.

agony N. pain, torment, suffering, anguish, torture.
Ant. comfort, health, peace, happiness.

agrarian ADJ. rural, farmlike, countrified, bucolic.
Ant. urban, metropolitan.

agree V. settle, concur, approve, join.
Ant. disagree, oppose, contradict.

agreeable ADJ. charming, cooperative, friendly, pleasant.
Ant. unpleasant, disagreeable, incongruous.

● **agreement** N. pact, understanding, treaty, bond. *The legislators signed a pact to keep the peace.*
Ant. disagreement, opposition, discordance.

ahead ADJ., ADV. early, forward, before.
Ant. late, after, behind.

aid V. help, support, assist.
Ant. obstruct, hinder, block.

aide N. assistant, helper.

ail N. ill, sick; —V. worry.
Ant. healthy, well.

ailing ADJ. sickly, ill, sick.
Ant. healthy, well.

ailment N. disease, sickness, illness.
Ant. heartiness, good health.

aim N. objective, goal, endeavor, aspiration.
Ant. neglect, oversight, carelessness.

aimless ADJ. purposeless, directionless.
Ant. aspiring, determined, purposeful.

air N. style, appearance, manner, atmosphere, firmament, sky; —V. make known.
Ant. hide, stifle, conceal.

airless ADJ. stifling, breathless, still.
Ant. exposed, ventilated, circulating.

airplane N. jet, airliner, aircraft, plane.

airy N. breezy, windy, atmospheric.
Ant. stifling, dead, stagnant.

aisle N. corridor, passage, passageway, gangway.

ajar ADJ. askew, loose, partly open.
Ant. sealed, secure, closed tight.

akin ADJ. related, affiliated, associated, alike.
Ant. different, unrelated.

à la mode ADJ. fashionable, modern.
Ant. outdated, antiquated, old.

alarm N. fear, terror, apprehension, panic.
Ant. comfort, calm, security.

alarming ADJ. fearful, frightful, terrifying.
Ant. calming, comforting, assuring.

alarmist N. terrorist, scaremonger.
Ant. pacifier.

alert ADJ. wakeful, wide awake, active, prepared, attentive.
Ant. tired, asleep, lethargic.

alias N. pen name, pseudonym, nom de plume.

alibi N. excuse, explanation, justification, pretext.
Ant. witness.

alien N. foreigner, stranger, immigrant; —ADJ. foreign.
Ant. native; appropriate, friendly.

• **alienate** V. estrange, transfer, separate, distance. *His actions may estrange some of his supporters.*
Ant. befriend, relate, correspond.

align V. line, ally.
Ant. disjoint, split, misalign, distance.

alike ADJ. similar, comparable, identical.
Ant. dissimilar, unlike, different.

alive ADJ. existing, living, live, animated.
Ant. dead, deceased, lifeless.

all ADJ. whole, entire; —ADV. purely.
Ant. some, part, none, nothing.

all-around ADJ. versatile, general.
Ant. specific, inflexible.

allay V. calm, soothe, alleviate.
Ant. aggravate, intensify, provoke.

allegation N. claim, assertion, statement.
Ant. denial, objection, negation.

allege V. claim, assert, state, present, set forth.
Ant. deny, protest, object.

allegiance N. homage, loyalty, devotion, fidelity.
Ant. disloyalty, treason, treachery.

alleviate V. lessen, relieve, mitigate.
Ant. intensify, aggravate.

alliance N. confederation, federation, union,
coalition, league.
Ant. secession, hostility, separation.

allied ADJ. unified, aligned, confederated.
Ant. separated, hostile, unconnected.

allocate V. allot, distribute, give, disburse.
Ant. retain, withhold, confiscate.

allot V. distribute, apportion, divide, allocate.
Ant. retain, deny, refuse.

allow V. permit, authorize, concede, acknowledge.
Ant. refuse, deny, forbid.

allowable ADJ. permissible, bearable, endurable.
Ant. impermissible, forbidden.

allowance N. allotment, concession, advantage,
permission.
Ant. disapproval, intolerance, inadmission.

alloyed ADJ. mixed, combined, impure, adulterated.
Ant. clear, pure, unadulterated, unmixed.

• **all right** ADJ. fine, satisfactory; —ADV. yes, certainly.
The presentation was satisfactory but not exciting.
Ant. unsatisfactory; no.

allude V. refer, indicate, suggest, bring up.
Ant. state, quote, specify.

allure V. draw, attract, lure, captivate.
Ant. repel, discourage, dissuade.

allusive ADJ. suggestive, indicative.
Ant. direct, easy.

ally V. align, confederate, join; —N. confederate,
coalitionist, friend.
Ant. foe, enemy, adversary.

almighty ADJ. omnipotent, all-powerful, supreme.
Ant. weak, feeble, frail, puny.

• **almost** ADV. nearly, practically, approximately,
somewhat. *The stadium was nearly filled by showtime.*
Ant. exactly, perfectly, completely.

alms N. donation, charity, assistance, contribution.

aloft ADV. above, up, in the air.
Ant. aground, beached, ashore, stranded.

alone ADJ. isolated, solitary, sole, lonely.
Ant. accompanied, together.

aloof ADJ. uninterested, distant, withdrawn, separate.
Ant. interested, down-to-earth, involved.

aloud ADV. out loud, audibly, distinctly.
Ant. silently, inaudibly, indistinctly, quietly, mutely,
noiselessly.

already ADV. earlier, even.
Ant. after, later.

• **also** ADV. as well, in addition, further, too,
additionally. *The pets needed vitamins as well.*

alter V. modify, adjust, change.
Ant. retain, keep, preserve.

alteration N. modification, adjustment, change.
Ant. preservation, continuation.

altercation N. disagreement, fight, dispute, squabble.
Ant. peace, tranquility, harmony, serenity, calm.

alternate V. rotate, switch, interchange.
Ant. dominate, continue, hoard.

alternative N. selection, possibility, choice.
Ant. obligation, compulsion.

altitudinous ADJ. high, lofty.
Ant. low.

altogether ADV. completely, wholly, entirely.
Ant. partly, somewhat, partially.

altruism N. benevolence, kindness, charity, generosity.
Ant. hatred, envy, malevolence.

always ADV. perpetually, constantly, eternally.
Ant. never, not at all.

amalgam N. mixture, blend, combination.
Ant. division, separation.

amass V. accumulate, gather, collect.
Ant. disperse, waste, dissipate.

amateur N. beginner, novice, nonprofessional.
Ant. professional, master, expert.

amateurish ADJ. unskilled, nonprofessional.
Ant. professional, skilled, expert, masterful.

amaze V. surprise, astonish, astound.
Ant. bore.

amazement N. surprise, astonishment.
Ant. coolness, indifference, composure.

• **amazing** ADJ. surprising, astonishing, astounding,
fabulous. *His astonishing feats were legendary among
magicians.*
Ant. average, boring, normal.

ambassador N. emissary, representative, diplomat,
envoy.

ambience N. environment, air, surroundings,
atmosphere.
Ant. vacuum, desert.

ambiguity N. unsureness, vagueness, equivocation.
Ant. clarity, explicitness.

ambiguous ADJ. unsure, unclear, obscure, vague,
unexplicit.
Ant. explicit, clear, definite.

ambition N. goal, aim, objective, desire.
Ant. indifference, satisfaction, laziness.

ambitious ADJ. aspiring, eager, driven, motivated.
Ant. satisfied, content, indifferent.

ambivalent ADJ. unsure, hesitant, indecisive.
Ant. sure, decisive, unambiguous.

amble v. walk, stroll.
Ant. run, dash, sprint, rush.

ambrosial ADJ. delicious, tasty.
Ant. sour, plain, distasteful.

ambush v. surprise, attack.
Ant. alert, forwarn.

ameliorate v. improve, make better.
Ant. detract, destroy, aggravate.

amenable ADJ. receptive, obedient.
Ant. disobedient, unreceptive.

amend v. better, correct, improve, fix, repair, revise.
Ant. spoil, harm, impair.

amendment N. revision, improvement.
Ant. deterioration, corruption.

amends N. compensation, restitution, reparation.

amenities N. courtesies, proprieties, civilities, comforts, facilities.
Ant. basics, essentials.

amiable ADJ. pleasing, lovable, likable, gentle.
Ant. rude, morose, ill-humored.

amicable ADJ. friendly, harmonious.
Ant. unpleasant, unfriendly, rude.

amiss ADV. wrong, awry.
Ant. right, in order.

amnesty N. forgiveness, release, reprieve.
Ant. unforgiveness.

amorous ADJ. affectionate, tender, loving.
Ant. cold, loveless, cool.

amount N. quantity, total, sum.

amour N. love, passion, amourness.
Ant. hate, dislike.

ample ADJ. full, generous, abundant.
Ant. lacking, insufficient, sparse.

amplify v. increase, magnify, intensify, enlarge, expand.
Ant. condense, reduce, decrease.

amplitude N. size, bulk, scope.
Ant. smallness, tininess.

amputate V. remove, sever, separate, cut off.
Ant. join, affix, fasten, connect, link.

amuse V. please, entertain, interest, distract.
Ant. bore, annoy, tire, irritate.

amusement N. diversion, entertainment, distraction.
Ant. tedium, boredom.

analogy N. similarity, likeness, resemblance,
correspondence.
Ant. dissimilarity, unlikeness.

analysis N. investigation, classification, breakdown,
examination, review.
Ant. combination, synthesis, assembly.

• **analyze** V. investigate, examine, inspect. *This study
will investigate the causes of early hair loss.*
Ant. generalize, overlook, synthesize.

anarchy N. disorder, rebellion, commotion, terrorism.
Ant. order, regulation.

anathema N. hate, curse.
Ant. blessing, love.

ancestor(s) N. descendant, predecessor, forerunner.
Ant. child, children, future generations.

ancestral ADJ. hereditary, inherited.
Ant. earned, acquired.

ancestry N. descent, origin, lineage, parentage.

anchor V. fix, fasten.
Ant. detach, loosen.

ancient ADJ. archaic, old, antique, aged.
Ant. modern, new.

ancillary ADJ. auxiliary, supplemental.
Ant. adversarial, opposing.

anecdote N. narrative, story, account.

anemic ADJ. sickly, pale, unhealthy.
Ant. healthy, sanguine, well, stout.

anesthetic N. opiate, sedative, painkiller.

angel N. innocent, sponsor, patron, seraph,
archangel.
Ant. devil, demon.

angelic ADJ. heavenly, innocent, pure, beatific.
　Ant. devilish, guilty, satanic, mischievous, evil.

anger N. wrath, rage, resentment, exasperation.
　Ant. patience, calm, good nature.

angle N. bias, hint, point of view.
　Ant. plane, line.

angry ADJ. upset, furious, enraged, mad.
　Ant. calm, patient, gentle.

anguish N. torment, agony, pain, distress.
　Ant. comfort, joy.

angular ADJ. thin, bony, emaciated, gaunt.
　Ant. plump, curved, graceful.

animal N. beast, creature; —ADJ. physical, carnal.
　Ant. spirit, mental; spiritual.

animate V. enliven, inspire, invigorate, stimulate;
　—ADJ. alive, lively.
　Ant. thwart; sluggish, inanimate.

animosity N. anger, ill will, hostility, bitterness.
　Ant. friendliness, kindliness, affability.

annals N. records, history.
　Ant. predictions.

annex V. add, join, append, affix; —N. addition,
　supplement.
　Ant. subtract, detach.

annihilate V. obliterate, nullify, exterminate, destroy.
　Ant. save, preserve.

annotation N. commentary, elucidation, revision.

announce V. advertise, tell, notify, proclaim.
　Ant. suppress, conceal, hold.

annoy V. irritate, harass, bother, trouble.
　Ant. please, soothe, aid.

annul V. cancel, abolish.
　Ant. restore, ratify, begin.

anomaly N. abnormality, variation, alteration.
　Ant. normality.

anonymity N. obscurity, hiddenness.
　Ant. fame, celebrity, visibility.

answer v. respond, reply, acknowledge, retort.
Ant. question, ask, differ.

antagonism N. animosity, antipathy, opposition, conflict.
Ant. agreement, harmony, accord.

antecedent N. cause, precedent, past.
Ant. result, subsequent, future.

anterior ADJ. past, advance.
Ant. future, next, posterior.

anticipate v. expect, forebode, foresee, forecast.
Ant. wonder, doubt.

anticlimax N. disappointment, letdown, comedown.
Ant. fulfillment, climax, culmination, achievement.

antidote N. remedy, cure, palliative.
Ant. malady, illness, sickness.

antipathy N. hatred, repulsion, repugnance, aversion, antagonism.
Ant. respect, admiration, sympathy.

antipode N. opposite, reverse, contrary.
Ant. similar, same.

antiquated ADJ. old-fashioned, ancient, antique.
Ant. new, modern, à la mode.

antique ADJ. old-fashioned, old, ancient, antiquated.
Ant. modern, new, recent.

antiseptic ADJ. clean, sterile.
Ant. dirty, germ-ridden, filthy.

antisocial ADJ. isolated, alienated, selfish, rebellious.
Ant. sociable, friendly, affable, gregarious, outgoing.

antithesis N. opposite, contrary.
Ant. similarity, sameness, thesis.

antonymous ADJ. contrary, opposite.
Ant. similar.

anxiety N. unease, worry, anguish, disquiet, apprehension, dread.
Ant. certainty, calm, security.

anxious ADJ. concerned, worried, apprehensive, troubled.
Ant. calm, certain, sure.

anyway ADV. nevertheless, in any case.

apart ADJ. unique, solitary; —ADV. independently,
aside.
Ant. together.

apartment N. condominium, dwelling, residence.

apathy N. indifference, passiveness, lethargy,
sluggishness.
Ant. passion, emotion, sympathy.

ape V. imitate, mimic, emulate.

aperture N. hole, entrance, inlet.
Ant. closure, wall.

apex N. point, climax, height.
Ant. depth, nadir, base.

aplomb N. confidence, balance.
Ant. unassuredness, apprehension, uncertainty.

apocalypse N. revelation, prophecy, oracle, vision.
Ant. deception, concealment.

apogee N. climax, apex, zenith.
Ant. base, bottom.

apology N. justification, excuse, confession,
acknowledgment.
Ant. accusation, disapprobation, censure.

apostasy N. defection, unfaithfulness, faithlessness.
Ant. faithfulness, loyalty.

apostle N. missionary, follower, disciple.
Ant. dissenter.

apotheosis N. exultation, transformation.
Ant. defeat, denial.

appall V. shock, horrify, frighten, dismay.
Ant. enervate, activate, please.

apparatus N. outfit, equipment, device.

apparel N. clothing, dress, clothes.

• apparent ADJ. evident, distinct, plain, obvious. *The
error was evident for the auditor.*
Ant. uncertain, doubtful, unclear.

apparition N. ghost, spirit.
Ant. reality, body, person, actuality.

appeal V. petition, request, plead, implore.
Ant. retract, deny, revoke.

• appearance N. aspect, look, image, presence. *The school had the look of a rundown hotel.*
Ant. leaving, departure, absence.

appease V. calm, soothe, pacify.
Ant. perturb, aggravate, provoke.

appellation N. name, moniker, title.

append V. add on, affix, join.
Ant. separate, sever, undo, disunite.

appendage N. branch, limb, extremity, member.
Ant. whole, body, entire, entity.

appertain V. belong, apply, concern.
Ant. disinterest.

appetite N. longing, craving, desire, hunger.
Ant. anorexia, denial, renunciation.

applaud V. praise, cheer, clap.
Ant. condemn, disapprove, reproach, ignore.

applause N. clapping, cheering, approval.
Ant. condemnation, disapproval, booing.

appliance N. device, apparatus, mechanism.
Ant. nonapplication, nonuse.

applicable ADJ. suitable, proper.
Ant. inept, unusable.

applicant N. candidate, aspirant.
Ant. employer, hirer, master.

application N. employment, utilization, implementation.
Ant. laziness, inattention.

apply V. employ, use, utilize.
Ant. neglect.

appoint V. designate, name, select, assign.
Ant. strip, dismiss.

appointment N. engagement, nomination, designation.
Ant. dismissal, firing, termination, demotion.

apportion V. assign, allot, distribute, allocate, ration.
Ant. monopolize, withhold.

appraise v. evaluate, estimate, consider.
Ant. guess.

appreciable ADJ. perceptible, noticeable.
Ant. depreciable, disparagable.

appreciate v. realize, comprehend, thank, prize.
Ant. scorn, reproach, depreciate, disparage.

appreciation N. liking, responsiveness, gratefulness, gratitude.
Ant. disapproval, malevolence, hatred.

apprehend v. get, capture, arrest, seize.
Ant. lose, release.

apprehensive ADJ. uneasy, fearful, anxious, afraid.
Ant. composed, confident, unafraid.

apprise v. inform, advise, acquaint.
Ant. conceal, hide.

approach v. address, approximate.
Ant. depart, leave, distance.

approachable ADJ. friendly, accessible, warm, easy-going.
Ant. cold, distant, unfriendly.

approbation N. praise, approval, acceptance.
Ant. scorn, rejection, disapproval.

appropriate v. assume, seize, take; —ADJ. proper, correct, suitable.
Ant. inept, wrong, inappropriate.

appropriation N. grant, usurpation, funding.
Ant. withholding, denial.

approval N. justification, endorsement, acceptance, consent.
Ant. rejection, disapproval, censure.

approve v. accept, endorse, ratify, validate.
Ant. reject, disapprove, censure.

approximate v. estimate, approach; —ADJ. close, similar, inexact.
Ant. exact, detailed.

• approximately ADV. almost, practically, nearly, about, roughly. *She created almost one thousand costumes during her career.*
Ant. completely, entirely, exactly.

apt ADJ. suitable, appropriate, proper.
Ant. improper, unsuitable, inappropriate.

aptitude N. talent, gift, ability.
Ant. difficulty, disliking.

arable ADJ. suitable for farming, fertile.
Ant. arid, parched, infertile, barren.

arbitrary ADJ. random, whimsical, personal, subjective.
Ant. relative, objective, reasoned.

arbitrate V. judge, adjudicate, referee, mediate.

arcane ADJ. mysterious, mystic, secret, unknown.
Ant. clear, definite, ordinary.

archaic ADJ. old-fashioned, antiquated, outdated.
Ant. modern, new, updated.

arched ADJ. bend, curved, bowed, unstraight.
Ant. straight.

archetypal ADJ. typical, universal.
Ant. specific, personal, individual.

archetype N. original, type, model.

arctic ADJ. frigid, cold.
Ant. warm, temperate, tropical.

ardent ADJ. eager, intense, enthusiastic, passionate.
Ant. unenthusiastic, apathetic, cool.

ardor N. passion, enthusiasm.
Ant. indifference, coolness.

arduous ADJ. difficult, hard, burdensome, laborious.
Ant. simple, easy.

area N. region, territory, subject, realm.

arena N. area, scene, locale, stadium.

arguable ADJ. debatable, disputable.
Ant. agreeable, indisputable, inarguable.

argue V. dispute, discuss, debate, quarrel.
Ant. agree, harmonize, accord.

• **argument** N. discussion, debate, dispute, quarrel. *The neighbors joined in a heated discussion of the issue.*
Ant. agreement, harmony, pact.

argumentative ADJ. quarrelsome, contentious, combative.
Ant. passive, unaggressive.

arid ADJ. dry, barren, boring.
Ant. damp, humid, moist, wet.

arise V. begin, rise, get up, emerge, appear.
Ant. finish, disappear, sink.

aristocratic ADJ. elite, noble, royal.
Ant. poor, common, lowborn, plebeian.

arm N. branch, division; —V. equip, supply.
Ant. disarm.

armistice N. truce, treaty.
Ant. war, aggression, battle.

aroma N. fragrance, scent, smell.
Ant. stench, stink.

around ADJ. nearby, surrounding, encircling, about.
Ant. distant, faraway.

arouse V. excite, stimulate, awaken, inspire.
Ant. calm, pacify, alleviate.

arraign V. accuse, indict.
Ant. release, excuse.

arrange V. group, distribute, place, order, assort.
Ant. disturb, confuse, disarrange.

arrant ADJ. shameless, flagrant.
Ant. tactful, subtle.

array N. assortment, order, arrangement; clothes, dress.
Ant. V. disorder, disarray, disorganization.

arrest V. apprehend, seize, halt, capture.
Ant. release, activate, let go.

arrival N. appearance, success.
Ant. disappearance, departure.

arrive V. come, attain, appear, reach.
Ant. depart, leave.

arrogance N. loftiness, disdain, presumption, pride, superiority.
Ant. humility, humbleness.

arrogant ADJ. proud, insolent, disdainful, overbearing, presumptuous.
Ant. meek, humble, servile.

art N. craft, cunning, expertise.

artful ADJ. deft, skillful, dexterous, crafty.
Ant. artless, rude, plain.

article N. object, element.

articulate ADJ. vocal, eloquent, well-spoken.
Ant. silent, taciturn, bluff.

artifice N. trick, art.
Ant. honesty, sincerity, organism.

artificial ADJ. synthetic, manufactured, unnatural.
Ant. genuine, real, natural.

artisan N. craftsman, artist.

artistic ADJ. tasteful, creative, inventive.
Ant. artless, graceless.

artless ADJ. naive, honest, candid, unsophisticated, rustic.
Ant. artful, sly, deceptive, cunning, crafty.

ascend V. advance, progress, climb, rise.
Ant. fall, lower, descent.

ascendancy N. dominance, control.
Ant. submission, yielding.

ascendant ADJ. ruling, dominant.
Ant. submissive, obeying.

ascension N. rise, ascent.
Ant. descent, decline, fall.

ascent N. rise, progress, climb, ascension.
Ant. descent, fall.

• **ascertain** V. determine, figure out, discover, evaluate.
The researcher was unable to determine the source of the pollution.
Ant. assume, guess, presume.

ascribe V. attribute, blame.
Ant. release, acquit.

ashen ADJ. gray, white, pale, pallid, wan.
Ant. rosy-cheeked, flushed, glowing, blushing.

ask V. question, demand, request, appeal, interrogate.
Ant. answer, respond, deny, reply, refuse.

askance ADV. skeptically, quizzically.
Ant. encouragingly, positively.

askew ADJ. disordered, out of place, awry.
Ant. orderly, arranged, neat, systematic.

asleep ADJ. sleeping, dormant, inactive.
Ant. awake, active, alert.

aspect N. appearance, look, expression.

asperity N. difficulty, hardship.
Ant. ease, simplicity.

aspiration N. dream, ambition, hope.
Ant. surrender, disdain.

aspire V. hope, try, desire, seek, crave.
Ant. give up, disdain.

assail V. revile, attack.
Ant. leave, retreat, ignore.

assault N. attack, aggression.
Ant. retreat, ignore.

assemble V. collect, gather, convene.
Ant. disperse, split, scatter, disassemble.

assembly N. congress, body, congregation, gathering.
Ant. dispersal, disunity.

assent V. agree, allow, concur, approve.
Ant. deny, refuse, dissent.

assert V. affirm, declare, insist, state.
Ant. contradict, deny, reject.

● **assertion** N. affirmation, statement, declaration. *His statement will certainly be challenged in court.*
Ant. rejection, contradiction, denial.

assertive ADJ. emphatic, aggressive.
Ant. passive, relaxed.

● **assess** V. estimate, judge, evaluate, guess, determine. *It may be difficult to estimate the extent of the damage.*

assessment N. tax, estimate, evaluation, appraisal.

assets N. resources, capacity, profits, possessions.

assiduous ADJ. applied, persistent, devoted, industrious, diligent, hardworking, ambitious.
Ant. casual, lazy, random.

assignment N. task, responsibility, duty.

assimilate V. habituate, conform, absorb, liken.
Ant. repel, split.

assist V. help, support, aid.
   Ant. hinder, impede, deter.

● **assistance** N. help, support, aid. *The town appreciated the help of nearby villages.*
   Ant. hindrance, deterrence, discouragement.

assize N. law, rule.

associate V. unite, combine, ally, attach, affiliate.
   Ant. separate, part, disassociate.

assortment N. collection, melange, variety, mixture.
   Ant. specific, singularity, purity.

assuage V. relieve, pacify, make better.
   Ant. agitate, perturb, irritate.

● **assume** V. infer, suppose, feign, pretend, take on, appropriate. *Do not infer that the problem was his fault.*
   Ant. relinquish, doubt.

assumption N. postulate, theory, hypothesis, conjecture, guess.
   Ant. proof, certainty.

assurance N. guarantee, promise, pledge, courage, confidence.
   Ant. uncertainty, distrust, denial.

assure V. promise, guarantee, pledge.

astonish V. surprise, startle, astound.
   Ant. calm, bore.

astound V. shock, amaze, startle, frighten, astonish.
   Ant. bore, calm.

astral ADJ. highest, grand.
   Ant. petty, lowly.

astray ADV. missing, lost, off track.
   Ant. located, placed, sited, positioned, in place, accounted for.

astute ADJ. shrewd, sensible, reasonable, intelligent.
   Ant. candid, naive, inexperienced, unsophisticated.

asylum N. home, cover, refuge.

atheism N. disbelief, agnosticism, incredulity.
   Ant. theism, belief, faith.

atmosphere N. environment, flavor, air, ambience.
   Ant. vacuum.

atrium N. court, entry, doorway, courtyard.

atrocious ADJ. outrageous, horrible, awful, unspeakable.
Ant. wonderful, kind, benevolent, good.

atrocity N. outrage, offense, horror.
Ant. beauty, wonder.

attach V. secure, fasten, connect, add.
Ant. loosen, disconnect, remove.

attack V. assault, violate, assail, abuse, criticize.
Ant. defend, protect, withdraw, retreat.

attain V. accomplish, obtain, gain, achieve, reach.
Ant. fail, abandon, surrender.

attempt V. endeavor, experiment; —N. effort.
Ant. accomplish, attain; success, certainty.

attend V. frequent, serve, wait on, tend, follow, accompany.
Ant. miss, skip.

attendant N. helper, accompaniment, servant.

• **attention** N. notice, concentration, diligence, care.
The lesson required close concentration.
Ant. disregard, neglect.

attentive ADJ. aware, mindful, observant.
Ant. bored, distracted, unaware.

attenuate V. thin, enervate, dilute.
Ant. calm, purify, thicken.

attest V. confirm, testify, certify.
Ant. deny, disprove.

attire N. dress, apparel, clothing.

• **attitude** N. disposition, manner, view, position. *His disposition rarely changed.*

attract V. lure, draw, hold interest, appeal.
Ant. repulse, repel.

attraction N. enticement, fascination, lure, affinity.
Ant. repulsion.

attribute V. assign, credit, refer, ascribe; —N. characteristic, quality.

attribution N. assignment, credit, ascription.

attrition N. penitence, atonement, remorse, loss.
Ant. gain.

attune V. harmonize, adjust.
Ant. disrupt, disjoint.

atypical ADJ. abnormal, unusual.
Ant. normal, typical, usual.

audacious ADJ. bold, intrepid, daring, brazen.
Ant. humble, reserved, restrained.

audacity N. arrogance, rashness, boldness,
impudence.
Ant. forbearance, humility, patience, restraint.

audience N. hearing, public, listeners.

augment V. increase, intensify, add to.
Ant. decrease, abate, reduce.

augur N. prophet; —V. predict, anticipate, prophesy.

august ADJ. grand, exalted.
Ant. humble, lowly.

aurora N. dawn, dawning.
Ant. sunset, dusk, night.

auspices N. patronage.
Ant. neglect.

auspicious ADJ. opportune, favorable.
Ant. inauspicious, unfavorable.

austere ADJ. severe, stern, harsh, simple, plain.
Ant. kind, mild, meek.

austerity N. strictness, rigor, severity, harshness.
Ant. lenience, kindness, flexibility.

authentic ADJ. genuine, veritable, true, legitimate,
reliable.
Ant. false, unnatural, inaccurate.

authenticate V. validate, verify, certify, guarantee.
Ant. falsify, corrupt.

authenticity N. truthfulness, validity, genuineness,
realness, legitimacy.
Ant. fraudulence, unreliability, illegitimacy.

author N. dramatist, novelist, poet, originator, writer.

authoritarian ADJ. despotic, dictatorial, tyrannical, authoritative, dominant, commanding, powerful, standard, official.

authority N. rule, jurisdiction, control, supremacy, command, power.

• **authorize** V. permit, empower, allow. *Our bylaws permit only one term for the president.*

autocracy N. absolutism, dictatorship, despotism. *Ant.* democracy, freedom.

autograph V. sign; —N. signature.

automatic ADJ. routine, regular, expected, usual. *Ant.* irregular, unusual, manual, nonroutine.

autonomous ADJ. free, independent, self-governing. *Ant.* manipulated, governed, dominated.

autumn N. fall.

auxiliary ADJ. assisting, secondary, supplemental. *Ant.* main, chief.

avail V. help, serve, use, benefit. *Ant.* hinder, hurt, oppose.

• **available** ADJ. obtainable, ready, accessible. *They purchased the best skis obtainable.* *Ant.* unobtainable, inaccessible, unavailable.

avarice N. greed, self-seeking. *Ant.* selflessness, giving.

avenge V. settle, pay back, repay, vindicate. *Ant.* pardon, forgive.

avenue N. way, street, road, lane.

aver V. assert, claim, avow. *Ant.* disavow.

average ADJ. typical, ordinary, common, undistinguished; —N. mean, median, norm. *Ant.* extraordinary, unusual, exceptional; maximum, minimum.

averse ADJ. indisposed, unwilling, reluctant. *Ant.* willing.

aversion N. disgust, loathing, dislike, hatred. *Ant.* favor, attachment, liking.

avert V. turn away, prevent, avoid.
Ant. cause, turn toward.

avid ADJ. eager, voracious, greedy.
Ant. relaxed, lazy, calm.

avocation N. hobby, leisure activity.
Ant. vocation, profession, occupation, job, career, calling.

• **avoid** V. dodge, elude, escape, shun. *The thief was able to elude his pursuers.*
Ant. encounter, face, confront.

avoidance N. escape, evasion, dodging.
Ant. encountering, confronting.

avow V. assert, acknowledge.
Ant. deny, reject.

await V. expect, anticipate, remain.

awake V. alert, stimulate, arouse, wake; —ADJ. aware.
Ant. unaware, asleep.

award V. honor, give, bestow, recognize.
Ant. withdraw, withhold, reject.

aware ADJ. alert, mindful, sensible, cognizant.
Ant. unconscious, unaware, inattentive.

away ADV. aside; —ADJ. distant, absent, gone.
Ant. near, close.

awe N. wonder, admiration, respect, fear.
Ant. calmness, familiarity, pose.

• **awful** ADJ. terrible, abominable, dreadful. *We disliked the dreadful conclusion to the movie.*
Ant. wonderful, superb, excellent.

awkward ADJ. difficult, cumbersome, inconvenient, lumbering, inept.
Ant. graceful, skillful, lithe, coordinated.

axiom N. rule, precept, proposition.
Ant. absurdity, contradiction, nonsense.

B

babble N. chatter, gibberish, nonsense.

baby N. infant, newborn, babe.
Ant. adult, grown-up, senior.

back N. posterior, end, rear; —V. assist, support, help, endorse, finance.
Ant. fore, front, face.

backbiting ADJ. slanderous.
Ant. helpful, charitable.

backbone N. spine, courage, bravery, guts.
Ant. spineless, timid, fearful, cowardly, gutless.

backbreaking ADJ. burdensome, difficult, hard.
Ant. easy, simple.

backfire V. rebound, bounce back.
Ant. succeed, work.

background N. history, experience.
Ant. foreground, conspicuous, position.

backlog V. hoard, stockpile, reserve.

backside N. bottom, buttocks, behind.

backsliding N. lapse, slippage.
Ant. advancing, progressing.

backtrack V. back up, go back.
Ant. advance, go forward, progress.

backup N. auxiliary, supplement, substitute.
Ant. primary.

backward ADJ. behind, dull, stupid; —ADV. in reverse order.
Ant. forward, precocious, ahead.

bacteria N. germs, microorganisms, microbes.

bad ADJ. harmful, unpleasant, evil, wrong, corrupt.
Ant. good, worthy, virtuous.

badge N. decoration, emblem, cross.

badger V. provoke, harass, torment, taunt.
Ant. encourage, assist, help.

badly ADV. unfavorably, ineffectively, poorly.
Ant. well, right, competently.

bad-mannered ADJ. impolite, rude.
Ant. polite, courteous, respectful.

bad-tempered ADJ. ill-tempered.
Ant. gentle, kind.

baffle V. confound, outwit, frustrate, elude.
Ant. facilitate, assist.

bag V. sack, catch, arrest, trap.

baggage N. suitcases, pack, equipment, luggage.

bail N. bond, deposit, surety.

bait V. entice, captivate, lure, tease, pester.
Ant. reject, repel.

bake V. burn, toast, cook.
Ant. cool.

balance N. stability, proportion, equilibrium.
Ant. disproportion, imbalance.

balanced ADJ. sane, fair.
Ant. insane, unbalanced, unfair, disproportioned.

balcony N. deck, ledge, gallery, terrace.

bald ADJ. bare, hairless.
Ant. hirsute, hairy.

bald-faced ADJ. shameless, audacious.
Ant. respectful, honorable.

baleful ADJ. detrimental, harmful, injurious, destructive.
Ant. helpful, beneficial, positive.

balk V. stop, hesitate, check.
Ant. hasten, act, continue.

ballad N. song, poem.

balloon V. enlarge, swell, bulge.
Ant. shrivel, shrink.

balmy ADJ. gentle, soothing, mild.
Ant. tempestuous, stormy, cold.

ban V. prohibit, outlaw, forbid, censor.
Ant. allow, permit, legalize.

banal ADJ. overused, trite, insipid.
Ant. novel, fresh, original.

band N. association, group, gang.

bandage N. dress, wrapping, repair.

bandit N. villain, robber, crook, thug.

bandy V. exchange, give back.

bane N. poison, curse, ruin.
Ant. help, antidote.

bang V. blow, blast, slam, hit.

banish V. expel, dismiss, deport, ostracize.
Ant. welcome, forgive, receive.

bank N. shore, embankment.

bankroll V. finance, support, back.

bankrupt ADJ. ruined, broke.
Ant. wealthy, rich, secure.

banner N. flag, colors, pennant.

banquet N. feast, meal, entertainment.

bantam ADJ. tiny, small, dainty, feisty.
Ant. huge, immense, stout.

banter V. chatter, joke, humor, tease.

baptize V. bless, consecrate, christen.

bar N. barricade, hindrance, barrier, obstacle; saloon,
café, lounge; —V. prevent, impede, stop, hinder.

barbarian N. brute, ruffian, savage.
Ant. gentleman, gentlewoman, sophisticate.

bard N. poet, storyteller, muse, author.

bare ADJ. uncovered, naked, nude, empty,
unfurnished, barren, plain, scarce.
Ant. full, complete, covered, furnished.

• **barely** ADV. hardly, scarcely, almost, nearly,
approximately, just. *He felt hardly any pain during the
procedure.*
Ant. considerable, substantial, much.

bargain N. arrangement, deal, contract, agreement.

bark V. snap, crack, yelp.

baroque ADJ. elaborate, embellished, ornate.
Ant. plain, simple, unadorned.

barrage N. bombardment, shower, burst.

barren ADJ. bare, sterile, fruitless, unproductive,
empty, futile.
Ant. full, pregnant, fruitful, productive.

barricade N. fence, barrier, wall, obstacle.

barrier N. obstacle, fence, blockage, obstruction.

basal ADJ. radical, elementary.
Ant. advanced.

base ADJ. worthless, vile, corrupt, low; —N. theme,
basis, headquarters, complex, station.
Ant. elevated, worthy, esteemed, respected.

baseless ADJ. unjustifiable, groundless, unfounded,
empty.
Ant. justifiable, proven.

bash N. party, blast; —v. hit.

bashful ADJ. shy, modest, timid.
Ant. immodest, bold, arrogant, self-assured.

basic ADJ. essential, fundamental, primary,
elementary.
Ant. additional, supplemental, secondary, extra.

• basically ADV. essentially, mainly, chiefly,
fundamentally. *The company was essentially a one-
person operation.*
Ant. subordinately, additionally.

basin N. depression, watershed, sink, tub.
Ant. elevation.

basis N. foundation, ground, base, justification.

bask v. luxuriate, sun, loaf, enjoy.

bass N. low sound, deep tone.
Ant. soprano, tenor, alto, high, shrill.

bastard ADJ. illegitimate.
Ant. legitimate.

baste v. moisten; beat, thrash; sew.

batch N. set, bunch, cluster.
Ant. single, solitary.

bate v. subside, return.
Ant. continue, pursue.

bathe v. wash, cleanse, immerse, rinse.

bathos N. sentimentality, foolishness.
Ant. aloofness.

batter v. hit, strike, pummel.

battle N. combat, warfare, struggle, war.
Ant. peace, amnesty.

battlefield N. arena, front line, theater of battle, field.

batty ADJ. insane, crazy.
Ant. stable, sane.

bawd N. prostitute, whore.
Ant. innocent, virgin.

bay N. cove, harbor, gulf.

be v. exist, subsist, live.
Ant. die, expire.

beacon N. floodlight, fire, flare, bonfire.

beak N. bill, nose.

beam N. timber, girder; —v. gleam, glow, shine, glisten.

bear v. carry, transport, support, endure, tolerate, stand.
Ant. shun, avoid, refuse, reject.

bearing N. behavior, carriage, posture, reference, connection.
Ant. confusion, disorientation.

beast N. monster, fiend, brute, animal.

beat v. batter, hit, strike, hammer, defeat, surpass.

beatitude N. happiness, blessing.
Ant. melancholy, curse.

beau N. suitor, admirer, boyfriend, lover.

• **beautiful** ADJ. lovely, attractive, pretty, gorgeous, fair, handsome. *We admired the lovely roses.*
Ant. unattractive, plain, ugly, homely.

beautify v. revamp, do up, redecorate.
Ant. neglect, abandon, disregard, tear down, allow to fall into disrepair.

beauty N. attractiveness, loveliness.
Ant. ugliness, unattractiveness.

beckon V. call, summon, signal.
Ant. shun, refuse, reject.

become V. change, grow, suit, come to be.
Ant. remain.

becoming ADJ. proper, fitting, suitable, decent.
Ant. indecent, improper, unsuitable, unfitting.

bedazzle V. daze, amaze, stun.
Ant. bore, stultify.

bedeck V. adorn, decorate.
Ant. strip.

bedevil V. besiege, annoy.
Ant. please, aid.

bedlam N. mayhem, confusion, turmoil.
Ant. order, calm, serenity, harmony.

bedraggled ADJ. shabby, disheveled.
Ant. clean, neat, orderly.

befall V. chance, happen.

befit V. suit, fit.

before ADJ. prior, earlier, ahead; —ADV. sooner.
Ant. after, subsequent; later.

befriend V. look after, assist, take care of, make
friends with.
Ant. shun, ostracize, blackball.

befuddle V. daze, stun, confuse.
Ant. clarify.

beg V. plead, petition, implore, entreat, supplicate.
Ant. give, earn.

beget V. father, propagate.

beggar N. homeless person, poor person, needy
person, pauper, supplicant.

• **begin** V. initiate, start, commence. *She wanted to
initiate her business plans as soon as possible.*
Ant. end, finish, complete, terminate.

beginner N. novice, apprentice, amateur, initiate.
Ant. professional, expert, master.

beginning N. outset, source, origin, inception, start.
Ant. completion, end, termination, conclusion.

begrudge V. envy, resent.
Ant. comply, accept.

beguile V. deceive, fool.
Ant. bore, aid, help.

behave V. act, comport.
Ant. misbehave.

• behavior N. action, manners, comportment, conduct, attitude, demeanor. *Judge his values by his action.*
Ant. misbehavior, mischief.

behemoth N. giant, leviathan.
Ant. midget, dwarf.

behind ADJ., ADV. in back of, slow, late; —N. bottom.
Ant. ahead, before.

behold V. look at, see, perceive.
Ant. ignore.

being N. essence, nature, existence, actuality, thing.
Ant. nonexistence.

belated ADJ. late, overdue.
Ant. early, in advance, first.

belch V. burp, erupt.

belie V. refute, distort.
Ant. corroborate, clarify.

belief N. opinion, conviction, persuasion.

believable ADJ. plausible, credible.
Ant. implausible, unbelievable, incredible.

• believe V. accept, trust, credit, feel, deem. *They are willing to accept his explanation.*
Ant. mistrust, question.

belittle V. minimize, discredit, humiliate, diminish.
Ant. commend, exult, flatter.

bellicose ADJ. warlike, belligerent, military.
Ant. peaceful, pacifist, nonviolent.

belligerence N. hostility, aggression, bellicosity.
Ant. nonviolence, kindness, peacefulness.

bellow V. scream, roar, yell, shout.
Ant. whisper, murmur.

belly N. stomach, abdomen; —v. bulge, swell.

- **belong** V. pertain, fit, appertain, have to do with.
  These files pertain to the Smith case.

beloved ADJ. favorite, darling, loved, dear.
Ant. hated, neglected, despised.

belt N. area: —v. hit, strike.

bemoan V. lament, bewail, regret.
Ant. applaud, extol, praise.

bemuse V. daze, amaze, mesmerize.
Ant. bore, stultify.

benchmark N. standard, criterion, gauge.

bend V. curve, turn, bow, deflect, submit, yield.
Ant. straighten, refuse, reject.

benediction N. grace, blessing.
Ant. curse, malediction.

benefaction N. donation, benevolence, contribution.
Ant. malevolence.

benefactor N. patron, donor, backer.

beneficence N. donation, benevolence, contribution.
Ant. malevolence.

- **beneficial** ADJ. helpful, useful, good, favorable. *Her expertise proved helpful to our efforts.*
  Ant. harmful, detrimental, damaging.

benefit N. advantage, profit, favor, service.
Ant. disadvantage, disservice, hindrance.

benevolence N. kindness, tenderness, humanity, charity.
Ant. cruelty, unkindness, malevolence, envy, hatred.

benign ADJ. harmless, favorable, benevolent.
Ant. harmful, malevolent, cancerous, unfavorable.

bent ADJ. curved, crooked, arched.
Ant. straight.

bequeath V. give to, leave, hand down.
Ant. take, seize.

berate V. bawl out, criticize.
Ant. honor, praise.

bereave V. deprive, take away, withdraw.
Ant. give, donate.

berth N. place, position.

beseech V. implore, ask, beg, appeal.
Ant. answer, give.

beset V. attack, annoy, surround.
Ant. soothe, retreat, help, rescue.

• besides ADV. additionally, furthermore, moreover, in
addition. *In addition, the team needed new uniforms.*
Ant. solely, singularly.

besiege V. blockage, beset, harass, surround.
Ant. retreat, relieve.

besmirch V. tarnish, slander, defame.
Ant. eulogize, laud, extol.

best ADJ. optimal, optimum, largest; —N. elite.
Ant. smallest, lowest, worst.

bestial ADJ. fierce, animalistic.
Ant. calm, subdued, spiritual.

bestow V. award, give, present, donate.
Ant. take, seize.

bet V. gamble, wager, stake.

betray V. expose, reveal, be treacherous.
Ant. safeguard, protect.

betrothal N. engagement, promise.

better ADJ. superior, preferable.
Ant. worse, inferior.

bevel N. slant, angle, slope, inclination.

beverage N. drink, libation.

bevy N. group, assembly, collection.
Ant. solitaire.

beware V. look out, be cautious, take care, be careful.

bewilder V. puzzle, mystify, confuse.
Ant. aid, clarify, bore.

bewitch V. captivate, charm, enchant, dazzle.
Ant. repulse, bore.

bias N. prejudice, inclination, partiality.
Ant. impartiality, fairness, justice.

bicker V. dispute, argue, quarrel.
Ant. agree, harmonize.

bid v. offer, propose, direct, order; —N. proposal, invitation, offer.
Ant. enjoin, prohibit.

bide v. remain, pause, delay.
Ant. start, expedite.

big ADJ. immense, large, enormous, important, gigantic, huge.
Ant. small, tiny, diminutive, minuscule.

bigotry N. prejudice, intolerance, bias.
Ant. tolerance, openmindedness.

bill N. charge, invoice, account.

binary ADJ. double, polar.
Ant. single, solitary.

bind v. fasten, tie, affix, commit.
Ant. loosen, free, untie.

binge N. rampage, orgy, spree.

birth N. ancestry, onset, beginning, childbirth, labor, start.
Ant. death, end, termination.

birthright N. right, prerogative, inheritance, legacy.

bisect v. divide, intersect, sever.
Ant. join, affix, connect, link.

bit N. fragment, scrap, particle.
Ant. whole, entirety.

bite v. chew, eat, sting; —N. mouthful, morsel, snack.

biting ADJ. acidic, pungent, bitter, cutting.
Ant. sweet, soothing, aromatic, fragrant.

bitter ADJ. acidic, acrid, sour, biting.
Ant. pleasant, sweet, agreeable.

• bizarre ADJ. fantastic, eccentric, strange, unusual. *His eccentric clothing aroused many questions.*
Ant. usual, normal, expected, common.

black ADJ. dark, dirty, evil, gloomy, ebony, jet.
Ant. white, clean.

blackball v. ostracize, drive out.
Ant. welcome, accept, embrace.

blacken v. stain, dirty, smear, tarnish, darken.
Ant. whiten, clean, erase.

blade N. edge, knife.

• blame V. condemn, criticize, reprove, accuse,
  censure. *Do not condemn the person before the trial.*
  Ant. exonerate, commend, praise.

blameless ADJ. innocent, exemplary.
  Ant. guilty.

blanched ADJ. pale, white.
  Ant. darkened, stained.

bland ADJ. neutral, plain, gentle.
  Ant. pungent, biting, hot, spicy.

blank ADJ. vacant, bare, void, expressionless.
  Ant. filled, occupied, animated.

blare V. scream, yell, glare.
  Ant. whisper, murmur.

blasphemy N. sacrilege, profanity.
  Ant. reverence, worship, praise.

blast N. explosion, detonation, blowout.

blatant ADJ. shameless, obvious, brazen, flagrant.
  Ant. hidden, subtle, sly, unnoticed.

blaze N. inferno, fire, flame.

bleach V. whiten, pale.
  Ant. blacken, darken, smear.

bleak ADJ. austere, drab, unwelcoming.
  Ant. cheerful, sanguine, optimistic, rosy.

bleary ADJ. unclear, exhausted.
  Ant. clear, sharp.

bleed V. ooze, flow from, exude.

blemish n. stain, flaw, detect, mark, spot.
  Ant. decoration, ornament, purity.

blend V. mix, combine, harmonize.
  Ant. extract, precipitate, separate.

bless V. thank, sanctify.
  Ant. curse, malign.

blight N. disease, affliction, sickness; —v. destroy,
  damage, ruin.
  Ant. advancement, growth; help.

blind ADJ. sightless, unseeing, dull, unperceptive.
  Ant. sighted, perceptive, seeing.

blink V., N. wink, twinkle, flicker, flash.
Ant. stare.

blithe ADJ. jolly, happy, joyful, animated, gay.
Ant. miserable, unhappy, cheerless.

bloat V. inflate, fatten, distend, blow up.
Ant. deflate, empty.

blockade V. block, attack; —N. barrier, wall.
Ant. escape, free, release.

blockhead N. dullard, idiot, jerk, dope.
Ant. genius.

blond ADJ. fair, flaxen.
Ant. dark, brunette.

blood N. bloodshed, gore, murder; heritage, ancestry.

bloodcurding ADJ. horrible, frightening, awful.
Ant. harmless, peaceful, calm.

bloodless ADJ. pale, insensitive.
Ant. ruddy, sanguine, passionate.

bloodline N. lineage, ancestry.

bloodshed N. massacre, slaughter, warfare.
Ant. peace, tranquility.

bloodstained ADJ. bloody, smeared.

bloody ADJ. bloodstained, murderous, cruel.
Ant. bloodless.

bloom V. blossom, flower.
Ant. wilt, die, fade.

blossom V. flower, flourish, bloom.
Ant. wilt, wither, shrink, fade.

blot V. stain, smear, spot, blemish, flaw.
Ant. clean, cleanse, whiten, restore.

blotch N. spot, blemish, splotch, red mark.

blow V. slap, hit, shock, stroke; explode, inflate.
Ant. embrace, caress.

blowhard N. braggart, boaster.

blowout N. explosion, blast.

blowup N. outburst, blast.

bludgeon V. intimidate, beat, pummel, assault.
Ant. embrace, caress.

blue ADJ. azure; depressed, unhappy, sad, melancholic.
Ant. happy, glad, mirthful.

blue-blooded ADJ. noble, aristocratic, royal.
Ant. common, poor, lowly.

blueprint N. design, plan.

blues N. gloom, depression.
Ant. happiness, elation, mirth.

bluff N. cliff, escarpment; —v. ruse, challenge; —ADJ. impolite, bold, rude, frank, outspoken, open.
Ant. polite, reserved, polished, courteous.

blunder N. error, mistake, faux pas.
Ant. success.

blunt ADJ. dull, direct, impolite, rude.
Ant. tactful, subtle, polite.

blur V. dim, obscure, stain, smudge.
Ant. clear, illuminate.

blurt V. exclaim, shout.
Ant. whisper, murmur.

blush V. color, redden.
Ant. pale, whiten.

board V. harbor, take, lodge.
Ant. exit, leave.

boast V. brag, exaggerate.
Ant. belittle, depreciate, speak modestly.

bodily ADJ. personal, physical, corporal.
Ant. spiritual, ethereal.

body N. group, assembly, quantity; cadaver, corpse.
Ant. singular; spirit, soul.

boggle V. stagger, bewilder, surprise.
Ant. clarify, explain.

bogus ADJ. false, worthless, phony, sham.
Ant. bona fide, authentic, genuine, legitimate.

boil V. bubble, simmer, stew, cook.
Ant. freeze.

boisterous ADJ. vociferous, noisy, loud, rowdy.
Ant. serene, calm, pacified.

bold ADJ. fearless, brave, daring.
Ant. timid, fearful, cowardly, shy.

bold-faced ADJ. impudent, shameless.
Ant. respectful, honorable.

bolster V. support, sustain, help.
Ant. hurt, harm.

bombardment N. barrage, bombing.

bombastic ADJ. sonorous, rhetorical, overdone.
Ant. subtle, quiet, subdued.

bona fide ADJ. legitimate, honorable, genuine,
authentic.
Ant. bogus, false, worthless, phony, sham,
illegitimate.

bonanza N. jackpot, prize, gold mine.

bond N. tie, attachment, convenant, commitment,
contract.

bonny ADJ. good, beautiful.
Ant. unattractive, ugly.

bonus N. gift, reward, bounty.
Ant. fine, penalty, levy.

booby trap N. pitfall, trap, lair.

book N. work, publication, text, novel, tome.

bookish ADJ. studious, pedantic, scholarly.
Ant. illiterate, unschooled.

boom N. rumble, blast, thunder, roar, prosperity.

boon N. advantage, fortune, luck, benevolence.
Ant. disadvantage, impoverishment.

boor N. barbarian, philistine, boob, clown.
Ant. aristocrat, sophisticate.

boost V. promote, elevate, lift, increase.
Ant. lower, hinder.

boot V. eject, dismiss.
Ant. welcome, accept.

booty N. plunder, reward, treasure, bounty.

bop V. blow, hit.
Ant. embrace, caress.

border N. edge, periphery, frontier, boundary, limit.
Ant. interior, center, inside.

• **bore** V. tire, weary, fatigue; drill, perforate. *An interminable lecture can tire even the most interested student.*
Ant. interest, amuse, amaze, stimulate.

boredom N. ennui, tedium, tiredness.
Ant. excitement, stimulation, amusement, interest.

borrow V. use, have access to, have use of, have a loan of.
Ant. repay, pay back, return, reimburse, settle up.

bosom N. heart, chest, breast, feelings.

boss N. director, employer, supervisor, chief, leader.
Ant. employee, worker, subordinate.

botch V. fumble, wreck, ruin, mix up, mess up.
Ant. succeed, perfect.

bother V. disturb, irritate, annoy.
Ant. solace, aid, comfort.

bottom N. base, depth; —ADJ. lowest, undermost.
Ant. top, height, pinnacle, zenith.

bounce V. rebound, jump, spring, eject.

bound N. bounce, limit, boundary, border; —ADJ. destined, compelled.
Ant. extended, enlarged, liberated.

boundary N. border, frontier, limit, outline.
Ant. interior, inside, center.

bountiful ADJ. plentiful, generous, fulsome.
Ant. lacking, empty.

bouquet N. fragrance, compliment, nosegay.

bout N. contest, match, fight.
Ant. agreement, harmony.

bow V. bend, stoop, yield, give in, succumb.
Ant. stand, refuse.

bowdlerize V. censor, edit, revise.
Ant. free, liberate.

box N. predicament, flap; carton, crate.

boy N. youngster, kid, youth.
Ant. elder, adult, man, grown-up.

boycott v. blackball, strike, avoid.
Ant. support.

boyfriend n. beau, friend, male companion, significant other.

brace v. support, crutch, prop.

bracket n. class, category; support, prop.

brag v. boast, exaggerate.
Ant. deprecate, depreciate.

braggart n. bragger, blowhard.

brain n. mind, intelligence, sense, intellect.

brainstorm n. inspiration, idea.
Ant. stagnation, block.

branch n. division, part, limb, offshoot.
Ant. whole, entire, trunk.

brand n. manufacture, kind, trademark; —v. mark, stamp.

brandish v. flourish, display.

brash ADJ. tactless, presumptuous, brazen.
Ant. tactful, subtle, subdued.

brave ADJ. fearless, heroic, brave-hearted, steadfast, courageous, valiant.
Ant. cowardly, timid, fearful.

brawl n. riot, dispute, disturbance, fight.
Ant. peace.

brawn n. strength, muscle.
Ant. weakness, frailty.

brazen ADJ. shameless, impudent, rude, bold.
Ant. modest, shy, retiring.

breach v. break, rupture, transgress, trespass.
Ant. repair, restore, restoration.

bread n. food, living, money.

breadth n. expanse, width.
Ant. length.

break v. shatter, smash, fracture, split; disobey, collapse; —n. breach, interruption.
Ant. repair, mend, join.

breakable ADJ. fragile, delicate.
Ant. unbreakable, indestructible.

breakage N. destruction, wreckage, damage.
Ant. building, construction.

breakdown N. failure, collapse, decay; analysis.

breakneck ADJ. fast, speedy, quick.
Ant. slow, calm, easy.

breakout N. escape, flight, getaway.

breast N. heart, chest, bosom.

breath N. inhalation, respiration, exhalation.

breathe V. respire, inhale, exhale.

breathless ADJ. airless, amazed.
Ant. calm, relaxed.

breed V. father, create, conceive, bear, propagate.

breeze N. wind, air, zephyr.
Ant. stagnation, still.

brevity N. succinctness, concision, terseness.
Ant. wordiness, verbosity, length, expansion,
elaboration, amplification.

bribe N. payoff, inducement.

bridal N. wedding, marriage.

bridle V. restraint, control, check.
Ant. free, liberate, loosen.

bridge N. span, viaduct, overpass.

• brief ADJ. temporary, short, concise, succinct. *A
temporary electrical outage delayed our departure.*
Ant. long, involved, permanent.

bright ADJ. shining, brilliant, radiant, luminous.
Ant. dull, obscure, dim, dark, gloomy.

• brilliant ADJ. radiant, bright, shining; gifted,
intelligent, talented. *The radiant diamond brought
gasps of admiration from onlookers.*
Ant. dark, dull, dim, stupid.

brim N. margin, border, edge, lip.
Ant. interior, center.

brimming ADJ. full, bordering, verging.
Ant. empty.

bring V. carry, take, bear; cause.
Ant. set down, abandon, give, send.

brink N. verge, limit, border, edge.
Ant. interior, center, heart.

brisk ADJ. energetic, lively, agile.
Ant. calm, reserved, lethargic.

bristle V. teem, anger.
Ant. calm, subdue.

brittle ADJ. delicate, thin, fragile, weak, breakable.
Ant. strong, durable, unbreakable.

broach V. introduce, open, raise, bring up, put forth.
Ant. close, retract, pull back.

broad ADJ. wide, large, sizable, considerable,
expansive, liberal, progressive, open-minded.
Ant. thin, narrow, refined.

broad-minded ADJ. liberal, unprejudiced, tolerant,
open-minded.
Ant. close-minded, intolerant, prejudiced.

broil V. burn, cook.

broke ADJ. poor, impoverished.
Ant. wealthy, rich.

broken-down ADJ. shabby, old.
Ant. new, remodeled, rehabilitated.

broker N. go-between, agent.
Ant. principal.

bromide N. cliché, saying.

brood N. offspring, young, litter; —V. worry, dwell
on.
Ant. forget, ignore.

brook N. branch; stream, creek.

brotherhood N. friendship, fellowship, community,
camaraderie.
Ant. hatred.

browbeat V. intimidate, threaten.
Ant. console, help.

browse V. scan, skim, glance at.
Ant. study, examine.

bruise v. wound, injure.
Ant. heal, help.

bruit v. noise, advertise.
Ant. quiet, calm.

brush v. shave, skim, graze; whisk, broom, scrub.

brusque ADJ. abrupt, rough, blunt, curt.
Ant. personable, courteous, gentle.

brutal ADJ. savage, barbaric, mean, cruel.
Ant. sensitive, kind, gentle, rational.

brutalize v. attack, injure.
Ant. help, aid, heal.

bucket N. pail, container.

buckle v. clasp, fasten; collapse, give way, fail, yield.
Ant. unbuckle, loosen, unfasten; withstand.

bucolic ADJ. rustic, country.
Ant. modern, new.

buddy N. associate, friend, pal, fellow.
Ant. enemy, stranger, foe, opponent.

budget N. quantity, projection, money, allowance.

buffet N. cabinet, counter, sideboard; —v. beat, slap, hit.

buffoon N. fool, clown, joker, comedian.

bug N. germ, defect; —v. annoy, irritate, bother.
Ant. leave, let alone.

• build v. assemble, construct, erect, make. *The children learned to assemble their own playhouse.*
Ant. destruct, destroy, tear down.

building N. edifice, house, structure.

built-in ADJ. constituent, incorporated, inherent, innate, natural.
Ant. unincorporated, unnatural.

bulge N. lump, swelling, enlargement; —v. swell, balloon, protrude.

bulk N. magnitude, quantity, size, volume.

bulky ADJ. huge, massive, oversized, clumsy, awkward.
Ant. delicate, small.

bull N. nonsense, stupidity.
Ant. rationale, logic.

bulldoze V. push, intimidate.

bullheaded ADJ. obstinate, stubborn, difficult.
Ant. flexible, compliant, reasonable.

bully V. intimidate, harass; —N. persecutor, heckler, tormentor.

bum N. hobo, drifter, beggar.

bumbling ADJ. unskillful, awkward, clumsy.
Ant. skilled, adept.

bump V. hit, strike, knock, collide.

• **bunch** N. group, crowd, cluster, bundle. *A group of teenagers stood in line for tickets.*
Ant. single, solitaire.

bundle N. packet; —V. bunch, package, group.
Ant. separate, distinguish.

bungle V. botch, mess up.
Ant. succeed, fix.

buoyant ADJ. floating, airy, cheerful, bright, gay, lighthearted.
Ant. morose, dark, melancholy.

burden V. worry, trouble, load, laden.
Ant. disburden, unencumber, unload.

burgeon V. rise, bloom.
Ant. sink, wilt.

burglarize V. rob, thieve, break in.

burial N. interment, entombment, funeral.

burlesque N. mockery, satire.
Ant. encomium, praise, laudation.

burly ADJ. husky, muscular, robust, hefty.
Ant. skinny, scrawny, weak, puny.

burn V. blaze, blame, fire, bake.
Ant. extinguish, put out.

burning ADJ. pressing, imperative; blazing, afire.
Ant. inessential, unnecessary.

burnish V. gloss, polish, buff.
Ant. stain, darken.

burrow N. hole, den, tunnel.

burst V. explode, pop, blow up.
Ant. implode.

bursting ADJ. eager, full, exploding.
Ant. unenthusiastic.

bury V. conceal, cover, hide, inter.
Ant. uncover, reveal.

• business N. firm, company, concern, corporation. *Her firm offered excellent health benefits.*
Ant. unemployment, hobby, avocation.

businesslike ADJ. efficient, serious, methodical.
Ant. inefficient, unprofessional, amateurish.

businessperson N. dealer, agent, employee, manager.

bust V. break, ruin, arrest; —N. failure; statue, chest, bosom.
Ant. fix, restore.

bustle V. hurry, rush, stir.
Ant. sit, wait.

• busy ADJ. hardworking, engaged, occupied, crowded.
The hardworking weavers produced six carpets per week.
Ant. unoccupied, indolent, inactive.

busybody N. snoop, gossip, interloper, intruder.

but ADV. still, however, moreover, besides, nevertheless, though; —CONJ. yet, unless, except, notwithstanding.

butcher V. annihilate, destroy, murder.
Ant. save, rescue.

butt N. end, bottom; —V. thrust, adjoin.
Ant. top, height.

buxom ADJ. chesty, voluptuous.
Ant. flat-chested, boyish.

buy V. obtain, purchase, acquire, believe.
Ant. sell.

buzz N. gossip, hum.

by ADJ. close to, near.
Ant. far, distant.

bygone ADJ. old-fashioned, passé.
Ant. modern, new, updated.

bypass v. skirt, avoid, go around.
Ant. confront, encounter, face.

by-product N. derivative, result, outcome.

byword N. motto, proverb, slogan.

C

cabinet N. cupboard, dresser, breakfront.

cache .v. hide, conceal; —N. storehouse, stockroom.
  Ant. reveal.

cackle V. laugh, shout, exclaim, tattle.

cacophonous ADJ. noisy, inharmonious.
  Ant. quiet, harmonious.

cadaver N. body, corpse.
  Ant. spirit, soul.

cadence N. rhythm, speed, beat.

cafe N. restaurant, coffee bar, snack bar.

cage V. enclose, trap.
  Ant. release, free, liberate.

cajole V. lure, beguile, humor, coax.
  Ant. repulse, repel.

calamity N. disaster, mishap, misfortune, distress.
  Ant. happiness, benefit, profit.

calculate V. figure, estimate, consider, weigh,
  compute.
  Ant. assume, guess, estimate.

calendar N. schedule, program.

call V. shout, exclaim, address, name, summon.
  Ant. listen, stifle, restrain.

callous ADJ. indifferent, insensible, unfeeling, hard.
  Ant. kind, sympathetic.

calm ADJ. collected, reserved, tranquil, quiet, sedate.
  Ant. fierce, angry, agitated.

calumniate V. libel, slander, defame, lie.
  Ant. praise, commend, sympathize.

camouflage V. disguise, cover, hide.
  Ant. reveal, uncover, show.

can V. know how to, dismiss, preserve.

cancel V. erase, delete, annul, abolish.
  Ant. uphold, approve, confirm.

candid ADJ. frank, honest, truthful, simple, straightforward.
Ant. insincere, shrewd, hidden.

candidate N. applicant, contestant, aspirant, hopeful.

candle N. taper, wick.

candy N. sweets, confection.

candor N. frankness, sincerity, openness.
Ant. insincerity, deceitfulness.

cane N. stick, pole, club, rod, staff.

canny ADJ. sharp, economical.
Ant. slow, dull.

canon N. regulation, standard, precept, rule, law.

canopy N. tent, awning, covering.

cant N. jargon, argot.

cantankerous ADJ. irritable, mean, bad-tempered.
Ant. good-natured, happy, sanguine, kindly, friendly.

canvass V. survey, campaign, solicit.

canyon N. arroyo, gorge, valley, ravine.

cap V., N. cover, top.
Ant. uncover, uncap.

- **capable** ADJ. skilled, competent, able. *One worker proved more skilled than the other.*
Ant. incapable, unable.

capacious ADJ. full, roomy.
Ant. narrow, confining.

- **capacity** N. content, aptitude, capability, faculty, talent. *The factory had the capability of doubling its production.*
Ant. incapacity, smallness, incompetence.

caper N. adventure, antic, prank, gambol.

capital ADJ. important, best, principal, first; —N. money, principal, property.
Ant. last, unimportant, trivial.

capitalism N. free enterprise, entrepreneurship.
Ant. communism, socialism.

capitalize v. finance, benefit.
Ant. forego, give up.

capitulate v. succumb, give in to.
Ant. withstand, refuse, hold out.

caprice N. fancy, whim.
Ant. necessity, essential.

capricious ADJ. fanciful, whimsical, odd, inconstant, inconsistent.
Ant. reliable, steady, dependable.

capsize v. turn upside down, overturn, upset.
Ant. stabilize, balance, steady.

captain N. leader, supervisor, director, commander.

captivate v. enthrall, charm, fascinate, enchant.
Ant. repel, offend, disgust, bore.

capture v. seize, catch, trap, take, apprehend.
Ant. release, free, lose.

carcass N. body, cadaver.

cardinal ADJ. fundamental, capital, principal, important, essential.
Ant. negligible, insignificant, minor.

care N. anxiety, worry, concern, attention, heed.
Ant. negligence, omission, carelessness.

career N. job, vocation, occupation, calling.

• careful ADJ. vigilant, cautious, concerned, meticulous.
It pays to remain vigilant after dark.
Ant. negligent, careless, unconcerned.

careless ADJ. unthoughtful, reckless, negligent, thoughtless, uncaring.
Ant. thoughtful, attentive, wary.

caress v. kiss, embrace, hug.
Ant. buffet, annoy, spurn.

carnage N. massacre, destruction, slaughter, havoc.

carnal ADJ. worldly, concupiscent, lascivious, physical.
Ant. moral, spiritual, intellectual.

carnivorous ADJ. meat-eating.

carouse v. revel, celebrate, party.

carp v. quibble, scold, nag, berate.
Ant. agree.

carpet N. rug, mat, flooring.

carry V. move, transfer, bear, bring.
Ant. drop, leave, put down.

case N. situation, circumstance, occurrence, instance, example, condition.

cash N. coinage, currency, notes.

cashier N. teller, bursar, banker.

cast V. throw, direct, toss, pitch.
Ant. catch, receive.

castigate V. call down.
Ant. praise, laud.

castle N. estate, kingdom, manor, chateau.
Ant. hovel, shack, shed, lean-to, bungalow.

castrate V. sterilize, emasculate.

• **casual** ADJ. careless, relaxed, negligent, unintentional. *His careless dress was inappropriate for the interview.*
Ant. calculated, deliberate, intentional.

casualty N. disaster; injured, wounded, victim, dead.
Ant. prosperity, good fortune, good health.

cataclysm N. flood, disaster, revolution.
Ant. calm, peacefulness.

catalyst N. leavening, yeast, accelerator.
Ant. hindrance.

catastrophe N. disaster, calamity, cataclysm, accident.
Ant. success, blessing, prosperity.

catch V. capture, grasp, seize, snare, trap.

categorical ADJ. definite.
Ant. lose, release, miss.

categorize V. class, assort, organize.

cater to V. humor, baby.
Ant. rebuff, reject.

catharsis N. cleansing, purification, purge.
Ant. sin, regression.

catholic ADJ. universal, wide-reaching, all-embracing.
Ant. parochial, narrow-minded, provincial, insular.

● **cause** N. origin, reason, motive, determinant, necessity, justification. *The origin of the problem lay in his eating habits.*
Ant. outcome, consequence, result.

caustic ADJ. harsh, disagreeable, malicious, mean, spiteful.
Ant. kind, gentle, caring.

caution N. care, acumen, foresight, wariness.
Ant. carelessness, heedlessness.

cave N. hole, cavern, grotto.

caveat N. warning.

cavern N. cave, grotto.

cavil V. quibble, argue, dispute.
Ant. agree, harmonize.

cavity N. depression, cave, hollow, opening.
Ant. swelling, elevation, bulge, protuberance.

cavort V. gambol, revel.

cease V. stop, terminate, end, quit, desist, discontinue.
Ant. continue, persist, begin.

ceaseless ADJ. neverending, continual.
Ant. temporary, short-term, ending, terminal.

celebrate V. honor, glorify, observe, commemorate.
Ant. ignore, dishonor, neglect.

celebrity N. star, idol, fame.
Ant. nobody, commoner.

celestial ADJ. heavenly, angelic, unearthly, ethereal.
Ant. earthly, terrestrial, mortal.

censor V. screen, suppress, edit, delete, ban.
Ant. publish, advertise, release.

censure V. deplore, blame, disapprove, criticize.
Ant. approve, praise, commend.

center N. middle, core, nucleus, heart.
Ant. edge, rim, brink, brim, periphery.

central ADJ. principal, dominant, fundamental, essential, focal, middle.
Ant. peripheral, secondary, incidental.

cerebral ADJ. mental, intellectual.
Ant. carnal, bodily.

ceremony N. service, ritual, rite.
Ant. informality.

certain ADJ. sure, assured, confident, reliable, positive.
Ant. uncertain, unsure, indefinite.

• **certainly** ADV. absolutely, definitely, surely. *The leader is absolutely committed to the new program.*
Ant. uncertainly, doubtfully, questionably.

certainty N. actuality, fact, sureness, truth.
Ant. uncertainty, doubt, unreliability.

certify V. authenticate, verify, validate, affirm, substantiate, guarantee.
Ant. discredit, negate, deny.

chafe V. rub, abrade, irritate.
Ant. soothe, pacify, calm.

chagrin N. embarrassment, irritation, annoyance, shame.
Ant. rapture, delight, triumph.

chain N. series, sequence, row, succession.

• **challenge** N. contest, rival, defiance, obstacle. *The two managers looked upon the job as a contest.*
Ant. acceptance, agreement, victory.

chance N. hazard, luck, fortune, fortuity, risk, opportunity.
Ant. inevitability, certainty, design.

• **change** V. modify, vary, alter, exchange; —N. alteration, modification, variation. *We can modify the design to reduce friction.*
Ant. steadiness, certainty, stability.

chant N. singing, song, hymn.

chaotic ADJ. confusing, tumultuous, anomalous.
Ant. organized, ordered, methodical, systematic.

character N. disposition, nature, personality, honesty, integrity, reference, reputation.

characterize V. distinguish, call.

charge V. accuse, blame, indict, attack, price, sell for.
Ant. excuse, absolve, retreat.

charisma N. attraction, charm, allure, influence.
Ant. unpleasantness, offensiveness.

charity N. giving, generosity, beneficence,
philanthropy.
Ant. selfishness, stinginess.

charm v. enchant, enthrall, beguile, please, fascinate.
Ant. disgust, repulse.

charming ADJ. captivating, delightful, ravishing,
fascinating, pleasing.
Ant. disagreeable, disgusting, offensive.

chart N., v. diagram, map, plan.

chary ADJ. wary, economical.
Ant. careless, generous, wasteful.

chase v. pursue, seek, track, stalk, hunt.
Ant. run, flee, elude.

chaste ADJ. simple, innocent, pure, neat,
uncorrupted.
Ant. corrupt, coarse, sinful, impure.

chastise v. punish, discipline, correct, reprimand.
Ant. reward, praise, forgive.

chastity N. purity, virtue, decency, modesty.
Ant. immodesty, impurity, indecency.

chatter v. converse, talk, rattle, babble, gab.

cheap ADJ. inexpensive, common, shabby, inferior.
Ant. costly, valuable, worthy.

cheat v. deceive, trick, con, swindle, defraud.
Ant. deal honorably, act with integrity.

check v. stop, examine, hinder, moderate.
Ant. allow, help, facilitate, release.

cheer N. happiness, cheerfulness, joy, merriment,
gaiety; —v. comfort, gladden.
Ant. sadness, melancholy, jeer, boo, discourage.

chew v. bite, nibble, masticate.

chic ADJ. fashionable, stylish, modish, elegant.
Ant. out of fashion, unattractive.

chide v. call down, scold, admonish, rebuke, criticize.
Ant. commend, praise.

chief ADJ. principal, paramount, essential, first;
—N. director, leader, boss.
Ant. secondary, minor; disciple, follower.

child N. youngster, juvenile, kid, youth, minor.
Ant. adult, grown-up.

childish ADJ. immature, infantile, childlike.
Ant. mature, sophisticated, adult.

childlike ADJ. babyish, immature, childish.
Ant. adult, grown-up, mature.

chilly ADJ. cool, cold.
Ant. hot, warm, balmy.

chime V. ring, clang, peal; —N. alarm, buzzer, bell.

chip N. piece, fragment, bit.
Ant. whole, entirety, totality.

chivalrous ADJ. gallant, brave, valiant, heroic,
courteous.
Ant. cowardly, timid, fearful.

choice N. selection, preference, alternative, option;
—ADJ. superior, exceptional, select.
Ant. voteless, choiceless, inferior.

choke V. gag, strangle, suffocate, stifle.

choose V. pick, select, elect, decide upon.
Ant. discard, refuse, decline.

chop V. cut, mince, hew.

chore N. work, task, duty.
Ant. relaxation, free time, leisure.

chronic ADJ. lingering, persistent, continuing,
habitual, sustained.
Ant. temporary, occasional.

chubby ADJ. fat, plump, hefty, overweight.
Ant. slender, slim, trim, thin.

chuckle V. laugh, giggle, snicker.

chunk N. block, hunk, large piece.

church N. faith, temple, synagogue, religion, theology.

churn V. boil, agitate.

cinema N. movie, show, theater.

circle N. disk, ring, society, clique, class.

circuit N. revolution, circle, course, orbit.

circulate V. flow, pass, move, travel.
Ant. clog, clot, coagulate.

circumscribe V. confine, limit, enclose, bound.
Ant. free, open, expand.

circumspect ADJ. heedful, careful, observant, discreet.
Ant. audacious, bold, careless.

circumstance N. situation, incident, occurrence,
happening, fact.

circumvent V. avoid, evade, dodge, thwart.
Ant. engage, take on, meet head-on.

citation N. recognition, ticket, notice.

cite V. name, summon, call, quote, mention.
Ant. ignore, neglect, disregard.

citizen N. native, subject, dweller, inhabitant, resident.
Ant. alien, non-native, foreigner.

city N. municipality, town, village, urban setting.

civic ADJ. public, civil, municipal.

civil ADJ. public, courteous, gracious, polite.
Ant. rude, impolite, uncivil, ungracious.

civilization N. culture, society.
Ant. nature, anarchy.

• claim V. contend, assert, maintain, declare. *They
contend that illness is hereditary.*
Ant. release, deny.

clamor N. shouting, noise, uproar, roar.
Ant. serenity, quiet, silence.

clan N. family, group.

clandestine ADJ. secret, hidden, concealed, covert.
Ant. open, unconcealed, overt.

• clarify V. define, explain, make clear, elucidate,
illuminate. *Please define your key terms.*
Ant. diffuse, complicate, muddle.

clarity N. lucidity, intelligibility, transparency.
Ant. opacity, murkiness, dullness, ambiguity,
unintelligibility.

clasp V. hold, clutch, hug, embrace; —N. buckle, hook.
Ant. release, unhook, let go.

class N. rank, order, classification, group, grade.

classic ADJ. vintage, typical, elegant, simple, refined.
Ant. modern, new, fresh, avant-garde.

clean ADJ. cleansed, purified, stainless, pure.
Ant. dirty, foul, impure.

clear ADJ. lucid, transparent, vivid, bright, apparent, obvious, definite, straightforward.
Ant. dim, obscure, dark.

cleave V. cut, divide, hew, chop.
Ant. join, affix, attach, link.

clergyman N. preacher, priest, chaplain, rabbi.

clerk N. assistant, helper, secretary.

clever ADJ. bright, capable, skillful, sharp, keen, quick.
Ant. slow, dull, awkward.

click V. snap, succeed, relate.

climate N. aura, atmosphere, environment.

climax N. peak, summit, culmination, pinnacle.
Ant. bottom, nadir, base, depth.

climb V. ascend, scale, rise.
Ant. descend, repel, descent.

cling V. hold onto, grip, hug, adhere to.
Ant. repel, fend off, ward off.

clinic N. medical facility, hospital, health center.

clock V. time; —N. watch, chronometer.

close ADJ. near, immediate, nearby, adjoining, adjacent, attached; —V. shut, conclude, finish, terminate, end.
Ant. far, distant, detached; open, release, begin.

closure N. end, conclusion, termination.
Ant. initiation, beginning, prelude, opening.

clothe V. dress, robe, cloak.
Ant. disrobe, undress, unclothe.

cloudy ADJ. indefinite, blurred, dim, obscure, overcast, sunless, gloomy.
Ant. clear, sunny, definite.

clown N. fool, comedian, jester, entertainer.

clumsy ADJ. awkward, ungainly, inept, ungraceful.
Ant. skilled, graceful, dexterous.

clutch V. hold, grasp, embrace, seize.
Ant. release, free, liberate, give up.

clutter N. mess, disorder, chaos.
Ant. order, organization, neatness, cleanliness.

coach N. mentor, trainer, teacher, instructor.

coarse ADJ. crude, rough, vulgar, unrefined.
Ant. refined, sophisticated, polite, civil.

coax V. cajole, entice, flatter, invite.
Ant. bully, force, deter.

coddle V. pamper, indulge, spoil.

coerce V. force, hijack.
Ant. convince, persuade.

cogent ADJ. valid, powerful, sound, persuasive.
Ant. weak, ineffective, unconvincing.

cogitate V. reason, consider, ponder, think.
Ant. neglect, ignore, forget.

cognizant ADJ. aware, alert.
Ant. asleep, unaware, unattentive.

cohere V. bond, join, conform.
Ant. refuse, revolt, break apart.

cohort N. follower, associate.
Ant. enemy, opponent.

coiffure N. hairdo, hairstyle.

coincide V. agree, correspond, synchronize, match, concur.
Ant. disagree, differ, clash.

cold ADJ. frigid, cool, distant, aloof, reserved, passionless.
Ant. hot, warm, passionate, zealous, balmy.

collaborate V. concur, cooperate, unite, conspire.
Ant. disagree, dispute.

collapse v. faint, give way, fail, break in.
Ant. rise, recover, revive.

collect v. obtain, summon, receive, assemble, compose.
Ant. spread, disburse, scatter, disperse, dispense.

collide v. crash, hit, bump.
Ant. miss, avert.

colloquial ADJ. conversational, informal, familiar.
Ant. formal, standard, correct.

color N. tone, tint, hue.

colorful ADJ. vivid, impressive, bright, picturesque.

colossal ADJ. gigantic, enormous, giant, huge, immense.
Ant. bland, unimpressive, dark.

comb v. brush, scour.

combat N. contest, battle, fight, struggle.
Ant. agreement, peace, truce.

• **combination** N. mixing, mixture, blend, association, union. *A mixing of three coffee types produced the most savory blend.*
Ant. detachment, separation, division.

combine v. mix, join, blend, connect.
Ant. detach, separate, divide.

combustible ADJ. flammable, explosive, burnable.
Ant. incombustible, fireproof, nonexplosive.

come v. advance, near, proceed, approach.
Ant. go, depart, leave.

comfort v. help, support, encourage, console.
Ant. torment, aggravate, irritate.

comical ADJ. laughable, amusing, funny, humorous.
Ant. sad, pathetic, sober.

command v. direct, order, instruct, lead.
Ant. comply, obey.

commemorate v. memorialize, celebrate, observe.
Ant. neglect, forget, dishonor.

commence v. start, begin, initiate, dawn.
Ant. cease, finish, end.

commend v. approve, praise, compliment, extol.
Ant. reprimand, admonish, rebuke.

comment n. remark, explanation, observation; —v.
observe, note, remark.

commerce n. business, trade, exchange.

commiserate v. feel, sympathize, empathize.
Ant. neglect, ignore, overlook.

commit v. perform, carry out, entrust, authorize,
delegate.
Ant. cease, stop, rest.

- common ADJ. mutual, shared, joined, familiar,
ordinary, everyday, average, normal, acceptable,
inferior. *Our mutual interests are best served by
cooperation.*
Ant. unusual, rare, peculiar.

commotion n. tumult, uproar, upheaval.
Ant. serenity, calm, peacefulness, order, harmony.

communal ADJ. common, joint, public, shared.
Ant. separatist, individual.

communicable ADJ. contagious, infection, catching.
Ant. noninfectious.

- communicate v. relate, express, convey, impart, tell,
disclose. *The adventurer was eager to relate his tale.*
Ant. suppress, conceal, withhold.

community n. public, society, city, town, village.

compact ADJ. packed, compressed, thick, tight; —n.
bargain, agreement, pact; —v. consolidate,
combine, compress.
Ant. diffuse, slack, loose.

companion n. friend, partner, colleague, associate.
Ant. stranger, antagonist, enemy.

- company n. establishment, business, firm, visitor,
guest, companionship, assembly, group. *The
establishment will open for business next week.*
Ant. solitude, seclusion, loneliness.

compare v. match, contrast, liken.
Ant. vary, differentiate, modify.

compassion n. pity, sympathy, kindness, tenderness.
Ant. injustice, cruelty, indifference.

compensate V. balance, recompense, reimburse, pay.
Ant. forfeit, deprive, confiscate.

- compete V. contend, contest, rival, oppose. *The athletes will contend for the prize.*
Ant. support, aid, collaborate.

competent ADJ. able, skilled, qualified, sufficient.
Ant. inept, inadequate, incompetent.

competitor N. opponent, contender, rival, contestant.
Ant. friend, ally, collaborator.

complacent ADJ. lazy, uncaring, laid back, assured, satisfied, content.
Ant. restless, dissatisfied, uneasy.

complain V. protest, fret, grumble, gripe.
Ant. commend, praise, applaud.

complaisant ADJ. obliging, amiable.
Ant. unlikable, difficult, disobedient.

complement N. supplement, completion, accompaniment.

complete ADJ. thorough, whole, finished, entire; —V. accomplish, effect, realize, conclude.
Ant. partial, deficient, incomplete, lacking; neglect, abandon, ignore, give up.

complex ADJ. compound, involved, complicated, intricate, perplexing.
Ant. simple, easy, uncomplicated, obvious.

complexity N. difficulty, complication, intricacy.
Ant. simplicity, ease, effortlessness.

compliant ADJ. obedient, obliging.
Ant. difficult, disobedient, rebellious.

compliment V. praise, recommend, felicitate, congratulate.
Ant. criticize, reprehend, reproach.

component N. element, part, piece.
Ant. whole, complex.

compose V. create, write, make, form.
Ant. destroy, break, ruin, excite, agitate.

composite ADJ. complex; —N. combination, mixture.
Ant. diverse.

- **comprehend** V. grasp, understand, perceive, know.
  He failed to grasp the importance of the message.
  Ant. misunderstand, misinterpret, err.

  compress V. squeeze, crowd, reduce, contract.
  Ant. stretch, expand, increase.

  comprise V. make up, contain, constitute, include,
  involve.
  Ant. want, lack, exclude.

  compromise N. conciliation, settlement, agreement;
  —v. agree, concede, conciliate.
  Ant. disagreement, quarrel, altercation.

- **compute** V. count, calculate, add, figure. *Please count
  the number of envelopes needed for the mailing.*
  Ant. estimate, guess, surmise.

  comrade N. associate, friend, companion.
  Ant. adversary, enemy, opponent.

  concave ADJ. hollow, sunken.
  Ant. protruding, convex.

  conceal V. cover, hide, cache.
  Ant. uncover, expose, open.

  concede V. compromise, acknowledge, admit, give in,
  yield.
  Ant. refuse, contradict, deny.

  conceit N. egotism, vanity, self-esteem, pride.
  Ant. modesty, humility, diffidence.

- **conceive** V. imagine, understand, invent, grasp. *Can
  you imagine a wingless airplane?*

  concentrate V. condense, focus, converge.
  Ant. disperse, weaken, dissipate.

- **concept** N. idea, theory, thought. *Her idea led to the
  eventual vaccine.*

- **concern** N. interest, regard, worry, anxiety. *He won
  friends by showing interest in them.*
  Ant. indifference, calm.

  concise ADJ. brief, condensed, pointed, short.
  Ant. redundant, lengthy, diffuse, repetitive.

  conclude V. terminate, end, finish, settle.
  Ant. begin, commence, start, introduce.

concoct V. develop, make up, invent, devise, fabricate.

concrete ADJ. real, tangible, solid, particular.
Ant. intangible, abstract, immaterial.

condemn V. denounce, convict, sentence, reprobate.
Ant. forgive, pardon, exonerate.

condense V. thicken, compact, shorten.
Ant. expand, increase.

● condition N. status, state, position, situation, necessity, requirement. *The status of the spacecraft will not be known for another hour.*

condone V. forgive, pardon, allow, excuse.
Ant. punish, condemn, forbid.

conduct V. manage, direct, guide, regulate; —N. demeanor, behavior, attitude.
Ant. forsake, abandon, relinquish.

conduit N. channel, pipe, instrument, means of expression.

confederate N. ally, associate; —v. join, unite.
Ant. opponent, enemy, opposition.

confer V. talk, consult, discuss, deliberate, donate, bestow.

confide V. share, entrust, whisper.
Ant. distrust, mistrust.

confidential ADJ. private, classified, restricted, intimate.
Ant. open, public, unrestricted.

confine V. bound, limit, imprison, restrict.
Ant. release, free, expand.

confirm V. substantiate, corroborate, validate, approve, affirm.
Ant. cancel, abrogate, annul.

confiscate V. seize, appropriate, take.
Ant. return, restore, give back.

conflict N. clash, friction, contention, difficulty.
Ant. peace, harmony, tranquility.

conform V. submit, yield, follow, agree.
Ant. rebel, disagree, dissent.

confound v. confuse, perplex, bewilder, puzzle, baffle.
Ant. enlighten, illuminate, inform.

confront v. encounter, face, accost.
Ant. avoid, evade.

● confuse v. bewilder, confound, perturb, mistake, mix up. *The evidence may bewilder even the most expert detective.*
Ant. enlighten, inform, illuminate.

congenial ADJ. gracious, friendly, agreeable, grateful.
Ant. disagreeable, unfriendly, unsympathetic.

congest v. fill, crowd, choke, clog.
Ant. empty, relieve.

congregate v. gather, assemble, meet, collect, flock.
Ant. scatter, disperse, separate.

conjecture N. guess, speculation, presumption, hypothesis, theory.
Ant. fact, certainty, truth.

● connect v. attach, associate, relate, unite. *Be sure to attach the safety latch.*
Ant. disconnect, disjoin.

connive v. plot, plan.

conquer v. gain, triumph, overcome, defeat.
Ant. lose, surrender, give up, yield.

● conscious ADJ. aware, sensible, awake, purposeful, intentional. *He was aware of this important responsibility.*
Ant. asleep, ignorant, unaware, insensible.

consecrate v. sanctify, devote.
Ant. desecrate, ignore.

consecutive ADJ. sequential, next, succeeding, subsequent, ensuing.
Ant. random, alternate.

consensus N. unanimity, opinion, group feeling.
Ant. disagreement.

consent N. permission, acceptance, agreement; —v. permit, allow, agree.
Ant. deny, refuse, withhold.

- **consequence** N. result, impact, effect, importance, significance. *As a result of her actions, the child was saved.*
  Ant. cause, source, origin.

  conservative ADJ. right-wing, orthodox, reactionary, conventional, traditional.
  Ant. liberal, left-wing, unorthodox.

  conserve V. preserve, save, keep, retain.
  Ant. waste, discard.

- **consider** V. reflect upon, study, deliberate, inspect, examine. *I hope you will study your choices more thoroughly.*
  Ant. ignore, neglect, dismiss.

- **considerable** ADJ. much, important, big, great, noteworthy, worthwhile. *There was much work to be done.*
  Ant. insignificant, unimportant, little, minor.

- **consideration** N. kindness, thoughtfulness, esteem, empathy; payment, deposit. *Her kindness won many friends for the company.*
  Ant. carelessness, disregard, neglect.

  consist V. lie, reside, dwell, exist.

- **consistent** ADJ. invariable, constant, unchanging, same. *The scientists reached invariable results, no matter what the temperature.*
  Ant. random, inconsistent, unreliable.

  consolation N. comfort, solace, sympathy.
  Ant. discouragement, condemnation, discomfort.

  conspicuous ADJ. prominent, obvious, noticeable, visible.
  Ant. invisible, tactful, inconspicuous.

  constant ADJ. stable, invariable, steady, permanent.
  Ant. unreliable, inconstant, variable.

  constitute V. compose, form, create, organize, appoint, authorize, delegate.

  construct V. make, build, form, erect, produce.
  Ant. destroy, break, demolish.

  construe V. interpret, explain, translate.
  Ant. confuse, mislead.

consult v. discuss, confer.

consume v. devour, waste, exhaust, destroy, annihilate.
Ant. collect, store, gather.

contact N. meeting, contingence, touch; —v. reach, touch.
Ant. avoid.

contagious ADJ. communicable, catching, spreading.
Ant. noninfectious.

contain v. hold, embody, encompass, compose, have.
Ant. release, let go.

contaminate v. poison, spoil, dirty, pollute.
Ant. clean, purify, cure.

contemplate v. ponder, consider, reflect, meditate.
Ant. disregard, neglect, reject.

contemporary ADJ. concurrent, coexistent, existing, related, simultaneous, present.
Ant. outdated, old, unrelated.

contempt N. disrespect, hatred, derision, scorn.
Ant. respect, praise, regard, admiration.

contend v. compete, argue, oppose, fright.
Ant. cease, halt, abandon.

contest N. fight, dispute, challenge, competition; —v. oppose, challenge, dispute.
Ant. calm, peace; relinquish, resign, forsake.

continual ADJ. eternal, timeless, unending, everlasting.
Ant. interrupted, uncertain, broken.

continue v. go on, resume, sustain, persist, advance, proceed.
Ant. complete, stop, finish.

contract v. shorten, diminish, condense, reduce; —N. agreement, promise, covenant.
Ant. lengthen, enlarge, extend.

contradict v. dispute, resist, oppose, deny.
Ant. agree, verify, endorse.

contrary ADJ. opposite, conflicting, adverse, antagonistic.
Ant. similar, homogeneous, like.

contrast V. differentiate, differ, distinguish; —N. distinction, difference, incongruity.
Ant. similarity, agreement, likeness.

contribute V. donate, share, give, help.
Ant. neglect, withhold, ignore, oppose.

● control N. authority, management, administration, command; —V. direct, manage, administer, dominate, rule. *The student president had the authority to hire several assistants.*
Ant. abandon, relinquish, quit.

controversy N. quarrel, dispute, argument.
Ant. agreement, patience, forbearance.

convene V. assemble, meet.
Ant. adjourn, disperse, scatter.

● convenient ADJ. accessible, handy, available. *The right tools were easily accessible for the job.*
Ant. unsuitable, inaccessible, useless.

convention N. meeting, conference, assembly.

conventional ADJ. accepted, customary, usual, conforming.
Ant. informal, irregular, unusual.

conversation N. talk, discussion, chat, chatter, intercourse, dialogue.

converse V. talk, speak, visit.

convert V. transform, transfigure, change, alter, modify.
Ant. retain, keep, maintain.

convey V. express, communicate, impart, transfer, transmit.
Ant. preserve, keep, retain.

conviction N. sureness, belief, position.
Ant. disbelief, apostasy.

convince V. persuade, satisfy, assure.
Ant. warn, dissuade, deprecate.

cook V. prepare, boil, broil, fry, bake.

cool ADJ. calm, nonchalant, distant, reserved, cold, remote.
Ant. warm, sunny, passionate, responsive.

- cooperate V. collaborate, unite, help, combine. *The writers decided to collaborate on the project.*
  Ant. delay, impede, obstruct, prevent.

coordinate V. match, harmonize, adapt, organize.
Ant. disorganize, disrupt.

cope V. deal with, handle, get by.
Ant. panic, lose control.

copy N. imitation, simulation, reproduction, duplicate; —V. simulate, reproduce, duplicate.
Ant. original; invent, produce.

cordial ADJ. polite, gracious, friendly, amiable.
Ant. unfriendly, hostile, inhospitable.

corpulent ADJ. fat, overweight, flabby, heavy, hefty.
Ant. slender, slim, slight, thin.

correct V. edit, amend, rectify; —ADJ. right, accurate, proper, respectable, appropriate.
Ant. indecent, wrong, inappropriate.

correlate V. associate, relate, compare.
Ant. differ, diverge, disparage.

correspond V. compare, agree, coincide.
Ant. diverge, differ.

corroborate V. certify, confirm, prove, affirm.
Ant. disprove, refute, oppose.

corrupt ADJ. unscrupulous, perverse, debased, low, degenerate, dishonest.
Ant. sound, pure, honorable.

cost N. value, price, charge, expense, sacrifice.

counsel V. advise, guide, admonish, inform.
Ant. withhold, misinform, misadvise, conceal.

count V. calculate, number, compute, enumerate.
Ant. guess, estimate.

counterfeit ADJ. fraudulent, false, bogus, phony.
Ant. true, genuine, real.

country N. state, territory; —ADJ. provincial, rustic.
Ant. urban, metropolitan.

courage N. boldness, fearlessness, bravery, valor, heart.
Ant. fear, timidity, cowardice.

course N. heading, direction, bearing.

court N. enclosure, quad, yard, atrium.

courtesy N. graciousness, respect, civility, politeness.
Ant. impoliteness, rudeness, discourtesy, incivility, disrespect.

courtly ADJ. gracious, gallant, ceremonious.
Ant. crude, rude.

courtship N. dating, romance.

cover V. hide, cap, conceal, shroud, mask.
Ant. reveal, expose, uncover.

covet V. envy, desire, want.
Ant. renounce, relinquish.

cowardly ADJ. timid, shy, afraid, weak.
Ant. brave, courageous, bold.

crack V. split, break, snap, fissure.

cram V. crowd, stuff, fill, overfill.
Ant. empty.

cramp V. constrain.
Ant. liberate, free.

crash N. collision, wreck, smash; —V. collide.
Ant. avert, evade.

crave V. lust, desire, want, long for.
Ant. renounce, relinquish, give up.

crawl V. creep, slide, worm.
Ant. stand, walk.

craze N. fashion, enthusiasm, fad; —V. derange.

crazy ADJ. insane, enthusiastic, foolish, mad.
Ant. sane, well-balanced.

crease V. line, fold.

create V. make, produce, compose, invent, originate.
Ant. destroy, ruin, dismantle.

creation N. invention, conception, formation, establishment.
Ant. destruction, demolition, desolation, annihilation, obliteration.

• **creative** ADJ. inventive, original. *She suggested an inventive ending for the play.*
Ant. unimaginative.

credible ADJ. believable, authentic, conceivable.
Ant. unbelievable, inconceivable, incredible.

credit N. belief, trust, faith, recognition, attribution;
—V. believe, attribute.
Ant. discredit.

creep V. sneak, crawl, steal, skulk, slip.

crime N. wrongdoing, offense, felony, violation,
misdeed.
Ant. innocence, virtue, goodness.

criminal ADJ. illegal, wrongful, unlawful; —N. crook,
fugitive, outlaw, gangster.
Ant. honest, good, virtuous.

cripple V. injure, maim, mutilate, disable.
Ant. cure, heal.

• crisis N. emergency, juncture. *The citizens met the
emergency with courage.*

critic N. reviewer, commentator, judge.
Ant. admirer, fan.

crooked ADJ. curved, winding, twisting, tortuous.
Ant. straight, direct, honest.

cross V. traverse, mix; —ADJ. annoyed, irritable,
cranky.
Ant. miss, avoid; complaisant, agreeable.

crowd N. group, multitude, legion, assembly.

crown N. tiara, coronet, top, climax.
Ant. bottom, pit.

• crucial ADJ. decisive, critical, essential. *His decisive
actions ensured victory.*
Ant. subsidiary, minor, secondary.

crude ADJ. rude, uncouth, rough, unsophisticated.
Ant. refined, elegant, sophisticated, polished.

cruel ADJ. mean, pitiless, brutal, merciless.
Ant. kind, merciful, compassionate.

crunch V. grind, chew.

crush V. smash, break, squeeze, mash.
Ant. restore, repair.

cry V. sob, yell, shout, weep.
Ant. laugh.

culminate V. end, climax, finish, result in, terminate.
Ant. start, begin, commence, undertake.

culprit N. villain, bandit, offender, wrongdoer.

cultivate V. grow, produce, develop, raise.
Ant. neglect, deteriorate, depress.

cultural ADJ. civilizing, refining, enlightening.
Ant. wild, ignorant, vulgar.

culture N. civilization, refinement, breeding, education.
Ant. ignorance, unsophistication, vulgarity.

cure V. remedy, heal; —N. medicine.
Ant. malady, illness, sickness.

curiosity N. interest, inquisitiveness, prying, nosiness.
Ant. boredom, indifference.

curse N. misfortune, evil, jinx, invective; —V. damn, accurse, swear.
Ant. blessing, benediction, advantage.

curt ADJ. short, blunt, direct, succinct, brief.
Ant. loquacious, garrulous, expansive, verbose, wordy.

curve V. bend, crook; —N. arch, arc, bow.
Ant. straighten.

custom N. ritual, habit, practice, manner.
Ant. difference, irregularity, deviation.

cut V. slice, chop, carve.

cutback N. decrease, reduction, curtailment.
Ant. increase, supplement, expansion.

cycle N. circle, process, circuit.

cynical ADJ. ironic, pessimistic, satirical, contemptuous, sardonic, sarcastic.
Ant. optimistic, hopeful, pleasant.

D

dabble v. experiment, play at, try one's hand at.

dainty ADJ. delicate, fine, petite, elegant.
Ant. clumsy, inelegant, unpleasant.

damage N. harm, injury, breakage, destruction.
Ant. improvement, benefit, advantage.

damn v. curse, condemn, swear.
Ant. cherish, bless, praise.

damp ADJ. moist, humid, wet, dank, soggy.
Ant. dry, arid.

dance v. step, foot it, gambol; —N. ball, party.

danger N. hazard, threat, peril, risk.
Ant. safety, security, certainty.

dangerous ADJ. unsafe, risky, hazardous.
Ant. safe, nonthreatening, secure, protected.

dangle v. hang, suspend, swing.

dare v. risk, brave, defy, challenge.
Ant. retire, fear.

daring ADJ. adventurous, brave, bold, intrepid.
Ant. withdrawn, timid, timorous, fearful, shy,
hesitant.

dark ADJ. dim, murky, obscure, black, somber.
Ant. illuminated, light, bright.

darling ADJ. dear, favorite, beloved, precious.
Ant. disliked, hated, unwanted.

dash v. rush, run, smash, break.
Ant. amble, stroll.

data N. evidence, information, statistics, facts.

dawn N. daybreak, sunrise, morning, birth.
Ant. dusk, evening, sunset, disappear.

daze v. confuse, stun, dazzle, blind.
Ant. clarify, show.

dead ADJ. deceased, insensible, demised, lifeless,
perished, departed, numb, exhausted.
Ant. living, alive, existing.

deadlock N. stalemate, impasse, standstill, logjam.

deal N. transaction, agreement, affair; —v. barter, distribute, allocate.
Ant. retain, hold, keep.

dear ADJ. darling, favorite, beloved, expensive, costly.
Ant. worthless, common, inexpensive.

death N. decease, demise, passing, fatality.
Ant. existence, being, life.

debase v. humble, dishonor, impair, corrupt, demean.
Ant. enhance, improve, elevate.

debate v. dispute, contend, argue.
Ant. agree, concur, acquiesce.

debauch v. seduce, corrupt, defile, pervert.
Ant. purify, clean.

debilitated ADJ. infirm, run-down.
Ant. able, working.

debris N. trash, rubbish, wreckage.

debt N. arrears, liability, deficit, charge.
Ant. excess, assets.

decadence N. deterioration, decay, retrogression.
Ant. progress, advancement, flourishing.

decay v. deteriorate, decompose, go bad, spoil, rot.
Ant. growth, development, vigor.

deceit N. fraud, dishonesty, cunning, guile.
Ant. truth, openness, honesty.

deceive v. mislead, fool, delude, beguile, cheat.
Ant. help, advise, counsel.

decent ADJ. correct, proper, clean, appropriate, acceptable.
Ant. lewd, improper, obscene.

deception N. treachery, deceit, subterfuge, ruse.
Ant. honesty, truthfulness, veracity.

• **decide** v. conclude, determine, judge, resolve, settle.
We may conclude that the project is too expensive.
Ant. postpone, defer, hesitate.

declare V. say, proclaim, affirm, claim, announce, assert.
Ant. deny, retract, silence.

decline V. fade, deteriorate, decay, ebb.
Ant. improve, increase, strengthen.

decorate V. adorn, ornament, paint, enhance.
Ant. simplify, strip.

● **decrease** V. lessen, diminish, abate, decline. *Her absence will lessen our chances of success.*
Ant. heighten, expand, increase.

dedicate V. devote, commit, consecrate.

deduction N. elimination, subtraction, discount; conclusion, judgment.
Ant. addition, supplement.

deep ADJ. bottomless, abysmal, profound, low.
Ant. shallow, superficial, frivolous.

defeat N. failure, beating, rebuff, destruction.
Ant. triumph, success, victory.

defect N. flaw, error, imperfection, fault, shortcoming.
Ant. completeness, improvement, faultlessness.

defend V. guard, shield, protect, justify, vindicate.
Ant. leave, abandon, forsake.

defer V. delay, postpone, remit, adjourn.
Ant. accelerate, hasten, expedite.

deficient ADJ. lacking, incomplete, defective, flawed, insufficient.
Ant. satisfactory, adequate, ample.

deficit N. lack, shortfall, debit, dearth.
Ant. surplus, profit, credit, plenty.

● **definite** ADJ. certain, decided, clear-cut, precise, unambiguous, positive, certain, fixed, limited. *The time and date of the meeting are certain.*
Ant. vague, uncertain, undefined.

defraud V. deceive, beguile, cheat, swindle.
Ant. support, repay, contribute.

defunct ADJ. nonworking, obsolete, outdated.
Ant. operational, up-to-date, useful, valid, current.

defy V. oppose, dare, disobey, brave, challenge.
Ant. obey, yield, accept, agree with.

degrade V. demote, humble, debase.
Ant. reward, honor, respect, elevate.

degree N. proportion, rank, order, stage, grade, magnitude.
Ant. numbers, size, mass.

dejected ADJ. unhappy, depressed, discouraged, sad.
Ant. cheerful, gay, merry, happy.

delay V. set back, detain, postpone, hesitate, slow; —N. deferment, suspension.
Ant. acceleration, advancement, expedition.

delete V. erase, drop, cancel, remove.
Ant. establish, initiate, propagate.

deliberate V. reason, ponder; —ADJ. intentional, planned, considered, unhurried, calculated, careful.
Ant. repudiate, reject, unintentional, sudden, careless.

delicate ADJ. dainty, fragile, fine, weak, gentle.
Ant. coarse, rough, indelicate.

delicious ADJ. delightful, palatable, tasty, pleasing, tasteful, toothsome, savory.
Ant. disagreeable, unpalatable, distasteful.

delight N. joy, enjoyment, pleasure; —V. enchant, please, gladden, cheer.
Ant. sorrow, pain, misery.

delinquent ADJ. careless, reckless, irresponsible.
Ant. careful, responsible, painstaking.

- **deliver** V. carry, convey, give, present. *Please carry our best wishes to your parents.*
Ant. bind, restrain, limit.

delude V. deceive, fool, beguile, lead astray, corrupt.
Ant. inform, enlighten.

- **demand** V. insist upon, ask for, request, require, involve, necessitate. *The customer should insist upon fair treatment.*
Ant. present, offer, reply.

demeanor N. behavior, manner, attitude, bearing, air.
Ant. unmannerliness, misbehavior.

demented ADJ. manic, frantic, uncontrolled, crazy.
Ant. sane, stable, well-balanced, rational, normal.

demise N. death, end, decease.
Ant. birth, beginning.

democratic ADJ. popular, self-governing, autonomous.
Ant. despotic, tyrannical.

demonstration N. exhibition, presentation, display, show.
Ant. concealment, misrepresentation, confusion.

demote V. reduce, downgrade, lower.
Ant. promote, elevate, heighten, upgrade.

demure ADJ. modest, coy, prudish, shy, bashful.
Ant. immodest, shameless, impudent.

denial N. rejection, refusal, contradiction, negation.
Ant. confession, acknowledgment, confirmation.

denote V. designate, intend, imply, signify.
Ant. ignore, forget.

denunciate V. blame, accuse, condemn.
Ant. commend, praise, applaud.

deny V. refuse, repudiate, contradict, reject.
Ant. affirm, acknowledge, confess.

depart V. go, leave, deviate.
Ant. linger, stay, remain.

● **depend** V. rely upon, expect, rest upon. *The adult children still rely upon their parents for support.*

depict V. represent, portray, describe, illustrate.
Ant. caricature, confound, distort.

deplorable ADJ. shameful, disgraceful, regrettable, unfortunate.
Ant. delightful, triumphant, cheerful.

deposit V. place, lay down, precipitate, put.
Ant. erode, withdraw.

depreciate V. devalue, lower, belittle, cheapen, reduce.
Ant. increase, add to, magnify, raise.

depressed ADJ. melancholic, low, dejected, unhappy, sad, deprived, impoverished, underprivileged.
Ant. cheerful, stimulated, happy, mirthful.

deprive V. rob, strip, bereave, deny.
Ant. assist, enrich, restore.

depth N. profundity, drop, deepness.
Ant. shallowness, height.

derive V. obtain, get, acquire, take.
Ant. terminate, issue, conclude.

descend V. drop, fall, sink, deteriorate.
Ant. ascend, mount, climb.

• **describe** V. explain, represent, relate, recount, communicate. *Please explain again how you redesigned the room.*
Ant. misrepresent, falsify, distort.

desert V. abandon, defect, quit, leave.
Ant. remain, stay, dwell.

design V. draw, chart, plan, create; —N. project, plan, intention, idea.

designate V. indicate, specify, call, note.

desolate ADJ. empty, deserted, unhappy, miserable.
Ant. populated, full, fertile, pleasant.

despair N. hopelessness, desperation, misery, despondence.
Ant. ambition, hope, confidence.

despise V. hate, condemn, dislike, scorn, distain.
Ant. love, cherish, praise, respect.

destroy V. demolish, wreck, annihilate, break, kill.
Ant. construct, restore, build.

destruct V. demolish, annihilate, wreck.
Ant. build, construct, restore.

detach V. disengage, dismantle, separate, divide.
Ant. attach, combine, unite.

detail N. element, particular, item, circumstance; —V. itemize, tell, report.
Ant. entirety, whole.

detain V. hold, arrest, delay, keep, restrain.
Ant. release, free, liberate.

detect v. perceive, discover, catch, expose, determine.
Ant. overlook, miss, omit.

deter v. prevent, dissuade, stop, hinder, halt.
Ant. encourage, persuade, advise.

deteriorate v. erode, decay, degenerate, crumble, disintegrate, decline.
Ant. renew, improve, refurbish.

- **determine** v. judge, discover, ascertain, resolve, decide. *He will judge the success of our efforts.*
Ant. hesitate, falter, doubt.

detest v. despise, hate, abominate, abhor.
Ant. admire, respect, love.

detriment N. damage, injury, harm, disadvantage.
Ant. favor, advantage, benefit.

devastate v. waste, desolate, ravage, ruin, wreck.
Ant. restore, renew, replenish.

- **develop** v. produce, generate, mature, elaborate, unfold, evolve. *The team must produce a workable plan soon.*
Ant. conceal, shorten, repress.

deviate v. swerve, diverge, err, depart.
Ant. continue, converge, remain, stick to.

devise v. make, plan, prepare, invent, design.
Ant. muddle, disarrange, fumble.

devotion N. adoration, sincerity, piety, observance, adherence.
Ant. indifference, apathy, carelessness.

dialect N. vernacular, argot, slang, accent, provincialism.
Ant. standard speech, official language.

dictate v. impose, prescribe, decree, speak, tell.
Ant. implore, plead.

dictator N. authoritarian, oppressor, tyrant, ruler.
Ant. subservient, pawn.

die v. decease, perish, demise, expire, subside, fade.
Ant. grow, live, exist.

differ v. vary, disagree, disaccord, dissent.
Ant. correspond, resemble, agree.

- **difference** N. inequality, variation, disparity, distinction, discrepancy. *We noted a grave inequality in economic opportunity.*
  Ant. similarity, agreement, harmony.

  different ADJ. variant, unlike, perverse, dissimilar, distinctive.
  Ant. similar, agreeable, harmonious, corresponding.

  diffident ADJ. shy, modest, timid, bashful.
  Ant. brazen, bold, brash.

  digest V. assimilate, absorb, consume, eat; —N. summary, synopsis, précis.
  Ant. complicate, confound, expand.

  dignify V. honor, exalt, elevate, grace.
  Ant. insult, shame, condemn.

  dignity N. distinction, honor, elevation, nobility, elegance, eminence.
  Ant. lowliness, degradation.

  digress V. deviate, depart, diverge, stray, wander, err.
  Ant. preserve, advance, continue.

  diligent ADJ. industrious, alert, studious, assiduous.
  Ant. apathetic, lazy, indifferent.

  dilute ADJ. watered down, watery, weak, diluted; —V. thin, weaken, cut, reduce.
  Ant. concentrated, rich, thickened.

  dim ADJ. shaded, obscure, dull, dark, unclear.
  Ant. brilliant, bright, clear.

  diminish V. lessen, reduce, weaken.
  Ant. increase, augment, amplify, enhance.

  diminutive ADJ. small, petite, minuscule, minute.
  Ant. large, big, great, hefty.

  dip V. dunk, immerse, submerge, fall, drop.
  Ant. remove, extract, rise.

  dire ADJ. fateful, critical, dreadful, awful, grievous.
  Ant. unimportant, lighthearted, minor.

- **direct** V. guide, conduct, govern, supervise, control; —ADJ. immediate, frank, straightforward. *Please guide the guests to the nearest exit.*
  Ant. beguile, deceive, mislead, indirect.

dirty ADJ. soiled, foul, impure, unclean, filthy, polluted.
Ant. clean, neat, moral, decent.

disable V. immobilize, cripple, paralyze, prostrate.
Ant. strengthen, impower.

disagree V. dispute, argue against, differ, oppose, deviate.
Ant. agree, concur, have the same opinion.

disappear V. evaporate, vanish, fade, depart, dissolve.
Ant. materialize, appear.

disappoint V. frustrate, discontent, let down, delude, foil.
Ant. please, satisfy, cooperate.

disapprove V. object, refuse, disfavor, frown upon.
Ant. sanction, approve.

disaster N. catastrophe, accident, tragedy, misfortune, cataclysm.
Ant. fortune, prosperity, blessing.

disburse V. distribute, pay, expend.
Ant. deposit, collect, receive.

discharge V. issue, unload, empty, emit, send out, demobilize, dismiss.
Ant. keep, retain, hold.

disciple N. follower, believer, student, pupil.
Ant. enemy, opponent, competitor.

disclose V. expose, reveal, communicate, uncover, show.
Ant. withhold, disguise, conceal.

discordant ADJ. incongruous, inharmonious, harsh, grating.
Ant. harmonious, peaceful, concordant, agreeable.

discourage V. depress, dishearten, dissuade.
Ant. encourage, aid, persuade.

● **discover** V. determine, find, reveal, ascertain, learn.
We wanted to determine how the pets escaped.
Ant. conceal, hide, cover.

discreet ADJ. cautious, delicate, conservative, prudent, wary, careful.
Ant. reckless, thoughtless, imprudent.

discrete ADJ. separate, individual.
Ant. joined, together, connected.

● **discuss** V. consider, deliberated, talk over. *Next week the members will consider the proposal.*

disengage V. detach, break, undo, loosen, free.
Ant. tie, bind, attach.

disgrace N. shame, reproach, dishonor.
Ant. honor, dignity, esteem.

disgraceful ADJ. dishonorable, shameful, disreputable, ignominious, embarrassing.
Ant. respectful, dignified, exalted.

disguise V. cover, cloak, mask; —N. costume, facade.
Ant. unmask, reveal, uncover.

disgust N. repugnance, loathing, repulsion, aversion.
Ant. respect, approval, admiration.

dishonest ADJ. false, deceitful, unfaithful, lying, corrupt.
Ant. honest, upright, scrupulous.

disintegrate V. deteriorate, breakup, ruin, destroy.
Ant. integrate, form.

dismay N. terror, shock, fear, horror.
Ant. assurance, confidence, intrepidity.

dismiss V. release, discharge, let go, eject, drop.
Ant. keep, maintain, preserve.

disobey V. defy, disregard, ignore, resist, rebel.
Ant. obey, accept, submit, yield.

disorganized ADJ. disordered, messy, chaotic.
Ant. ordered, organized.

disoriented ADJ. confused, unsettled, bewildered.
Ant. oriented, clearheaded, lucid.

disparage V. belittle, lower, discredit.
Ant. acclaim, recommend, compliment.

disparity N. inequality, difference, gap.
Ant. similarity, equality.

dispel V. disperse, spread, scatter, dismiss.
Ant. gather, collect, increase.

disperse V. distribute, dispel, scatter, spread.
Ant. gather, collect, concentrate.

dispirited ADJ. discouraged, dejected, downhearted, pessimistic.
Ant. optimistic, cheerful, sanguine, hopeful, bouyant.

displace V. disturb, misplace, unseat, derange, disarrange.
Ant. adjust, arrange, sort.

display V. reveal, express, show, expose.
Ant. conceal, hide, cover.

disposal N. elimination, discard, dumping, arrangement.
Ant. concealment, holding, retention.

dispose V. arrange, incline, bias, adjust, settle, get rid of.
Ant. hold, retain, secure.

disposition N. character, sentiment, nature.

dispute V. argue, debate, wrangle, discuss.
Ant. agree, concur, share the same opinion.

disregard V. ignore, discount, forget about.
Ant. remember, pay attention to, attend to, regard, hold in regard, focus on, emphasize.

dissipate V. scatter, diffuse, spread, waste.
Ant. concentrate, accumulate, conserve.

dissolve V. vanish, evaporate, melt, destroy, fade.
Ant. assemble, concentrate, unite.

dissonant ADJ. inharmonious, incongruous, harsh, grating.
Ant. melodic, harmonious, musical.

distance N. remoteness, stretch, length, expanse; coldness, detachment.
Ant. proximity, convenience; warmth, sympathy.

distinct ADJ. separate, apparent, different, individual, diverse, various.
Ant. similar, same, confused, unclear.

distinguish V. divide, separate, discriminate, characterize, differentiate, discern.
Ant. combine.

distort V. misrepresent, belie, pervert, deform.
Ant. balance, explain, straighten.

distract V. occupy, amuse, divert, bewilder, derange, confuse.
Ant. placate, reassure, pacify.

distress N. worry, anguish, grievance, pain, agony, hurt, misery, anxiety.
Ant. satisfaction, comfort, pleasure.

• **distribute** V. hand out, dispense, deal, spread, arrange. *Two students will hand out flyers at the door.*
Ant. store, collect, preserve.

distrustful ADJ. dubious, suspicious, doubting, suspect, mistrustful.
Ant. confident, trustful, believing.

disturb V. annoy, disrupt, disorder, agitate, displace, bother.
Ant. pacify, appease, calm.

diverse ADJ. various, general, distinct, different.
Ant. similar, identical, same.

divide V. separate, section, part, partition.
Ant. connect, combine, unite, join.

divine ADJ. holy, godly, heavenly, celestial.
Ant. earthly, worldly.

division N. partition, separation, section, piece, branch.
Ant. union, oneness, agreement.

divorce V. divide, unmarry, split; —N. dissolution.
Ant. marriage, connection, linkage.

divulge V. reveal, disclose, let slip.
Ant. keep secret, hold in confidence.

dizzy ADJ. dazzled, giddy, bewildered, light-headed, vertiginous, confused.
Ant. sober, sure.

doctrine N. tenet, precept, principle, teaching, theory, belief, dogma.
Ant. heresy, skepticism, falsehood.

document N. article, paper, report, manuscript, certificate.

dominant ADJ. controlling, prevailing, ruling, primary, commanding.
Ant. subordinate, humble, modest.

dominate v. control, prevail, command, rule, lead.
Ant. follow, retire, serve.

donation N. contribution, gift, benefaction, offering, charity.

doom N. fate, destiny; —v. condemn, sentence, ordain.
Ant. hope, choice; redeem.

dote on v. adore, spoil, treasure.
Ant. ignore, rebuff.

double N. duplicate, copy, twin, counterpart; —ADJ. repeated, duplicated.
Ant. lone, single, unique.

doubt N. concern, question, distrust, qualm, skepticism.
Ant. belief, faith, trust.

downpour N. thundershower, cloudburst, torrent.

drag v. draw, pull, trail, tow.
Ant. push, speed, expedite.

drain v. exhaust, deplete, empty, tap.
Ant. fill.

dramatic ADJ. spectacular, theatrical, sensational.
Ant. mundane, boring.

draw v. picture, depict, sketch; attract, pull.
Ant. reject, rebuff, repel.

dread N. fear, anxiety, apprehension, terror, fright.
Ant. confidence, courage, bravery.

dream N. illusion, vision, reverie, ideal, aspiration.
Ant. reality, fact, actuality.

dress v. clothe, attire, don; —N. clothing, clothes, garments, attire.
Ant. disarray, undress, strip.

drink v. imbibe, swallow, guzzle, sip, absorb, ingest; —N. beverage, refreshment.

drive v. push, propel, shove, run, control, direct; — N. journey, ride, energy, effort, force.
Ant. discourage, hinder, restrain.

droll ADJ. amusing, funny, humorous.
Ant. boring, dull, sad.

droop V. sink, slouch wilt, sag.
Ant. thrive, grow.

drop V. descend, fall, omit, delete, eliminate; —N.
drip, droplet, globule.
Ant. rise, continue, pursue.

drug N. pharmaceutical, medicine, remedy, opiate,
palliative.

drunk ADJ. inebriated, crapulous, loaded, besotted,
high, tight.
Ant. sober, dry.

dry ADJ. dehydrated, parched, arid, thirsty, dull,
boring, bare.
Ant. moist, wet, humid.

dual ADJ. paired, binary, twofold.
Ant. single, solitary.

dubious ADJ. doubtful, ambiguous, distrustful,
unclear, suspicious, problematic.
Ant. sure, certain, definite.

duck V. evade, dip, avoid.
Ant. stand, jump, face.

due ADJ. payable, owed, outstanding, unpaid,
scheduled, anticipated, deserved.
Ant. paid.

dull ADJ. tiresome, boring, tedious, witless.
Ant. vivacious, lively, interesting.

dumb ADJ. ignorant, dull, stupid, worthless, mute,
speechless.
Ant. intelligent, witty, smart.

duplicate V. replicate, copy, reproduce, double; —N.
facsimile.
Ant. example, original, prototype.

durable ADJ. sturdy, robust, resilient.
Ant. weak, frail, feeble, flimsy.

• **duty** N. responsibility, purpose, function, job. *Each job
involves an important responsibility.*
Ant. disloyalty, irresponsibility, treachery.

dwelling N. home, domicile, house, habitation.

E

eager ADJ. willing, anxious, ready, keen, impatient.
Ant. apathetic, diffident, uninterested.

early ADJ. beginning, initial, primitive, ancient, untimely, premature; —ADV. ahead, beforehand, in advance.
Ant. late, tardy; afterward.

earn V. merit, deserve, gain, collect.
Ant. steal, beg, take.

earnest ADJ. determined, serious, grave, eager.
Ant. frivolous, careless, negligent, inconsiderate.

earth N. world, planet, globe, dirt, ground, soil.
Ant. outer space, universe, heavens.

ease N. comfort, tranquility, relaxation, facility, skillfulness.
Ant. difficulty, strife, discomfort.

• **easy** ADJ. simple, effortless, elementary, comfortable; —ADV. leisurely. *The kit came with simple instructions.*
Ant. complicated, difficult, hard.

eat V. devour, consume, bite, swallow.

ebb V. recede, subside, decrease.
Ant. increase, revive, improve.

eccentric ADJ. strange, idiosyncratic, unusual, odd, weird.
Ant. common, usual, normal.

echo N. reverberation, repercussion; mimic, imitator; —V. reflect, rebound, repeat, imitate.

• **economical** ADJ. thrifty, prudent, frugal, wary. *His thrifty habits allowed him to save a great deal of money.*
Ant. wasteful, generous, expensive.

ecstasy N. pleasure, delight, joy, bliss, rapture.
Ant. sorrow, despair, hopelessness.

edge N. corner, rim, boundary, margin, brink, border.
Ant. interior, center, area.

edgy ADJ. nervous, anxious, excited, irritable.
Ant. calm, serene, quiet.

edible ADJ. eatable, comestible.
Ant. inedible.

- educate V. teach, instruct, inform, tutor, train. *Few instructors could teach as well as he.*
Ant. misinstruct, miseducate.

effect N. result, consequence, impact, aftermath, outcome, influence, effectiveness, efficiency.
Ant. beginning, cause, origin.

effective ADJ. efficient, productive, practical, forceful.
Ant. ineffective, useless, inadequate.

effeminate ADJ. feminine, womanly, delicate.
Ant. masculine, virile, robust.

- efficiency N. capability, proficiency, effectiveness, practicality, pragmatism. *She had a down-to-earth sense of pragmatism about accomplishing her daily tasks.*
Ant. incompetency, inadequacy, weakness.

effort N. struggle, exertion, endeavor, strain, striving.
Ant. neglect, ease, failure.

egocentric ADJ. egotistical, individualist, individualistic, selfish, self-centered.
Ant. altruistic, self-giving, humble, unassuming.

egotist N. narcissist, egoist.
Ant. altruist.

eject V. expel, banish, dismiss, jump, send out, bail out.
Ant. accept, take in, receive, include.

elaborate ADJ. intricate, complicated, ornamented, decorated.
Ant. common, ordinary, plain.

elated ADJ. happy, joyful, overjoyed, ecstatic, euphoric, jubilant.
Ant. saddened, depressed, gloomy.

elder ADJ. older, senior.
Ant. junior, younger, youthful.

elect V. vote, choose, select, ballot.
Ant. cancel, reject, refuse.

elegant ADJ. cultivated, graceful, delicate, exquisite, refined.
Ant. crude, rough, unrefined.

element N. component, part, factor, item, detail, point.
Ant. compound, whole, nonessential.

elevate V. lift, boost, raise, heighten, amplify.
Ant. lower, denounce, condemn.

eligible ADJ. suitable, worthy, qualified, fit.
Ant. unqualified, ineligible, unsuitable.

• **eliminate** V. remove, omit, eradicate, excrete, purge.
The company goal was to remove all barriers to proper quality control.
Ant. restore, replace, maintain.

elite ADJ. upper class, privileged, select few.
Ant. common, plebian, ordinary, usual.

eloquent ADJ. articulate, fluent, fecund, powerful, passionate, vocal.
Ant. hesitant, silent, slow.

elude V. avoid, evade, escape, dodge, lose.
Ant. confront, encounter, invite.

emaciated ADJ. starved, withered, gaunt, sunken.
Ant. plump, chubby, well-fed, overweight, hefty.

emancipate V. free, release, unfetter.
Ant. imprison, enslave, fetter, bind.

embarrass V. perturb, confuse, faze, mortify, fluster.
Ant. comfort, inspire, encourage.

embezzle V. steal, misappropriate, misuse, cheat.

embody V. manifest, externalize, personify, typify, represent.
Ant. disperse, exclude, disintegrate.

embrace V. contain, accept, adopt, include, grasp, hug.
Ant. ignore, reject, release.

embroil V. involve, complicate.
Ant. absolve, release, deliver.

emergency N. crisis, urgency, difficulty, predicament.
Ant. deliverance, stability, solution.

eminent ADJ. prominent, celebrated, renowned, famous, distinguished.
Ant. unknown, obscure, humble.

emit v. give, release, discharge, shed.
Ant. conceal, retain, withhold.

emotion N. feeling, affection, sentiment.
Ant. insensibility, apathy, impassivity.

• **emphasize** v. underline, stress, accentuate, point out.
He wanted to stress two important goals.
Ant. downplay.

• **employ** v. hire, use, apply, engage, retain. *She wanted to hire three day laborers.*
Ant. fire, terminate, release, disengage.

empower v. authorize, enable, delegate, permit, license.
Ant. revoke, dismiss, disenfranchise.

empty ADJ. void, vacant, hollow, forsaken, abandoned, destitute.
Ant. full, complete, occupied.

emulate v. follow, imitate.
Ant. neglect, differ.

• **enable** v. authorize, empower, allow, permit. *This document will authorize him to take action.*
Ant. prevent, remove, oppose.

enchant v. charm, captivate, enrapture, fascinate.
Ant. exorcise, repel, offend, disgust.

enclose v. surround, fence, cage.
Ant. release, loosen, free.

encounter v. meet, face, confront; —N. confrontation, battle, clash.
Ant. elude, avoid; retreat, agreement, union, truce.

encourage v. support, inspire, hearten, cheer, stimulate, promote.
Ant. depress, dissuade, deride.

endanger v. threaten, jeopardize, imperil, expose, risk.
Ant. guard, protect, defend.

endeavor v. try, attempt, make an effort.
Ant. give up, surrender, yield, capitulate.

endless ADJ. interminable, perpetual, continuous, eternal, infinite, ceaseless.
Ant. limited, transient, passing.

endurance N. strength, stamina, persistence, diligence, patience.
Ant. weakness, faltering, tiredness.

endure V. bear, tolerate, accept, withstand, continue, take.
Ant. refuse, subside, fail.

energetic ADJ. dynamic, vigorous, determined, industrious, forceful.
Ant. lethargic, inactive, weak.

enforce V. implement, invoke, execute, effect.
Ant. dismiss, disregard, renounce.

engage V. occupy, involve, attract, commission, hire, employ.
Ant. release, discharge, cancel.

enhance V. promote, intensify, improve, flatter.
Ant. reduce, diminish, assuage.

enigma N. mystery, riddle, puzzle.

enjoy V. savor, appreciate, relish, admire.
Ant. grieve, hate, abhor.

• **enlighten** V. inform, illume, illuminate, educate, teach. *The book can inform you about space travel.*
Ant. delude, mislead, bewilder.

enormous ADJ. huge, giant, gigantic, outrageous, colossal, immense.
Ant. minute, small, insignificant.

enrage V. anger, madden, infuriate, incense, provoke, exasperate.
Ant. calm, soothe, pacify.

enrich V. augment, supplement, enhance.
Ant. impoverish, detract, weaken, deprive.

enslave V. enchain, yoke, bind.
Ant. emancipate, free, unbind, release.

ensure V. promise, guarantee, assure.

enter V. start, join, penetrate, intrude, post.
Ant. exit, depart, leave.

enterprise N. venture, undertaking, project, company, business.
Ant. incapacity, indolence, inactivity.

entertain V. amuse, capture, interest, divert.
Ant. bore, fatigue, depress.

enthusiasm N. passion, zeal, eagerness, fervor.
Ant. lethargy, dullness, ennui.

entice V. tempt, attract, charm, allure, draw.
Ant. repel, reject, scare.

entirely ADV. completely, wholly, solely.
Ant. partially, incompletely, partly.

entry N. entrance, admission, insertion.
Ant. exit, outlet, departure.

enumerate V. number, itemize, count, list.

enunciate V. state, pronounce.
Ant. stifle, silence.

envelop V. wrap, surround, blanket, enclose, cover.
Ant. unwrap, reveal, uncover.

- **environment** N. habitat, surrounding conditions, vicinity, climate, atmosphere. *The mice seemed to enjoy their new habitat.*

envy N. jealousy, covetousness, enviousness.
Ant. generosity.

epidemic N. illness, plague, outbreak, scourge.

epitomize V. review, capture, represent.
Ant. misrepresent.

- **equal** ADJ. same, equivalent, even, identical. *The parents wanted to give both children the same advantages.*
Ant. unlike, unequal, disproportioned.

equitable ADJ. fair, equal, honest, impartial, just.
Ant. biased, inequitable, injust.

equivocal ADJ. ambiguous, uncertain, indefinite, doubtful, enigmatic.
Ant. clear, evident, obvious.

eradicate V. exterminate, abolish, destroy, decimate, nullify, annihilate.
Ant. secure, establish, propagate.

erase V. obliterate, cancel, annihilate, remove.
Ant. create, write, replace.

erect ADJ. straight, vertical, rigid, upright.
Ant. slouching, crooked, prone, supine.

erotic ADJ. passionate, sexual, sensual, fervent, carnal, amorous, lustful, concupiscent.
Ant. passionless, cold, spiritual.

erudite ADJ. sage, wise, learned, well-educated.
Ant. illiterate, ignorant, uneducated.

escalate V. increase, magnify.
Ant. lessen, decrease, reduce.

escape V. elude, run away, flee, avoid.
Ant. capture, seize.

escort V. guide, protect, accompany, guard; —N. companion.
Ant. abandon, desert, maroon.

essay N test, composition, paper, thesis, dissertation, article.

essence N. substance, base, quintessence, heart.
Ant. accessory.

● **essential** ADJ. fundamental, vital, elemental, intrinsic, necessary, integral. *I think the speaker neglected one fundamental point.*
Ant. auxiliary, secondary, subsidiary.

● **establish** V. found, institute, base, install, settle, prove. *Next week they will found a nonprofit charitable organization.*
Ant. topple, destroy, overthrow.

esteem N admiration, respect, regard, appreciation, honor.
Ant. disrespect, contempt, disdain.

estimate V. assess, appraise, value, approximate, rate.
Ant. disregard, guess.

eternal ADJ. endless, perpetual, everlasting.
Ant. finite, temporary, brief.

eternity N. infinity, forever, endlessness, immortality.
Ant. transition, mortality.

ethical ADJ. good, honest, right, virtuous, moral, proper, decent, righteous.
Ant. unethical, corrupt, immoral.

evade v. avoid, dodge, lose, escape.
Ant. confront, face, acknowledge.

evaporate v. disappear, vanish, vaporize.
Ant. solidify, condense, crystallize.

evasive ADJ. equivocal, shifty, elusive, dishonest.
Ant. straightforward, honest, direct.

even ADJ. flat, level, smooth, straight, flush, equal,
uniform, regular, constant.
Ant. rough, uneven, irregular.

everyday ADJ. mundane, common, commonplace,
routine.
Ant. unusual, strange, uncommon.

• **evident** ADJ. apparent, plain, obvious, discernible,
visible. *The truth was apparent to all of us.*
Ant. puzzling, obscure, questionable.

evil N. nefarious, black, sinful, wrong.
Ant. good, honor, virtue.

evoke v. excite, elicit, summon, educe, draw.
Ant. repress, quiet, silence.

evolve v. develop, emerge, grow, elaborate.
Ant. regress, die.

exact ADJ. precise, accurate, close, strict, correct,
faultless.
Ant. false, inaccurate, unreliable.

exaggerate v. magnify, inflate, overstate, stretch.
Ant. lessen, understate, reduce.

exalt v. honor, praise, elevate, glorify.
Ant. humble, spurn, lower.

examine v. analyze, check, inspect, study, view.
Ant. ignore, disregard.

• **example** N. illustration, prototype, symbol, instance.
Perhaps this illustration will help make my point.

exceed v. surpass, overrun, overreach, excel, eclipse.
Ant. linger, lag, fail.

• **excellent** ADJ. superior, marvelous, splendid, great,
terrific, first, fine, wonderful. *The crew was made up
of superior athletes.*
Ant. poor, negligible, inferior, inadequate.

- **exceptional** ADJ. rare, outstanding, different, unusual.
  The guests brought a rare bottle of wine to the dinner party.
  Ant. frequent, common, usual.

  excess N. abundance, plethora, overabundance, surplus; —ADJ. profuse.
  Ant. poverty, lack, necessity.

  excessive ADJ. extreme, overabundant, undue, exorbitant, extravagant, immoderate.
  Ant. frugal, moderate, poor.

  exchange V. change, interchange, trade, swap.

  excite V. arouse, provoke, inspire, stimulate.
  Ant. pacify, soften, appease.

  exclaim V. cry, blurt, shout, call.
  Ant. whisper, murmur.

  excursion N. trip, tour, jaunt, expedition.

  excuse N. reason, apology, explanation; —V. forgive, justify, absolve, relieve.
  Ant. accuse, blame, convict, indict.

  execute V. perform, fulfill, enforce, effect, administer.
  Ant. omit, forget, fail.

  exercise N. activity, play, sport, practice, training.
  Ant. idleness, repose, relaxation.

  exertion N. endeavor, effort, attempt, exercise.
  Ant. laziness, lethargy, inaction.

  exhaust V. fatigue, tire, deplete, wear out, consume, finish.
  Ant. restore, invigorate, refresh.

  exhibit V. display, show, demonstrate.
  Ant. conceal, cover, hide.

  exist V. live, consist, be, subsist.
  Ant. die, cease, disappear.

  existing ADJ. present, alive, living, actual.
  Ant. dead, gone, fictional.

  expand V. increase, spread, elaborate, amplify, widen.
  Ant. condense, contract, abbreviate.

  expect V. envision, hope, await, anticipate.

- expectation N. anticipation, prospect. *In anticipation of his visit, the town leaders prepared a parade and banquet.*
  Ant. disbelief, discouragement, despair.

  expedite V. speed up, hasten, rush, facilitate, accelerate.
  Ant. slow, delay, hinder.

  expel V. eject, banish, remove, evict, oust.
  Ant. invite, admit, accept.

  expend V. spend, use, consume, exhaust.
  Ant. save, conserve, covet.

  expensive ADJ. costly, luxurious, classy, posh.
  Ant. cheap, inexpensive, economical, low-priced.

  experience V. feel, undergo, go through, live, encounter; —N. knowledge, training, event, occurrence.
  Ant. ignorance, immaturity, innocence.

  expert N. authority, master, specialist, professional.
  Ant. novice, amateur, apprentice.

- explain N. clarify, explicate, resolve, account for, interpret. *Please clarify the technical terms used in the manual.*
  Ant. bewilder, obscure, confuse, complicate.

  explanation N. definition, description, clarification, interpretation, account.
  Ant. confusion, complication.

  explode V. blow up, detonate, burst, blow.
  Ant. implode.

  exploit V. use, manipulate, abuse.
  Ant. help, conserve, save.

- explore V. investigate, inquire, examine, delve. *The researchers want to investigate the topic more thoroughly.*

  expose V. display, reveal, uncover, disclose.
  Ant. cover, hide, conceal.

- express V. convey, communicate, declare, state. *Please convey our gratitude to Mr. Evans.*
  Ant. conceal, stifle, silence.

  extend V. expand, widen, increase, spread, lengthen.
  Ant. decrease, curtail, abridge.

extent N. stretch, length, degree, size.

exterminate V. eradicate, kill, annihilate, destroy, rid, decimate.
Ant. generate, create, originate, produce.

external ADJ. outer, outside, peripheral.
Ant. inner, internal, inside, interior.

extinguish V. abolish, destroy, quench, douse, suppress.
Ant. kindle, light, initiate.

extra ADJ. additional, superfluous, another.
Ant. enough, sufficient.

extravagant ADJ. lavish, excessive, profuse, wasteful.
Ant. economical, parsimonious, reasonable.

extreme ADJ. utmost, furthermost, farthest, uttermost, greatest. *We devoted the utmost effort to the project.*
Ant. ordinary, moderate, sober.

extrovert N. outgoing person, assertive person.
Ant. introvert, shy person.

exuberant ADJ. buoyant, vivacious, high-spirited, effervescent, profuse.
Ant. austere, barren, defeated.

eye V. look, detect, discern, watch, gaze.

F

fabricate V. make, produce, manufacture, invent; fake, counterfeit, feign.
Ant. destroy, break.

face V. encounter, confront, meet, challenge.
Ant. retreat, evade, withdraw.

facile ADJ. easy, dexterous, ready, flexible, clever.
Ant. difficult, awkward, arduous.

facility N. ease, ability, fluency, skillfulness.
Ant. difficulty, ineptitude, awkwardness.

● **fact** N. certainty, truth, actuality, circumstance. *His retirement is a certainty, not supposition.*
Ant. falsehood, supposition, uncertainty, untruth.

● **factor** N. element, circumstance, part. *We counted on the element of surprise in announcing our plans.*

factual ADJ. truthful, accurate, realistic, based on evidence.
Ant. notional, speculative, hypothetical, imaginary.

faculty N. capacity, competence, talent, ability.
Ant. inability, incompetence, incapacity.

fade V. decline, deteriorate, dissolve, disappear.
Ant. recover, energize, strengthen.

fail V. collapse, break, falter, omit, fade.
Ant. win, obtain, succeed, triumph.

failure N. unsuccessfulness, neglect, default, shortage, deterioration.
Ant. achievement, success, recover.

faint ADJ. weak, muffled, inaudible, feeble, low, unclear; —V. pass out.
Ant. loud, clear, distinct, strong.

fair ADJ. impartial, unprejudiced, objective; light, blond; average, ordinary.
Ant. unreasonable, unjust, unfair; dark.

faith N. belief, creed, religion, persuasion.
Ant. disloyalty, suspicion, infidelity, unbelief.

faithful ADJ. devoted, loyal, allegiant, resolute, authentic, accurate.
Ant. wavering, capricious, unreliable.

fake V. counterfeit, simulate, pretend, feign, falsify, fabricate.
Ant. real, genuine, proven.

fall V. collapse, decline, drop, topple, plunge.
Ant. climb, ascend, rise.

fallacious ADJ. false, irrational, invalid, delusive, deceptive, erroneous.
Ant. certain, true, factual.

fallacy N. error, untruth, falsehood.
Ant. truth, certainty, axiom.

fallible ADJ. imperfect, weak, frail, unsound.
Ant. infallible, perfect, sound, faultless, strong.

• **false** ADJ. fallacious, delusive, deceptive, erroneous, untrue, dishonest. *They were accused of spreading fallacious rumors.*
Ant. true, accurate, correct, valid.

falsify V. fake, distort, lie, misstate, misrepresent.
Ant. establish, correct, validate.

familiar ADJ. conscious, aware, acquainted, informed; friendly, intimate, common.
Ant. unknown, foreign, unfamiliar.

family N. house, kindred, household, ancestry, lineage, loved ones.
Ant. stranger, alien.

• **famous** ADJ. eminent, popular, notorious, famed. *The eminent lawyer rose to speak.*
Ant. unknown, obscure, infamous.

fan N. enthusiast, follower, devotee.
Ant. antagonist, enemy, opponent.

fanatic N. extremist, enthusiast, devotee.
Ant. nonpartisan.

fancy N. notion, taste, humor; —ADJ. elaborate, ornate, deluxe, exclusive.
Ant. veracity, actuality, precision.

fantastic ADJ. incredible, fabulous, imaginary, unimaginable, unbelievable.
Ant. common, normal, conventional.

fare V. manage, go, eat; —N. ticket price.

farmer N. rancher, gardener, agriculturalist.

fascinate V. charm, attract, enthrall.
Ant. bore, stultify, displease, agitate.

fashion N. style, mode, vogue, craze; —V. make, adapt, mold, shape.

fast ADJ. speedy, quick, rapid, swift; —ADV. quickly.
Ant. slow, slothful, dull.

fasten V. tie, fix, attach, bind, connect.
Ant. detach, loosen, disconnect, release.

fat ADJ. obese, overweight, portly, corpulent, stout, weighty.
Ant. thin, light, slim, slender.

fatal ADJ. catastrophic, deadly, fateful, destructive.
Ant. wholesome, healthful, nourishing.

fate N. predestination, destiny, luck, chance, fortune.

fatigue N. exhaustion, weakness, weariness.
Ant. vigor, energy, force, strength.

fault N. flaw, weak spot, limitation, defect, deficiency.

faux pas N. mistake, misstep, gaffe, indiscretion.
Ant. manners, social graces, protocol, etiquette.

favor N. service, kindness, indulgence, courteousness; —V. esteem, prefer.
Ant. hinder, oppose, harm.

- **favorite** ADJ. preferred, favored, popular, liked; —N. darling. *Her preferred sport was tennis.*

fear N. dread, panic, alarm, trepidation, anxiety, fright.
Ant. courage, bravery, heroism.

fearful ADJ. alarming, dreadful, frightening, ghastly, terrible; anxious, nervous.
Ant. wonderful, pleasant, calm, fearless.

feast N. meal, banquet, festival.
Ant. hunger, fasting, abstinence.

feat N. trick, act, deed, performance, accomplishment.
Ant. failure, stagnation, inaction.

federation N. union, congregation, assembly, association.
Ant. isolation, alienation.

feeble ADJ. tenuous, weak, frail.
Ant. strong, vigorous, forceful.

● **feel** V. sense, know, experience, savor, touch, taste, perceive, *I sense that you are feeling uncomfortable.*

feeling N. sentiment, sensation, belief, intuition, impression, idea.
Ant. indifference, apathy, insensitivity.

feign V. fake, pretend, simulate.

feminine ADJ. femaleness, effeminacy, maidenly, womanly, delicate, tender.
Ant. manly, masculine, virile.

fertile ADJ. productive, prolific, fruitful, rich, abundant.
Ant. barren, unproductive, sterile.

fervent ADJ. passionate, earnest, enthusiastic, ardent, vehement.
Ant. impassive, adverse, hesitant.

feud N. fight, disagreement, quarrel, dispute.
Ant. harmony, serenity, peace, calm.

feverish ADJ. hot, fervid, overheated.
Ant. cool, calm.

fib N. lie, prevarication, falsehood, sham, pretense.
Ant. truth, honor, integrity.

fiction N. story, tale, fantasy, myth, dream.
Ant. reality, fact, history.

fidelity N. faithfulness, loyalty, devotion, commitment.
Ant. infidelity, unfaithfulness, faithlessness, disloyalty, betrayal.

fierce ADJ. violent, savage, ferocious, vicious, cruel.
Ant. harmless, gentle, tame.

fiery ADJ. spirited, hot, passionate, fervid, blazing.
Ant. monotonous, dull, uninteresting.

fight V. dispute, clash, battle, contend, struggle.
Ant. agree, accord, harmonize.

figure N. design, form, shape, pattern, outline.

fill V. pack, load, pile, satisfy, feed, charge, pervade.
Ant. exhaust, empty, drain.

filthy ADJ. rotten, foul, dirty, obscene, disgusting, abhorrent, squalid, vile.
Ant. clean, purified, unadulterated.

finale N. end, conclusion, culmination, climax.
Ant. prelude, prologue, introduction, beginning.

finance V. fund, subsidize, bank, back, capitalize.

find V. locate, discover, spot, detect, pinpoint.
Ant. misplace, lose, abandon.

fine ADJ. superior, excellent, delicate, subtle, thin.
Ant. rough, coarse, thick, unrefined, poor.

finish V. conclude, end, terminate, complete, close; —N. conclusion, completion, termination.
Ant. begin, start, initiate, commence.

fire N. flame, blaze; passion, enthusiasm, radiance, brilliance.
Ant. dullness, frigidity.

firm ADJ. solid, hard, strong, resolute, determined, sound, decisive, settled, flat, fixed.
Ant. weak, defective, irresolute.

first ADJ. primary, original, earliest, initial.
Ant. last, final, terminal.

fit ADJ. appropriate, suitable, proper, prepared, ready; —V. suit, match, adapt, become.
Ant. unsuitable, awkward, inadequate.

fitting ADJ. proper, just, appropriate, suitable.
Ant. unsuitable, improper.

fix V. fasten, tie, attach, mend, repair, adjust, pinpoint, decide, establish.
Ant. break, weaken, loosen.

flagrant ADJ. glaring, arrant, conspicuous, bold, outrageous.
Ant. restrained, mild, subtle.

flash V. shimmer, sparkle, gleam, blink, display.

flat ADJ. horizontal, recumbent, even, level, dull, tasteless, flavorless.
Ant. bubbling, flavorful, hilly, uneven, lively.

flattery N. compliment, adulation, praise, blandishment.
Ant. mockery, condemnation, ridicule.

flavor N. savor, taste, essence, atmosphere, aroma, quality.

• **flexible** ADJ. pliant, elastic, limber, bending, lithe. *A pliant sheet of plastic covered the opening.*
Ant. stubborn, unbending, rigid.

flirt V. toy, dally, coque, trifle, toy with, play with, tease.
Ant. ignore, reject, neglect.

flood N. deluge, torrent, inundation, overflow, cataclysm.
Ant. drought, aridity.

florid ADJ. flowery, ornate, elaborate.
Ant. plain, unadorned, simple, basic.

flourish V. thrive, bloom, prosper, grow, increase.
Ant. weaken, collapse, decay.

flow V. run, circulate, stream, pour, course.
Ant. prevent, cease, stagnate.

fluctuate V. change, vary, oscillate.
Ant. remain unchanged, stabilize, remain constant.

flush ADJ. flat, even, level; —N. blush; —V. empty, purge.
Ant. rough, uneven.

flutter V. hover, flicker, shake, tremble, oscillate.
Ant. remain, stand.

fly V. wing, sail, flap, dart, shoot, run, escape.
Ant. remain, stay, walk.

focus N. center, concentration, centrum, emphasis.

follow V. chase, pursue, imitate, ensue, heed, observe. *The dogs refused to chase the fox.*
Ant. ignore, disregard, elude, lead.

fond ADJ. affectionate, dear, tender, loving.
Ant. spiteful, hateful, disgusted.

food N. sustenance, nourishment, aliment, bread, edibles, comestibles, foodstuff.

fool N. imbecile, idiot, ass, moron, simpleton; —V. trick, deceive, delude, beguile.
Ant. genius; respect, clarify.

forbid V. ban, interdict, restrain, exclude, disallow.
Ant. allow, recommend, order.

forbidden ADJ. prohibited, banned, impermissible.
Ant. allowable, authorized, approved.

force N. vitality, power, vigor, muscle, energy; —V. pressure, compel, coerce.
Ant. weakness, incompetence; restrain.

foreign ADJ. strange, exotic, alien, external.
Ant. local, indigenous.

foretell V. prophesy, predict, divine.
Ant. ignore.

forget V. overlook, disregard, omit, neglect.
Ant. remember, recall, recollect.

forgive V. excuse, remit, pardon, condone, absolve.
Ant. charge, blame, accuse.

form N. shape, pattern, figure, format, cast; —V. mold, develop, shape, cast, pattern, constitute.
Ant. shapelessness, amorphism; ruin, destroy.

formal ADJ. ceremonious, ritualistic, orderly, methodical.
Ant. casual, ordinary, habitual.

formulate V. invent, devise, frame, draft, concoct.
Ant. guess, fumble.

fortify V. bolster, gird, strengthen, confirm.
Ant. weaken, distract, detract.

fortune N. fate, luck, chance, destiny; riches, wealth.
Ant. poverty, hardship, catastrophe.

forward V. send, advance onward; —ADJ. foremost, first, ahead, leading; arrogant, bold, impudent.
Ant. hinder, stop; last, final; reserved.

fragile ADJ. brittle, delicate, breakable, weak.
Ant. unbreakable, strong, tough.

fragrance N. perfume, scent, aroma, bouquet.

frail ADJ. fragile, delicate, infirm.
Ant. strong, potent, sound.

frank ADJ. direct, straightforward, open, honest, candid.
Ant. insincere, deceptive, hypocritical.

frantic ADJ. frenzied, wild, delirious, mad, hysterical.
Ant. calm, peaceful, composed.

free ADJ. independent, liberated, unrestrained, gratuitous; —v. release, liberate, emancipate.
Ant. enslaved, curbed, expensive; detain, arrest.

freedom N. independence, liberty, sovereignty.
Ant. slavery, dependence, captivity.

• **frequent** ADJ. recurrent, repeated, continual, many, common. *The child had recurrent nightmares.*
Ant. unusual, sporadic, occasional.

frequently ADV. usually, regularly, repeatedly, generally.
Ant. rarely, infrequently, seldom.

fresh ADJ. new, current, novel, healthy, green, different, recent.
Ant. stale, trite, respectful.

friend N. acquaintance, companion, comrade, colleague, pal.
Ant. enemy, adversary, antagonist, rival.

frighten V. intimidate, scare, terrify, terrorize, startle, alarm.
Ant. encourage, inspire, reassure.

frigid ADJ. cold, bitter, freezing, glacial, icy; passionless, unresponsive.
Ant. temperate, warm; responsive, amorous.

front N. facade, face, head, beginning, start.
Ant. back, rear, posterior.

frown V. scowl, glare, sulk, disapprove.
Ant. smile, beam, grin.

frustrate V. defeat, baffle, disappoint, hinder, halt.
Ant. satisfy, assist, facilitate.

• **fulfill** V. satisfy, execute, perform, complete, accomplish. *He decided to satisfy a longtime goal.*
Ant. ignore, omit, disappoint.

fumble V. botch, drop, muddle, grope, mess up.
Ant. succeed, catch, retain.

fun N. play, amusement, gaiety, enjoyment,
entertainment.
Ant. melancholy, sadness, boredom.

• **function** N. role, purpose, use, celebration, ceremony,
gathering; —v. work, operate, act, run, behave.
Your role in the company will be crucial.
Ant. idleness, unemployment; mismanage,
misconduct.

• **fundamental** ADJ. essential, elemental, basic,
principal, primary. *You have overlooked an essential
fact.*
Ant. auxiliary, subordinate, dispensable.

furious ADJ. raging, enraged, inflamed, angry, mad,
infuriated, ranting.
Ant. tranquil, pacific, calm.

furnish V. provide, give, equip, supply.
Ant. strip, dismantle.

futile ADJ. ineffective, unsuccessful, useless, fruitless.
Ant. productive, effective, beneficial.

• **future** ADJ. impending, approaching, coming,
imminent. *We cannot ignore impending pressures.*
Ant. past.

fuzzy ADJ. blurred, obscure, unclear, out of focus,
indistinct.
Ant. clear, obvious, distinct.

G

gadget N. contrivance, contraption, concern, gizmo, doodad.

gain V. acquire, get, recover, earn.
Ant. spend, lose, waste.

gallant ADJ. chivalrous, gracious, brave, valiant, courageous.
Ant. cowardly, fearful, contemptible.

gamble V. wager, bet, venture, speculate, stake.
Ant. invest, insure, safeguard.

game N. sport, pastime, amusement, recreation, fun.
Ant. work, drudgery.

gang N. mob, pack, band, group, crew.

gangster N. mobster, criminal, crook.

gap N. break, breach, interim, chase, opening.
Ant. closure, barrier, defense, impediment.

gape V. stare, gaze, gawk, ogle.

garish ADJ. gaudy, showy, ostentatious, flashy, vulgar.
Ant. sober, discreet, modest, cultured.

garment N. dress, clothes, attire, garb.

gasp V. pant, wheeze, heave.

gate N. entrance, entry, opening, door, doorway.

gather V. collect, accumulate, assemble, group, harvest.
Ant. spread, distribute, disperse, scatter.

gaudy ADJ. loud, showy, bold, tacky, tasteless, cheap.
Ant. refined, plain, tasteful, subdued.

gauge N. thickness, diameter, standard; —V. measure, evaluate, size, estimate.

gaunt ADJ. haggard, emaciated, wasted, thin.
Ant. stout, heavy, fat, corpulent, obese.

gay ADJ. happy, jovial, merry, gleeful; —N. homosexual.
Ant. morose, sullen, grouchy; straight.

gaze v. gape, stare, look intently.

- **general** ADJ. common, universal, expansive, widespread, diverse, comprehensive. *We acted for the common good.*
  Ant. rare, particular, infrequent.

- **generate** v. produce, develop, engender, cause. *The staff members produce dozens of letters each day.*
  Ant. destroy, degenerate.

generosity N. magnanimity, openhandedness, liberality.
Ant. selfishness, greed.

generous ADJ. unselfish, charitable, liberal, free, openhearted, magnanimous.
Ant. uncharitable, sparing, selfish.

genesis N. birth, beginning, creation, start.
Ant. death, end, destruction, termination.

genial ADJ. pleasing, gracious, kind, pleasant, amiable.
Ant. unfriendly, sorrowful, moody, unhappy.

genius N. mastermind, brain, intellect, whiz kid.
Ant. simpleton, moron.

genre N. type, sort, variety.

genteel ADJ. prim, polite, proper, polished, cultured, kind.
Ant. unrefined, rough, rude.

gentle ADJ. tender, soft, kind, mild, calm, soothing.
Ant. rough, mean, harsh.

genuine ADJ. reliable, sincere, honest, authentic, real.
Ant. false, misleading, erroneous.

germ N. microbe, bug, embryo, kernel, seed.
Ant. fruit, issue, end.

germinate v. sprout, grow, develop, take root.
Ant. wither, decay, devolve.

gesture N. sign, expression, signal, indication, motion.

get v. obtain, acquire, procure, receive, earn, attain, secure.
Ant. give, release, surrender.

ghastly ADJ. awful, terrible, shocking, hideous, horrid.
 Ant. pleasant, agreeable, appealing.

ghost N. shadow, specter, spirit, apparition, phantom.
 Ant. substance, reality, matter.

giant N. mammoth, behemoth; —ADJ. immense,
 massive, huge, enormous, monumental.
 Ant. dwarf, miniature, midget; tiny, microscopic.

giddy ADJ. lighthearted, frivolous, flighty, silly.
 Ant. serious, calm, solemn.

gift N. donation, present, gratuity, talent, aptitude.
 Ant. forfeit, loss, confiscation.

giggle V. laugh, snicker, titter.

gimmick N. contrivance, gadget, trick, wrinkle.

gird V. secure, fortify, support, bind.
 Ant. release, loosen, untie.

give V. present, furnish, supply, donate, impart,
 grant.
 Ant. take, withhold, withdraw.

glad ADJ. pleased, delighted, happy, gay, joyous,
 cheerful.
 Ant. dejected, sad, sorrowful, mourning.

glamorous ADJ. alluring, enchanting, sensational,
 attractive.
 Ant. dull, unattractive, plain.

glance V. glimpse, sight, view, look, appear.
 Ant. examine, scrutinize.

glare N. blaze, blare, glower, scowl, frown.

gleam V. shine, sparkle, glitter, flash.

glean V. garner, extract, cull, collect, harvest.
 Ant. plant, replace.

glib ADJ. articulate, fluent, vocal, suave, glossy.
 Ant. inarticulate, faltering, quiet.

glide V. flow, slip, slick, lapse.
 Ant. stick.

glisten ADJ. gleam, glint, shine.

glitter V. glisten, flash, sparkle, shimmer.

gloom N. dejection, depression, melancholy, sadness, unhappiness, blues.
Ant. joy, happiness, optimism, serenity.

gloomy ADJ. melancholy, sad, depressed, depressing, dark, dreary, dismal.
Ant. cheerful, sparkling, blithe.

glorious ADJ. splendorous, sublime, magnificent, majestic, superb, beautiful.
Ant. odious, shameful, infamous.

glum ADJ. gloomy, morose, sullen, sour, sad, dismal.
Ant. happy, cheerful, buoyant, glad.

go V. depart, leave, proceed, run, walk, travel, stride.
Ant. come, enter, appear.

goad V. spur, prod, provoke.

go-between N. intermediary, mediator, broker, middleman.
Ant. principal.

• **good** ADJ. pleasing, flawless, perfect, sound, whole, pleasant. *The pleasing sounds of violins drifted through the restaurant.*
Ant. evil, sinful, dishonest, depraved.

gossip N. murmur, hearsay, whispering, stories.
Ant. statement, declaration, news.

govern V. manage, control, command, administer, rule, lead.
Ant. exceed, obey, comply.

government N. administration, rule, direction, control.
Ant. anarchy, lawlessness, rebellion.

grab V. seize, grasp, catch, grip.
Ant. release, let loose.

grace N. elegance, ease, gracefulness, beauty, charm.
Ant. negligence, awkwardness, ungracefulness.

graceful ADJ. elegant, beautiful, smooth, harmonious, stylish, nimble, dexterous.
Ant. awkward, graceless, ungainly.

grade N. rank, level, stage; ascent; quality, class.
Ant. uniformity, plain.

gradual ADJ. continuous, slow, step-by-step, moderate, gentle.
Ant. abrupt, sudden, unanticipated.

grand ADJ. magnificent, majestic, splendid, sublime, superb, great.
Ant. humble, inferior, trivial.

grant N. allowance, gift, allocation, contribution; —v. concede, permit, yield, allow.
Ant. deny, withhold, oppose.

graphic ADJ. realistic, lifelike, vivid, photographic, illustrative, written.
Ant. obscure, confused, abstract.

grasp V. clutch, seize, grip, clasp, grab, take.
Ant. miss, slip, misunderstand.

grateful ADJ. thankful, appreciative, gratified, pleasant.
Ant. thankless, careless, ungrateful.

gratifying ADJ. enjoyable, satisfying, pleasant, agreeable.
Ant. annoying, disappointing, offensive.

gratuity N. tip, contribution, donation, offering.

grave ADJ. serious, severe, momentous, solemn, earnest.
Ant. comic, humorous, gay, flippant, inconsequential.

great ADJ. huge, majestic, large, big, gigantic, excellent, splendid, super.
Ant. low, unimportant, small, petty, ordinary.

greed N. covetousness, avarice, cupidity, avidity.
Ant. generosity, selflessness, altruism, extravagance, philanthropy.

greedy ADJ. avid, covetous, hungry, rapacious, stingy.
Ant. charitable, liberal, philanthropic.

greet V. welcome, salute, hail, receive.
Ant. bid adieu, say farewell.

grief N. sorrow, heartbreak, woe, sadness, mourning.
Ant. ecstasy, joy, pleasure.

grieve v. mourn, suffer, bemoan, lament, weep, sadden.
Ant. celebrate, rejoice.

grind v. crush, pulverize, sharpen, smooth.
Ant. assist, encourage, dull, roughen.

grip v. grasp, seize, hold, clutch.
Ant. loosen, release, untie.

gross ADJ. rough, obscene, vulgar; thick, enormous, fat, bulky.
Ant. thin, delicate, refined, attractive.

ground N. property, land, surface, earth, soil.
Ant. air, atmosphere, space.

group N. bunch, collection, assembly, gathering, set; —v. collect, gather, classify.

grow v. increase, enlarge, develop, produce, raise, cultivate.
Ant. decrease, lessen, vanish.

gruff ADJ. coarse, abrupt, rude, blunt.
Ant. courteous, respectful, affable.

grumble v. mutter, complain, fuss, protest.
Ant. agree, concur, harmonize.

guarantee v. attest, verify, certify, testify, assure; —N. warranty, assurance, promise, oath, pledge.
Ant. contradict, decry, disavow.

guard v. protect, watch, guide, keep, secure.
Ant. desert, forsake, abandon.

guardian N. custodian, keeper, warden, protector, trustee.

● **guess** v. suppose, presume, infer, suspect, assume.
I suppose two cakes will be enough for the party.
Ant. measure, count, calculate, ascertain.

guide v. lead, direct, show, escort, conduct; —N. conductor, escort, leader.
Ant. mislead, neglect, abandon.

guilty ADJ. corrupt, criminal, immoral.
Ant. faultless, innocent, pure.

H

habit N. custom, inclination, tendency, practice.
Ant. uncertainty, irregularity, nonconformity.

habitual ADJ. accustomed, customary, routine, usual.
Ant. infrequent, unusual, extraordinary.

haggard ADJ. worn, gaunt, fatigued, tired, exhausted.
Ant. exuberant, healthy, lively.

haggle V. bargain, deal, barter, trade, squabble.
Ant. consent, agree, concur.

hail V. welcome, greet, honor, address.
Ant. neglect, ignore, shun.

hairy ADJ. furry, woolly, fleecy.
Ant. bare, bald, shaven.

hallow V. sanctify, devote.
Ant. curse, blaspheme.

hallowed ADJ. sacred, holy, sanctified, consecrated, revered.
Ant. blasphemous, profane, unholy.

hallucination N. illusion, fantasy, delusion.
Ant. truth, reality, existence.

halt V. stop, falter, stand, arrest, hesitate.
Ant. advance, continue, proceed.

hamper V. prevent, obstruct, thwart, hinder.
Ant. help, facilitate, assist.

hand N. assistant, helper, aid, support; —V. pass, give, bequeath.
Ant. take, remove.

handicap N. disadvantage, advantage (in sports), hindrance, limitation.
Ant. advantage, benefit, asset.

handy ADJ. useful, helpful, convenient, skilled, clever, inventive, resourceful.
Ant. unskilled, clumsy, inept.

hang V. attach, suspend, swing, execute, lynch.

happen V. occur, take place, come about, ensue.

happiness N. joy, gladness, cheerfulness, bliss, contentment, rapture, peace.
Ant. sadness, misery, sorrow, grief.

• **happy** ADJ. joyous, glad, gay, cheerful, pleased, merry, fulfilled. *Congratulations on this joyous occasion.*
Ant. sad, disappointed, miserable, sorrowful.

harass V. annoy, irritate, besiege, tantalize, taunt, incense.
Ant. comfort, encourage, console.

harbor N. port, anchorage; —v. protect, shelter, shield, cover.
Ant. banish, expel, eject.

hard ADJ. tough, rugged, firm, strong, solid, severe, difficult, burdensome.
Ant. weak, pliable, easy, soft.

harden V. toughen, solidify, petrify; confirm.
Ant. melt, soften.

hardship N. difficulty, privation, adversity.
Ant. ease, luxury, plenty.

harm N. hurt, injury, damage, detriment.
Ant. benefit, good, blessing.

harmless ADJ. innocuous, innocent, benign, inoffensive, gentle, good.
Ant. malicious, injurious, hurtful.

harmonious ADJ. agreeable, concordant, congruous, amicable, melodious.
Ant. discordant, opposed, dissonant.

harmony N. consonance, accord, unity, agreement, kinship, peace, affinity.
Ant. dissonance, variance, alteration.

harsh ADJ. grating, discordant, rough, bleak, bitter.
Ant. kind, easy, gentle.

harvest N. gathering, reaping, crop, yield; —v. reap, gather.
Ant. plant, scatter, disperse.

hassle V. harass, aggravate, pester, annoy.

haste N. speed, hurry, rapidity, rush.
Ant. slowness, lethargy.

hasty ADJ. quick, abrupt, hurried.
Ant. watchful, deliberate, cautious.

hatch V. originate, plot, invent, produce.

hate V. despise, detest, abhor, loathe, resent,
disapprove.
Ant. befriend, love, approve.

haughty ADJ. proud, conceited, arrogant.
Ant. personable, interested, humble.

haul V. tow, pull, heave, tug.

haunt V. trouble, disturb, obsess, preoccupy.

have V. possess, own, hold, retain, contain.
Ant. lack, want, exclude.

haven N. refuge, sanctuary, asylum.

haze N. fog, mist, film, smoke, murk.
Ant. clarity, radiance, obviousness.

head N. commander, director, supervisor, boss; —V.
administer, direct, lead; —ADJ. chief, foremost, top.
Ant. pupil, disciple; follow, finish; bottom, base.

health N. healthiness, soundness, wholeness,
heartiness.
Ant. illness, sickness, disease.

healthy ADJ. robust, sound, strong, hearty, flourishing.
Ant. weak, ill, frail, sick.

heap N. pile, mass, bunch, pyramid; —V. pile,
mound, lump, load, shower.
Ant. diminish, lessen, contract.

hear V. detect, listen, perceive.
Ant. ignore, neglect.

heart N. core, essence, center, breast, bosom,
sentiment, sympathy.
Ant. exterior, outside, periphery.

heartless ADJ. callous, unfeeling, unkind.
Ant. kind, caring, gentle, sympathetic.

heat N. hotness, warmth, excitement, fervor.
Ant. cold, frigidity, lethargy.

heave V. throw, toss, boost, pull.
Ant. ebb, recede, lower.

heaven N. paradise, rapture, ecstasy, delight, bliss, happiness.
Ant. hell, torture, condemnation.

heaviness N. weight, gravity, ponderosity, heftiness.
Ant. lightness, unimportance, triviality.

heavy ADJ. weighty, massive, hefty, burdensome, cumbersome.
Ant. light, inconsequential, insignificant, happy.

hedge V. surround, equivocate, skirt, brush.
Ant. answer, meet, confront.

heedful ADJ. attentive, mindful, careful.
Ant. careless, inattentive, thoughtless.

heedless ADJ. inattentive, careless, unmindful, deaf.
Ant. careful, mindful, attentive.

hefty ADJ. severe, heavy, strong, tough.
Ant. light, easy, thin.

heighten V. intensify, increase, concentrate, elevate.
Ant. diminish, lower, reduce.

- **help** V. support, aid, assist, bolster. *Your support has meant so much to us all.*
Ant. hinder, oppose, retard.

- **helpful** ADJ. useful, supportive, assistive, effective, constructive, beneficial, practical. *Criticism is welcomed so long as it is useful.*
Ant. resistant, bothersome, annoying.

- **helpless** ADJ. powerless, feeble, dependent, weak, unprotected. *The company was powerless to prevent the takeover.*
Ant. powerful, strong, independent.

heritage N. birthright, legacy, inheritance, tradition.

hero N. celebrity, champion, idol.
Ant. coward, weakling.

- **hesitate** V. pause, waver, falter, delay. *Usually she will pause before stepping on stage.*
Ant. hasten, attack, continue.

hidden ADJ. secluded, blind, ulterior.
Ant. obvious, uncovered, open.

hide V. cover, obscure, conceal, disguise, protect, veil.
Ant. show, expose, reveal.

high ADJ. elevated, towering, tall, shrill, strong, heavy.
Ant. low, deep, inferior.

higher ADJ. superior, greater, senior, over, above.
Ant. lower, shorter.

hilarious ADJ. uproarious, sidesplitting, funny.
Ant. serious, somber, austere.

hill N. projection, rise, hillock, mound, eminence, prominence.
Ant. depression, gulf, valley.

• hinder V. prevent, impede, obstruct, hold back. *Your physical condition may prevent you from participating.*
Ant. aid, help, expedite, assist.

hint N. suggestion, clue, indication, allusion; —v. allude, imply, suggest.
Ant. cover, conceal, disguise.

hire V. employ, lease, rent, engage.
Ant. fire, discharge, retire.

history N. chronicle, story, account, past, record, archives.
Ant. allegory, myth, legend.

hit V. strike, punch, discover, find, slap.
Ant. caress, soothe.

hitch V. harness, tie, fasten; —N. hindrance, catch, obstacle.
Ant. untie, free, release; opening, help, opportunity.

hoard N. store, reservoir, inventory, stockpile; —v. amass, store, stock, gather.
Ant. donate, give, waste.

hoarse ADJ. harsh, rough, grating, husky.
Ant. melodious, smooth, tuneful.

hoist V. lift, raise, pull, elevate, erect.
Ant. lower, drop, let down

hold V. retain, keep, embrace, grasp, believe, think.
Ant. release, drop, relinquish.

hole N. orifice, opening, cavity, aperture, den, burrow, cave.
Ant. closure, blockade.

hollow ADJ. concave, empty, vacant, cavernous.
Ant. solid, firm, full.

holy ADJ. sacred, pious, religious, divine, blessed, devout.
Ant. profane, vicious, evil, wicked.

homage N. honor, respect, reverence, tribute, devotion.
Ant. treason, disobedience, treachery.

home N. dwelling, residence, house, lodging, habitat, refuge, sanctuary, asylum.

• **honest** ADJ. truthful, sincere, just, trustworthy, honorable, righteous, frank. *His truthful testimony influenced the grand jury.*
Ant. deceptive, unjust, ignoble.

• **honesty** N. straightforwardness, integrity, honor, rectitude, fairness. *Our response will depend upon your straightforwardness in this matter.*
Ant. trickery, artifice, fraud.

honor N. esteem, respect, deference, homage, reputation.
Ant. reproach, degradation, shame.

hoodwink V. dupe, deceive, take in, fool.

• **hope** V. aspire, desire; —N. expectation, belief, trust. *The two students aspire to become famous ballerinas.*
Ant. despondency, depression, despair.

• **hopeful** ADJ. optimistic, aspirant, confident; —N. aspirant. *Their optimistic attitudes help them succeed.*
Ant. despairing, dejected, inconsolable.

hopeless ADJ. impossible, incurable, useless, futile, desperate.
Ant. reassuring, enthusiastic, courageous.

horrible ADJ. ghastly, terrible, awful, dreadful.
Ant. wonderful, lovable, pleasing.

horror N. dread, terror, fear, abhorrence.
Ant. pleasure, fascination, delight.

horse N. stallion, mount, mare, steed, charger.

- **hostile** ADJ. unfriendly, contentious, inimical, argumentative. *Unfriendly forces surrounded the platoon.*
  Ant. friendly, diverting, agreeable.

hostility N. belligerence, aggression, antipathy, antagonism.
Ant. loyalty, neutrality, devotion.

hot ADJ. burning, scalding, torrid, flaming, blazing, passionate.
Ant. frigid, cold, calm, bland.

house N. residence, home, dwelling.

hover V. hang, linger, flutter, fly.
Ant. avoid, land, leave, settle.

howl V. yell, wail, cry, scream.
Ant. whisper, murmur.

hue N. tone, color, shade, tint.

- **huge** ADJ. enormous, large, big, gigantic, immense. *An enormous fossil was discovered in Montana.*
  Ant. small, tiny, miniature, diminutive.

hum V. whir, buzz, drone.

human N. mortal, man, person, creature, Homo Sapiens.
Ant. god, spirit, ghost.

humanitarian ADJ. compassionate, benevolent, merciful, humane.
Ant. brutal, uncivilized, savage.

humble ADJ. meek, docile, mild, modest, unassuming.
Ant. self-important, ostentatious, overbearing.

humiliate V. demean, disgrace, humble.
Ant. praise, applaud, encourage.

humor N. comedy, joking, amusement, wit, disposition, mood, sentiment; —V. placate, indulge, oblige, gratify.
Ant. dullness, stupidity; irritate, provoke.

humorous ADJ. funny, witty, amusing, comical.
Ant. dull, stupid, depressing.

hunch N. suspicion, feeling, premonition, intuition.
Ant. certainty, sureness, knowledge.

hunger N. desire, appetite.
Ant. satisfaction, surfeit, satiation.

hungry ADJ. starved, avid, famished, ravenous.
Ant. fed, satisfied, replete.

hunt V. pursue, chase, stalk, drive, search, probe, seek.

hurt V. wound, damage, injure, harm.
Ant. heal, assist, cure.

hush V. silence, quiet, repress, cover.
Ant. excite, amplify, encourage.

hustle V. hasten, rush, run, dash, hurry.
Ant. delay, procrastinate, stall.

hyperbole N. exaggeration, overstatement.
Ant. humility, understatement.

hypnotic ADJ. irresistible, mesmerizing, sleepy, quieting, lethargic.
Ant. exciting, shocking, reviving.

hypocrisy N. insincerity, delusion, falsehood, cant, sham.
Ant. reliability, truthfulness, honesty.

hypocritical ADJ. insincere, dishonest, two-faced, deceptive, sanctimonious, dishonorable.
Ant. trustworthy, frank, straightforward.

hypothesis N. theory, conjecture, speculation, supposition, postulate.
Ant. discovery, demonstration.

hypothetical ADJ. theoretical, speculative, imaginary, conjectural, symbolic.
Ant. proven, confirmed, indisputable.

I

icy ADJ. frigid, frozen, cold, frosty.
Ant. hot, fiery, passionate.

- idea N. concept, image, belief, opinion, meaning, significance. *Your concept for a new engine interests us.*
Ant. element, fact, reality.

ideal N. model, vision, dream; —ADJ. perfect, visionary, illusory, excellent, complete.
Ant. common, pragmatic, actual.

identical ADJ. equal, uniform, equivalent, same.
Ant. diverse, separate, opposite.

identify V. distinguish, recognize, characterize, sympathize, point out.
Ant. confuse, misinterpret, mistake.

identity N. personality, individuality, character, self.

idiot N. fool, moron, dope.
Ant. genius, wiseman.

idle ADJ. inactive, lazy, slothful, unemployed, unused.
Ant. active, energetic, ambitious, busy, occupied.

ignite V. spark, inflame, light, detonate.
Ant. quench, extinguish, dissuade, discourage.

ignorance N. illiteracy, innocence, unmindfulness.
Ant. knowledge, education, literacy.

- ignorant ADJ. illiterate, uneducated, stupid, unlearned, unlettered, shallow. *The illiterate man could not read the warning signs.*
Ant. schooled, knowledgeable, able.

ignore V. neglect, disregard, overlook, slight.
Ant. notice, pay attention to, recognize, acknowledge.

ill ADJ. sick, diseased, evil, bad, unhealthy.
Ant. healthy, well, vigorous.

ill-considered ADJ. unwise, precipitate.
Ant. planned, premeditated.

illegal ADJ. lawless, wrongful, unauthorized, forbidden, prohibited.
Ant. lawful, permissible, approved.

illegitimate ADJ. unlawful, illicit, illegal, improper, unlicensed, fatherless, bastard.
Ant. proper, correct, accepted.

illicit ADJ. unlawful, illegal, criminal, unethical.
Ant. authorized, right, legal.

illiterate ADJ. ignorant, unlettered, uneducated, unlearned.
Ant. literate, schooled, lettered, educated.

illness N. sickness, disease, malady.
Ant. health, strength, vigor.

illogical ADJ. unreasonable, superfluous, absurd, unsettled, inconclusive.
Ant. correct, sensible, logical.

ill-tempered ADJ. irritable, bad-tempered, grouchy, crabby, petulant.
Ant. calm, easygoing.

illuminate V. enlighten, illume, light up, clarify, explain, light.
Ant. obscure, cloud, darken.

illusive ADJ. delusive, illusory, hallucinatory.
Ant. factual, certain, real.

illustrate V. portray, express, depict, clarify.

image N. representation, likeness, double, idea, appearance.
Ant. reality, concretion.

• imagination N. conception, thought, fancy, fantasy, creativity. *His primary value to the company was his power of conception.*
Ant. actuality, reality, certainty.

imagine V. envision, conceive, picture, visualize, fantasize.

imbecile N. moron, idiot, simpleton.
Ant. genius, mastermind, whiz kid.

imbibe V. drink, absorb, sip.

imitate V. mimic, parody, mock, echo, copy.
Ant. create, originate, change, modify.

immature ADJ. young, precocious, childish.
Ant. adult, grown, mature.

- **immediate** ADJ. instantaneous, direct, primary, close, prompt. *An instantaneous temperature drop followed the storm.*
  Ant. later.

- **immense** ADJ. huge, enormous, gigantic, large. *Huge piles of grain awaited processing.*
  Ant. tiny, unimportant, insignificant.

  immoral ADJ. evil, wrong, impure, lecherous, indecent, unprincipled.
  Ant. holy, good, moral.

  immortal ADJ. endless, undying, eternal, perpetual, everlasting.
  Ant. transitory, earthly, mortal.

  immovable ADJ. fixed, anchored, stable, rooted, immobile.
  Ant. inconstant, yielding, mobile.

  impact N. collision, force, clash, percussion, shock.
  Ant. reflex, recoil, avoidance, miss.

  impartial ADJ. neutral, fair, nonpartisan, unprejudiced.
  Ant. prejudiced, biased, unfair.

  impatient ADJ. nervous, anxious, fretful, eager, restless.
  Ant. patient, forbearing, tolerant.

  impeccable ADJ. perfect, flawless, spotless, immaculate, faultless.
  Ant. defective, imperfect, messy.

  impede V. hinder, halt, stop, prevent, hamper, delay, block.
  Ant. assist, speed, advance, hasten.

  imperative ADJ. essential, unavoidable, critical, required, urgent.
  Ant. voluntary, optional, unnecessary.

  imperceptible ADJ. invisible, negligible, slight, subtle, insignificant.
  Ant. obvious, apparent, conspicuous.

  imperfect ADJ. defective, faulty, blemished, inadequate.
  Ant. faultless, complete, flawless.

impersonate V. portray, pose, imitate, act, represent.

impertinent ADJ. trivial, irrelevant, impudent, inapplicable.
Ant. respectful, obliging, courteous.

impetuous ADJ. impulsive, precipitate, rash, hasty, reckless.
Ant. patient, calm, considerate.

impious ADJ. irreverent, immoral, sinful, bad.
Ant. reverent, pious, moral, good, holy.

implausible ADJ. unbelievable, suspect, inconceivable, doubtful, questionable.
Ant. possible, real, believable, credible, plausible.

implement V. use, enforce, achieve; —N. instrument, device, tool.
Ant. neglect, set aside.

implicit ADJ. understood, unsaid, implied, tacit.
Ant. explicit, stated.

imply V. hint, indicate, suggest.
Ant. express, define, describe.

import N. substance, purport, amount, meaning, importance, significance.
Ant. insignificance, export.

• importance N. significance, import, weight, consequence, concern. *They misunderstood the significance of the discovery.*
Ant. worthless, triviality, pettiness.

• important ADJ. consequential, meaningful, influential, significant, substantial, weighty. *Two weeks of deliberation were required to consider the consequential matter.*
Ant. insignificant, small, worthless, inconsequential.

impose V. demand, inflict, require.

• impossible ADJ. infeasible, unworkable, impractical. *Your reforms may prove infeasible.*
Ant. easy, feasible, practical.

impotent ADJ. helpless, powerless, weak, frail, harmless.
Ant. powerful, strong, potent.

impractical ADJ. impossible, unworkable, infeasible, unattainable, unachievable, unrealistic.
Ant. feasible, workable, pragmatic.

impress V. engrave, pound, drive, excite, arrest, stir, move.
Ant. bore, lull, nonplus.

• impression N. interpretation, understanding, mark, feeling, effect, influence; indentation, print. *Please tell us your interpretation of the play.*

improper ADJ. inappropriate, unfit, unseemingly, unsuitable.
Ant. decent, correct, right.

• improve V. refine, amend, better, upgrade, repair, help. *We plan to refine the process before beginning production.*
Ant. decay, impair, worsen.

impudent ADJ. brazen, presumptuous, smart, audacious, arrogant, rude, disrespectful.
Ant. modest, courteous, retiring.

impulsive ADJ. spontaneous, rash, hasty, impatient, fiery.
Ant. restrained, thoughtful, sensible.

impure ADJ. unclean, defiled, corrupt, mixed, alloyed, crude.
Ant. immaculate, clean, pure.

inaccessible ADJ. unreachable, inconvenient, unattainable.
Ant. convenient, reachable, attainable.

inaccurate ADJ. wrong, incorrect, erroneous, false.
Ant. exact, precise, right.

inactive ADJ. still, idle, inoperative, motionless.
Ant. energetic, dynamic, active.

• inadequate ADJ. insufficient, incompetent, unqualified, incapable. *The agency has insufficient resources.*
Ant. sufficient, suitable, adequate.

inborn ADJ. inherent, natural, innate.
Ant. learned, acquired, taught.

incalculable ADJ. measureless, infinite, countless, limitless, enormous.
Ant. limited, finite, calculable.

incident N. evident, happening, occurrence, circumstance.

incisive ADJ. shrewd, perceptive, discerning, acute, penetrating.
Ant. slow, dull, obtuse.

incline V. lean, tend, slope, tilt, list.

income N. proceeds, earnings, revenue, pay.
Ant. expenses, expenditures, bills.

incompetent ADJ. inefficient, unqualified, unfit, incapable, unskilled, irresponsible.
Ant. proficient, skillful, experienced.

incomprehensible ADJ. unintelligible, impenetrable, unfathomable, incompetent.
Ant. understandable, intelligible.

incongruous ADJ. incompatible, inconsistent, conflicting, foreign, dissonant.
Ant. suitable, compatible, harmonious.

inconsistent ADJ. conflicting, incongruous, fluctuating, capricious, unsteady, incompatible.
Ant. uniform, steady, consistent.

inconspicuous ADJ. unobtrusive, obscure, unnoticed, retiring.
Ant. obvious, obtrusive, conspicuous.

inconvenience N. trouble, discomfort.
Ant. advantageousness, convenience.

incorrect ADJ. false, wrong, erroneous, inaccurate.
Ant. exact, right, correct.

- **increase** V. enlarge, amplify, expand, rise, augment, swell; —N. boost, enlargement, addition, augmentation. *They can enlarge the seating area by adding temporary bleachers.*
Ant. decrease, reduce, deplete.

incredible ADJ. astonishing, fantastic, fabulous, unbelievable, impossible.
Ant. realistic, believable, credible.

indecent ADJ. obscene, offensive, improper, shocking.
Ant. respectful, virtuous, decent.

indefinite ADJ. undetermined, general, indistinct, vague, unclear, obscure.
Ant. certain, sure, apparent.

indelicate ADJ. tactless, improper, unbecoming, offensive.
Ant. proper, unoffensive, tactful.

independence N. separation, freedom, sovereignty, self-reliance, autonomy, self-sufficience.
Ant. dependence, subservience, subordination, reliance.

• **indicate** V. designate, show, mark, testify, attest. *You should designate a second driver.*
Ant. confuse, perplex, conceal, hide.

indication N. sign, suggestion, hint, clue.

indifference N. apathy, insensitivity, insignificance, unimportance.
Ant. sympathy, concern, compassion.

indifferent ADJ. detached, nonchalant, cool, insensitive.
Ant. sympathetic, caring, sentimental.

indigenous ADJ. native, existing, innate, natural, inherent.
Ant. foreign, alien, imported.

indignation N. resentment, ire, crossness, anger.
Ant. serenity, calmness, good feelings, affability.

indignity N. insult, outrage, offense, disrespect, humiliation.
Ant. praise, esteem, honor.

indispensable ADJ. vital, necessary, essential.
Ant. unnecessary, pointless, gratuitous, needless.

indisposed ADJ. unwilling, reluctant, disinclined, sickly.
Ant. inclined, healthy, willing.

indisputable ADJ. unquestionable, certain, undeniable.
Ant. debatable, questionable, unsettled, controversial.

indistinct ADJ. hazy, dim, unclear, uncertain.
Ant. distinct, clear, lucid, certain.

• individual ADJ. particular, singular, separate,
different, unique, personal. *No one else has her
particular skills.*
Ant. universal, ordinary, regular.

indoctrinate V. instruct, teach, initiate, instill,
propagandize.
Ant. mislead, neglect, confuse.

indolent, ADJ. lazy, lethargic, slothful.
Ant. energetic, spirited, lively, vigorous, brisk.

indulge V. participate, satisfy, concede, cherish,
please, humor.
Ant. annoy, irritate, harass.

industry N. business, enterprise, diligence,
persistence.
Ant. negligence, idleness, sloth, play.

ineffectiveness N. ineffectuality, futility.
Ant. efficiency, success, potency.

• inefficient ADJ. wasteful, unproductive, inept,
incompetent, unskilled. *The whole city practiced
wasteful habits for garbage disposal.*
Ant. able, practical, efficient.

inept ADJ. unskilled, inefficient, awkward, clumsy,
unhandy.
Ant. able, competent, skilled.

inequality N. disproportion, disparity, irregularity.
Ant. regularity, justice, equality.

inexcusable ADJ. unjustifiable, unforgivable,
unpardonable, indefensible.
Ant. pardonable, forgivable, justifiable.

infallible ADJ. perfect, reliable, dependable,
foolproof.
Ant. fallible, imperfect, unreliable, undependable.

infamous ADJ. notorious, shocking, reprehensible,
despicable, abhorrent.
Ant. perfect, admirable, sublime, virtuous.

infamy N. notoriety, shamefulness, dishonorableness, disgracefulness, villainy.
Ant. fame, respect, adulation.

infant N. baby, child, young.
Ant. adult, grown-up.

infatuated ADJ. enamored, obsessed, enthralled, fascinated, beguiled.
Ant. prudent, sensible, fancy-free.

infect V. taint, transfer, poison, communicate.
Ant. clean, cleanse, sanitize, disinfect.

infer V. extract, conclude, deduce, gather, guess.
Ant. discover, prove, find.

inferior ADJ. common, mediocre, average, ordinary, second-rate.
Ant. better, superior, prime

infertile ADJ. sterile, barren, unfruitful, childless.
Ant. fertile, productive, fruitful, fecund.

infidelity N. unfaithfulness, disloyalty, betrayal.
Ant. faithfulness, loyalty, fidelity, trustworthiness.

infinite ADJ. eternal, boundless, endless, vast, incalculable.
Ant. limited, bounded, finite.

infinity N. eternity, limitlessness, inexhaustibility, boundlessness.

infirmity N. sickness, disease, malady, frailty, debility, decrepitude, illness.
Ant. vigor, force, strength.

inflated ADJ. exaggerated, enlarged, expanded, ostentatious, pretension.
Ant. compressed, condensed, shrunken.

inflexible ADJ. rigid, firm, stiff, tenacious, unalterable.
Ant. resilient, elastic, pliable.

inflict V. levy, impose.
Ant. retract, lift.

• **influence** N. effect, weight, leverage, sway, control, impress. *The effect of legislation far exceeded its original intent.*
Ant. pettiness, unimportance, weakness.

● **influential** ADJ. powerful, important, consequential, prominent. *A powerful legislator will speak on behalf of the bill.*
  Ant. weak, impotent, worthless.

inform V. enlighten, notify, educate, advise, relate.
  Ant. hide, cover, cache.

informal ADJ. easy, unofficial, regular, natural, conversational.
  Ant. ceremonious, precise, official.

infrequent ADJ. rare, occasional, unusual, scarce, uncommon.
  Ant. often, common, usual.

infuriate V. anger, madden, incense, exasperate.
  Ant. pacify, appease, soothe, calm.

ingenious ADJ. clever, imaginative, resourceful, original.
  Ant. ordinary, everyday, commonplace, expected, uninspired.

ingredient N. element, component, constituent, item.

inhabit V. occupy, populate, live in, make one's home in.
  Ant. abandon, leave, move away.

inhale V. breathe, breathe in, inspire.
  Ant. exhale, breathe out.

inheritance N. legacy, heritage, birthright, patrimony.

● **initial** ADJ. first, primary, beginning, outset, basic, early. *The first step is often the hardest.*
  Ant. subsequent, latter, later, furthermost.

initiate V. start, commence, introduce, begin, open.
  Ant. end, terminate, finish.

injure V. hurt, impair, harm, damage, blemish.
  Ant. cure, repair, heal.

injury N. injustice, damage, hurt, harm.
  Ant. benefit, blessing, favor.

innate ADJ. native, hereditary, built-in, inborn, constitutional.
  Ant. learned, taught.

innocent ADJ. pure, clean, uncorrupted, guiltless, ignorant.
Ant. guilty, reprehensible, delinquent.

inquire V. question, ask, explore, investigate.
Ant. answer, respond, reply.

inquiry N. study, probe, examination, inquest, investigation.
Ant. answer, confession, discovery.

inquisitor N. questioner, interrogator, inquirer.
Ant. suspect.

insane ADJ. crazy, mad, deranged, demented, maniacal, foolish.
Ant. sound, rational, well-adjusted, reasonable.

insanity N. madness, foolishness, mania, psychopathy, craziness, dementia.
Ant. stability, calm, lucidity, sanity.

● **insecure** ADJ. unsure, steady, shaky, unstable, nervous.
We all felt somewhat unsure about the unusual travel arrangements.
Ant. strong, assured, confident.

insensible ADJ. apathetic, stolid, unfeeling, insensitive, dull, unconscious.
Ant. feeling, aware, conscious.

insincere ADJ. artificial, dishonest, false, deceitful.
Ant. honest, truthful, straightforward, sincere.

insinuate V. infer, purport, hint, suggest, intimate.
Ant. evade, disguise, conceal.

insipid ADJ. banal, inane, flat, tasteless, unimaginative, bland.
Ant. savory, palatable, delicious, interesting.

● **insist** V. demand, urge, press, persevere, pressure.
A customer should demand courteous treatment.
Ant. beg, plead, request.

insolence N. impudence, rudeness, arrogance, defiance.
Ant. civility, courtesy, politeness.

inspect V. search, analyze, survey, examine, investigate.
Ant. ignore, overlook, neglect.

inspiration N. enthusiasm, elation, encouragement.
Ant. lethargy, apathy.

inspire V. stimulate, provoke, excite, encourage, prompt.
Ant. discourage, bore, rebuff.

instance N. example, occurrence, illustration, case.

instant N. moment, juncture, flash, point.

instigate V. activate, bring about, initiate, activate.

instinct N. intuition, feeling, insight, talent.
Ant. reason, acquisition, learning, will, education.

instruct V. educate, teach, command, counsel, direct.
Ant. misguide, pervert, ignore, miseducate.

instrument N. implement, device, tool.

insubstantial ADJ. insecure, tenuous, infirm, immaterial.
Ant. substantial, important, consequential, worthy.

insufficient ADJ. inadequate, scarce, sparse, incomplete.
Ant. ample, enough, plentiful.

insular ADJ. remote, local, provincial, protected.
Ant. universal, unprotected, well-known.

intact ADJ. good, whole, entire, complete, undamaged.
Ant. incomplete, defective, broken, fragmented.

integrate V. unify, consolidate, join, blend.
Ant. segregate, isolate, seclude.

integrity N. character, honesty, faithfulness, soundness.
Ant. corruption, dishonesty, infidelity.

intellectual ADJ. learned, intelligent, thoughtful, insightful, sharp, precocious.
Ant. inane, stupid, unlettered, irrational.

intend V. design, propose, mean, aim, conceive.

intense ADJ. furious, fierce, vehement, earnest, desperate.
Ant. lazy, inert, latent, slow.

intent N. meaning, intention, desire, object, motive.

- **interest** N. advantage, benefit, concern, portion.
  Further education may be to your advantage.
  Ant. default, indifference, bother, bore, displease.

  interfere V. obstruct, hinder, meddle, conflict, frustrate.
  Ant. aid, help, stand aside.

  internal ADJ. inner, domestic, inherent, interior, intrinsic.
  Ant. external, peripheral.

  interpret V. decipher, unravel, translate, render, play.
  Ant. misunderstand, misinterpret, pervert.

- **interpretation** N. explanation, commentary, rendition, performance, execution. *Few people accepted his explanation of the events.*
  Ant. perversion, caricature, distortion, misrepresentation.

  interrogate V. inquire, examine, ask, interpolate, probe.
  Ant. acknowledge, reply, answer.

  interrupt V. interfere, obstruct, suspend, stop, hinder.
  Ant. prolong, continue, sustain.

  intersperse V. spread, scatter, mix together.

  intimate ADJ. confidential, close, firsthand, familiar.
  Ant. distant, formal, cool.

  intimidate V. threaten, terrify, bully, frighten, browbeat.
  Ant. assist, inspire, praise.

  intolerant ADJ. bigoted, narrow, close-minded, prejudiced, biased.
  Ant. unbiased, impartial, lenient.

  intoxication N. elation, drunkenness, inebriation.
  Ant. soberness, levelheadedness.

  intricate ADJ. complex, involved, difficult, complicated.
  Ant. simple, easy, clear, uncomplicated.

  intrinsic ADJ. fundamental, essential, constitutional, innate, inherent, honest, true.
  Ant. extrinsic, nonessential, foreign.

introduce V. present, begin, initiate, originate, interpose, insert, preface.
Ant. conclude, part, end.

intrude V. infringe, break in upon, interlope, interrupt.
Ant. leave, withdraw.

intuition N. feeling, insight, instinct, impulse, guess.
Ant. reason, rationale, logic.

invasion N. aggression, intrusion, attack, raid, foray.
Ant. repulsion, defense, protection.

inventive ADJ. innovative, creative, new, ingenious, original.
Ant. outdated, antiquated, old, mundane.

investigate V. explore, examine, inspect, analyze, study.
Ant. answer, overlook, solve.

investigation N. exploration, examination, analysis, inspection, inquiry.
Ant. results, solution, neglect.

invitation N. inducement, encouragement, bid, solicitation, call.
Ant. repulsion, denial, rejection.

invite V. summon, ask, court, bid, solicitate.
Ant. repulse, reject, deny.

• **involve** V. implicate, entangle, include, entail, ensnare, imply. *Her testimony may implicate him in the robbery.*
Ant. disengage, extricate, separate.

irate ADJ. angry, exasperated, indignant.
Ant. happy, content, calm, at peace.

irregular ADJ. uneven, asymmetrical, abnormal, aberrant, inconsistent.
Ant. normal, even, consistent.

• **irrelevant** ADJ. inapplicable, extraneous, immaterial. *Your comments are interesting but inapplicable.*
Ant. appropriate, pertinent, fitting.

irresponsible ADJ. reckless, immature, careless, unreliable, foolish.
Ant. serious, trustworthy, accountable.

irritable ADJ. ill-tempered, sensitive, querulous, excitable.
Ant. tranquil, cool, composed.

irritate V. annoy, provoke, madden, disturb, inflame.
Ant. soothe, assuage, calm, placate.

isolate V. separate, imprison, seclude, segregate.
Ant. mingle, include, mix.

isolated ADJ. remote, solitary, secluded, quarantined.
Ant. populated, busy.

• issue N. point, subject, question, topic; offspring; —v. emanate, distribute, proceed. *I do not understand the point you are trying to make.*
Ant. beginning, inception; parent; repress, retain.

item N. piece, part, detail, topic.

itinerant ADJ. unsettled, roaming, arrant, nomadic.
Ant. located, permanent, settled.

J

jail N. prison, reformatory, penitentiary; —V. imprison, confine.
Ant, release, free.

jargon N. terminology, argot, slang, lingo.

jealous ADJ. envious, distrustful, doubtful, questioning, suspicious, possessive.
Ant. content, trusting, satisfied.

jeopardize V. endanger, threaten, imperil.
Ant. shield, protect, safeguard.

jerk V. pull, yank, twitch, shake, tug, wrench.

jinx N. hex, charm, spell, curse.
Ant. blessing, good luck, talisman.

jittery ADJ. nervous, excited, uneasy, edgy, anxious.
Ant. calm, relaxed, easy.

job N. employment, function, position, career, duty.
Ant. unemployment, idleness.

join V. couple, connect, enroll, enlist, combine.
Ant. sever, divorce, separate.

joint N. link, coupling, juncture.

joke N. wit, humor, wisecrack, gag, parody, prank.
Ant. seriousness, earnestness.

journey V. trek, travel, go, voyage; —N. voyage, trip, excursion.

jovial ADJ. gay, happy, glad, joyous, cheerful, lighthearted.
Ant. serious, sad, morose, melancholic, unhappy.

joy N. ecstasy, rapture, glee, happiness, cheer.
Ant. sorrow, melancholy, heartache, misery.

judge V. determine, arbitrate, decide, rule, decree.
Ant. defer, hesitate.

jumble V. shuffle, disorder, confuse.
Ant. arrange, classify, straighten.

jumbo ADJ. oversized, huge, gigantic, giant.
Ant. small, tiny, petit, diminutive, minute.

jump v. leap, bound, bolt, hurdle, spring.

junction N. gathering, meeting, convergence, coupling, joining, union.
Ant. divergence, separation, break.

jungle N. tangle, tropics, rain forest.
Ant. desert, wasteland.

just ADJ. right, deserved, appropriate, suitable, due.
Ant. unfair, wrong, partial.

justice N. fairness, equity, lawfulness, legality.
Ant. partiality, corruption, inequality.

• justify v. defend, warrant, explain, rationalize, confirm. *You may have to defend your point of view.*
Ant. reproach, accuse, blame.

jut v. protrude, extend, bulge, overhang.
Ant. cave, indent, collapse.

juvenile ADJ. young, childish, immature, adolescent.
Ant. old, adult, mature.

K

keen ADJ. clever, sharp, enthusiastic, acute, incisive.
Ant. thick, insensate, stupid, dull.

keep V. hold, retain, save, conserve.
Ant. relinquish, discard, abandon.

kernel N. seed, heart, germ, core.
Ant. exterior, shell, skin, chaff.

key N. answer, ticket, clue.

kick V. complain, break, boot.

kill V. murder, annihilate, finish, cancel, destroy, terminate.
Ant. protect, preserve, save.

kin N. relative, family, clan, kindred.
Ant. unknown, stranger, enemy, alien.

kind ADJ. tender, caring, good, benevolent, loving; —N. type, sort, variety, manner.
Ant. malignant, harsh, cruel.

kindle V. arouse, provoke, light, excite, ignite.
Ant. discourage, quench, douse.

kindness N. benevolence, grace, sympathy, goodness, generosity.
Ant. malevolence, bitterness, viciousness.

kindred N. family, family members, kin, relatives.

king N. monarch, ruler, sovereign, emperor.

kiss V. buss, smooch, smack, brush.

knock V. wrap, hit, tap, thump.

knot V. twist, tangle, snarl; —N. twist, loop; gathering, group.
Ant. untie, loosen, unfasten, untangle.

• **know** V. understand, feel, appreciate, acknowledge, comprehend. *Much of what the island natives understand cannot be translated.*
Ant. question, suspect, doubt.

knowledge N. learning, wisdom, understanding, education, information, intelligence.
Ant. darkness, ignorance, inexperience, engima.

L

label N. sticker, tag, mark, stamp; —V. call, mark, classify.

labor N. work, drudgery, employment, toil, strive, travail.
Ant. idleness, laziness, inactivity.

laborious ADJ. difficult, hard, burdensome, arduous, tiresome.
Ant. trivial, effortless, easy.

lag V. linger, delay, loiter, falter.
Ant. dash, hasten, quicken.

lair N. hole, den, burrow, hideout.

lame ADJ. disabled, crippled, sore.
Ant. able-bodied, healthy, fit.

land N. estate, acres, property, earth, homeland.
Ant. sky, sea, atmosphere, air, space.

language N. speech, dialect, tongue, jargon.

languid ADJ. limp, spiritless, passive, lethargic, slothful.
Ant. energetic, strong, eager, vigorous.

lapse N. slip, error, backsliding, relapse.

larceny N. theft, stealing, embezzlement, robbery.
Ant. reimbursement, compensation, return.

large ADJ. big, huge, enormous, massive, bulky, important.
Ant. slender, thin, small.

lash V. strike, drive, whip, beat, goad.
Ant. soothe, appease, reward.

lassitude N. exhaustion, stupor, apathy, lethargy, listlessness, fatigue.
Ant. lightness, energy, agility.

last ADJ. terminal, final, concluding, closing.
Ant. first, introductory, incipient.

late ADJ. overdue, tardy, delayed, slow, deceased.
Ant. early, prompt, timely, living.

latent ADJ. hidden, dormant, remissive, inactive.
Ant. apparent, exposed, evident.

later ADJ. subsequent, future, posterior; —ADV. after, next.
Ant. earlier, prior; before, sooner, previous.

latitude N. liberty, freedom, range, breadth, scope, extent.
Ant. longitude, constriction.

laud V. praise, honor, extol, esteem, merit.
Ant. blame, dishonor, revile.

laugh V. giggle, chuckle, snicker, cackle.
Ant. cry, weep, wail.

launch V. start, initiate, introduce, begin, drive, fire.
Ant. finish, land, close.

launder V. wash, cleanse, dry-clean.

lavish ADJ. exorbitant, profuse, luxurious, extravagant, abundant; —V. squander, shower.
Ant. empty, scarce; economize, withhold.

law N. measure, legislation, enactment, ordinance, edict, theorem, principle, axiom.
Ant. transgression, felony, violation, anarchy, chaos.

lawful ADJ. legal, legitimate, permitted, allowable, authorized.
Ant. illegal, prohibited, lawless.

lawless ADJ. illegal, disobedient, illicit, prohibited, lax, negligent, tolerant, careless, loose, unobservant.
Ant. permissible, legal, legitimate, responsible, careful.

lay V. set, place, put.
Ant. pick up, take.

laziness N. loafing, sloth, sluggishness, idleness, dormancy, lethargy.
Ant. industry, energy, vigor.

lazy ADJ. lethargic, sluggish, dormant, slow, inactive, slothful, sleepy.
Ant. sharp, quick, active, energetic.

lead v. guide, conduct, oversee, precede, direct, regulate.
Ant. obey, consent, conform.

leader N. chief, boss, director, guide, commander, conductor.
Ant. follower, worker, adherent.

league N. conference, union, class, alliance.

lean v. incline, tend, bend, slant, hang.
Ant. straighten.

leap v. jump, spring, vault, bound, romp.

learn v. gain, acquire, study, discover, master.
Ant. overlook, neglect, teach, educate.

leave v. go, part, quit, desert, vacate.
Ant. stay, remain, continue.

lecture N. talk, sermon, speech, homily.

legalize v. legitimize, allow, authorize, permit, warrant.
Ant. forbid, disallow.

legend N. myth, lore, fable, tradition.
Ant. fact, history, actuality.

legitimacy N. legality, truth, validity, authenticity.
Ant. invalidity, illegality, untruthfulness.

leisure N. rest, freedom, relaxation, vacation, ease.
Ant. duty, work, toil.

lend v. loan, advance, supply, give.
Ant. take, borrow.

length N. limit, extreme, reach, extent, distance.

lengthen v. prolong, extend, stretch, increase.
Ant. abbreviate, curtail, shorten.

lessen v. diminish, reduce, minimize, make less.
Ant. increase, supply, enhance, enrich.

let v. allow, permit, authorize, grant.
Ant. obstruct, prevent, keep.

lethal ADJ. deadly, fatal, toxic, life-threatening.
Ant. nonlethal, life-giving.

lethargic ADJ. sluggish, lazy, listless, slow, apathetic.
Ant. vital, energetic, lively.

letter N. note, epistle, missive, literalness.

level ADJ. flat, uniform, even, horizontal, smooth;
—V. destroy, flatten, demolish, equalize.
Ant. vertical, rugged, irregular; raise, erect.

levy V. charge; —N. tax, duty, draft.
Ant. collect, pay.

liable ADJ. accountable, responsible, susceptible,
subject to, likely, vulnerable.
Ant. excusable, freed, absolved.

liar N. perjurer, storyteller, fabricator.

libel N. defamation, vilification, slander.
Ant. truthfulness, candor, honesty.

liberal ADJ. progressive, left, fair, broad, generous.
Ant. narrow, greedy, intolerant, conservative.

liberty N. privilege, right, freedom, latitude, license.
Ant. oppression, slavery, bondage.

license V. warrant, permit, approve, authorize; —N.
liberty, permission.
Ant. withhold, limit, refuse.

lie V. fabricate, falsify, deceive, repose, recline.
Ant. rise, stand.

life N. existence, nature, vitality, duration, entity,
lifespan, longevity.
Ant. death, demise, decease.

lift V. elevate, raise, hoist, recall, revoke.
Ant. lower, decline, return.

light N. illumination, brightness, radiation; —V.
brighten, illuminate, animate, ignite, fire.
Ant. dark, shade, sadness, heaviness; extinguish,
darken.

light-headed ADJ. dizzy, giddy, vertiginous, silly, faint.
Ant. sober, clearheaded.

lighthearted ADJ. gay, happy, cheerful, glad.
Ant. somber, serious, stolid.

like V. admire, fancy, enjoy; —ADJ. analogous, similar,
equivalent.
Ant. different, divergent, unlike.

liken V. equate, compare, analogize, favor.
Ant. distinguish, diverge, separate.

likeness N. analogy, similarity, comparison, affinity.
Ant. dissimilarity.

- **limit** N. boundary, maximum, extreme, length; —V. restrict, confine. *It was necessary to place some boundary on their investigation.*
Ant. center, beginning.

limp V., N. hobble, stagger; —ADJ. soft, flexible, limber.
Ant. rigid, hard, stiff.

limpid ADJ. transparent, clear, translucent, pure, bright.
Ant. dark, opaque, cloudy.

line N. row, succession, file, cord, string, rope, program, policy.

linger V. hesitate, delay, loiter, remain, pause.
Ant. hurry, run, hasten.

link V. join, connect, combine, associate.
Ant. separate, divide, sever.

liquidate V. eliminate, annihilate, terminate, settle, pay, kill.
Ant. renew, refurbish, build.

list N. catalog, schedule, record.

listen V. hear, attend, mark, heed, hark, pay attention to.
Ant. neglect, disregard, ignore.

listless ADJ. languid, lethargic, lazy, limp.
Ant. energetic, vigorous, brisk, animated.

literacy N. reading ability.
Ant. illiteracy, inability to read.

literal ADJ. verbatim, actual, exact, true, rigorous.
Ant. deceiving, wrong, erroneous.

little ADJ. small, petite, unimportant, trivial, insignificant.
Ant. big, large, enormous.

livable ADJ. inhabitable, bearable, cozy, occupiable.
Ant. unbearable, uninhabitable, unlivable.

live V. reside, dwell, exist, be, survive, inhabit.
Ant. perish, die, depart.

lively ADJ. animated, vivacious, spirited, happy, active.
Ant. gloomy, dull, despondent.

livid ADJ. furious, angry, discolored, bruised.
Ant. serene, calm, content, at peace.

living N. support, sustenance, livelihood, alimony;
—ADJ. alive, existing.

load N. cargo, burden, weight; —V. charge, fill, heap.

loathing N. hate, disgust, abhorrence, disapproval,
condemnation.
Ant. admiration, esteem.

loathsome ADJ. offensive, filthy, abominable, foul,
obnoxious.
Ant. delightful, wondrous, beautiful.

local ADJ. limited, restricted, isolated, narrow, narrow-
minded, parochial, provincial.
Ant. universal, widespread, international.

locale N. scene, locality, environment.

locality N. place, region, location, area, vicinity.

locate V. find, discover, position, place, situate.
Ant. misplace, mislocate, lose.

location N. point, position, spot, place, site.

lofty ADJ. airy, elevated, exalted, towering, high.
Ant. shy, modest, diffident.

• **logic** N. reason, sense, rationality, coherence, validity.
Her speech appealed to reason more than emotion.
Ant. irrationality, fantasy, foolishness.

loiter V. stall, linger, idle, delay.
Ant. hurry, rush, hasten.

lone ADJ. separate, sole, solitary, deserted, secluded.
Ant. joined, accompanied, together.

lonely ADJ. depressed, friendless, lonesome, deserted,
desolate.
Ant. populated, crowded.

lonesome ADJ. alone, desolate, isolated, solitary.
Ant. befriended, cheerful.

long ADJ. lengthy, elongated, extended, tedious,
prolonged.
Ant. short, curt, brief.

longing N. dream, desire, yearning.
Ant. antipathy, apathy.

look V. survey, glance, see, regard, watch, observe.
Ant. disregard, miss, ignore.

lookout N. outlook, guard, observatory, sentry.

loose ADJ., ADV. untied, unrestrained, free, relaxed.
Ant. tight, bound, taut, precise.

loosen V. untie, undo, ease, unfasten.
Ant. fasten, tie, tighten.

loot N. booty, plunder; —v. plunder, ransack, steal, rob.

lore N. myth, tradition, folklore, superstition, fable.
Ant. history, truth, fact.

lorn ADJ. lonely, abandoned, solitary.
Ant. busy, populated, crowded.

lose V. misplace, mislay, waste.
Ant. find, recover, conquer, win.

lost ADJ. missing, gone, absent, vanished.
Ant. found, discovered.

lot N. plot, parcel; fate, fortune; gathering, assemblage, group.

loud ADJ. resonant, deafening, roaring, clamorous, noisy.
Ant. silent, soft, quiet, subdued.

love N. amour, passion, emotion, tenderness, friendship, devotion, attraction, warmth.
Ant. antipathy, loathing, hatred, hate.

low ADJ. deep, depressed, sunken, shameless, disgraceful, base.
Ant. high, elevated, prominent, respectable, honest.

lowly ADJ. humble, common, poor, unimportant, submissive.
Ant. worthy, proud, important.

loyal ADJ. faithful, devoted, trustworthy, steadfast.
Ant. treacherous, faithless, disloyal.

lucid ADJ. clear, serene, transparent, pure, rational, explicit, plain, evident.
Ant. murky, nebulous, confused, incomprehensible.

• **luck** N. fortune, chance, success, fate. *He had the good fortune to win the lottery.*
  Ant. defeat, bad fortune, ruin.

lucrative ADJ. rewarding, profitable, well-paid, beneficial.
  Ant. profitless, pointless, unrewarding.

ludicrous ADJ. foolish, ridiculous, absurd.
  Ant. sensible, reasonable, rational.

luminary N. dignitary, celebrity, star.
  Ant. nobody, commoner.

luminous ADJ. radiant, shining, glowing, incandescent.
  Ant. dark, opaque, dull.

lump N. hunk, chunk, clump, wad, clod, lug.

lurch V. tilt, roll, stumble, stagger, falter, reel, wobble.
  Ant. stand, continue.

lure V. tempt, attract, entice, bait, delude.
  Ant. repel, antagonize, disgust.

lurid ADJ. pale, horrible, ghastly, gruesome.
  Ant. banal, unimaginative, modest.

luscious ADJ. delightful, pleasing, delicious, satisfying, appetizing.
  Ant. sour, bitter, disagreeable, distasteful.

lush ADJ. succulent, abundant, fresh, opulent, profuse.
  Ant. barren, dry, sparse.

lust V. desire, hunger; —N. craving, thirst, passion, avarice.
  Ant. purity, restraint, chastity.

lustrous ADJ. eminent, glossy, shining, brilliant, bright, glowing.
  Ant. somber, drab, obscure.

lusty ADJ. vigorous, robust, strong, vital.
  Ant. weak, unhealthy, lethargic.

luxuriant ADJ. profuse, abundant, thick, fruitful, rich.
  Ant. thin, infertile, arid.

luxurious ADJ. opulent, plush, extravagant, posh, lavish.
  Ant. simple, plain, ascetic.

M

machine N. device, engine, apparatus, appliance, contraption.

mad ADJ. insane, foolish, angry, upset, wild, frenzied, enthusiastic.
Ant. sane, calm, lucid.

madden V. anger, infuriate, enrage, exasperate.
Ant. calm, placate, appease.

made-up ADJ. fictitious, invented, assumed.
Ant. real, truthful, nonfictional.

madness N. insanity, lunacy, psychosis, paranoia.
Ant. sanity, lucidity, rationality, serenity.

magic N. sorcery, wizardry, alchemy, enchantment, occultism, witchcraft.

magnanimous ADJ. generous, noble, exalted, charitable, honorable.
Ant. egotistical, selfish, vain.

magnetic ADJ. attractive, charismatic.
Ant. repellent, repulsive.

magnification N. amplification, enlargement, exaggeration.
Ant. reduction, understatement.

magnificent ADJ. excellent, sublime, outstanding, glorious, grand.
Ant. common, unimpressive, ordinary.

magnify V. amplify, enlarge, exalt, honor, exaggerate, aggrandize.
Ant. decrease, reduce, diminish.

magnitude N. degree, bulk, size, greatness, volume.
Ant. smallness, insignificance, mediocrity.

main ADJ. primary, principal, leading, foremost.
Ant. subordinate, secondary, minor.

maintain V. defend, claim, sustain, assert, justify.
Ant. discard, reject, abandon.

majestic ADJ. regal, grand, stately, royal, magnificent.
Ant. ordinary, common, humble.

make v. construct, form, do, fabricate, produce, prepare.
Ant. demolish, obliterate, destroy.

makeout v. discern, understand, recognize, perceive.
Ant. confuse, misunderstood, overlook.

maker N. originator, creator, builder.

maladroit ADJ. unskillful, clumsy, tactless, inept, awkward.
Ant. tactful, skillful, clever.

malady N. disease, illness, ailment, infirmity.
Ant. well-being, health.

male ADJ. manlike, masculine, virile.
Ant. female, feminine.

malevolent ADJ. evil, spiteful, malicious, mean, hateful.
Ant. tolerant, cordial, kind.

malfunction v. misbehave, act up, fail.
Ant. work, function.

malice N. hatred, spite, malevolence, resentment, bitterness.
Ant. charity, sympathy, benevolence.

malign v. slander, libel, defame, discredit.
Ant. compliment, celebrate, extol.

malleable ADJ. flexible, ductile, pliable, workable.
Ant. stiff, resolute, inflexible.

man N. male, mankind, human being.
Ant. woman, female.

• **manage** v. guide, conduct, rule, administer, get by, fend. *Frank can guide the company into the future.*
Ant. fumble, misconduct, fail.

management N. guidance, control, direction, administration, conservation.
Ant. staff, subordinates, employees.

manager N. executive, supervisor, boss, administrator, director.
Ant. employee, worker, subordinate.

maneuver N. movement, tactic, plot, procedure, artifice.

mania N. insanity, enthusiasm, rage, madness.
Ant. sanity, levelheadedness, calm.

maniac N. madman, lunatic, nut.

manifest V. show, embody, express; —ADJ. clear, apparent, evident, obvious.
Ant. concealed, hidden, difficult.

manifestation N. sign, display.

manipulate V. direct, control, exploit, conduct, handle, engineer.
Ant. aid, help, allow, guide.

• **mankind** N. humanity, people, men, men and women. *The future of humanity may be stake.*

man-made ADJ. artificial, synthetic, invented, manufactured.
Ant. natural, native, unadulterated.

manner N. custom, habit, behavior, style, bearing.

manners N. etiquette, civilities, behavior, demeanor, formalities.
Ant. misconduct, rudeness, vulgarity.

many ADJ. diverse, numerous, myriad, legion, several.
Ant. few, scarce.

may V., N. plot, chart, design, diagram, graph.

march V. walk, parade, step, stride, move.
Ant. stay, retreat, stop.

margin N. edge, border, limit, fringe, minimum.
Ant. interior, body, area, center.

marine ADJ. nautical, oceanic, seagoing, naval.
Ant. terrestrial, continental, earthly.

marital ADJ. matrimonial, nuptial, conjugal, espousal.
Ant. celibate, single, unmarried.

mark N. imprint, stamp, impression, symbol, dent, stain, scratch, mar.

marriage N. wedding, matrimony, conjugality, espousal, wedlock, union.
Ant. divorce, separation, celibacy.

married ADJ. wedded, espoused.
Ant. divorced, separated.

marry v. wed, espouse, mate.
Ant. divorce, separate.

martial ADJ. military, warlike, combative, belligerent.
Ant. humble, peaceful, submissive.

marvel N. sensation, wonder, prodigy, miracle.
Ant. bore, commonality.

marvelous ADJ. wondrous, phenomenal,
extraordinary, fabulous, amazing, astounding,
incredible.
Ant. ordinary, normal, insignificant.

mask v. disguise, cover, veil, hide, masquerade.
Ant. reveal, disclose, uncover.

masquerade v. pose, disguise, veil, trick.

mass N. bulk, body, total, whole, amount.
Ant. portion, part, factor.

masses N. commonality, people, magnitude, crowds.
Ant. aristocracy, nobility.

massive ADJ. immense, gigantic, weighty, huge, heavy,
colossal.
Ant. small, delicate, minute.

master N. expert, chief, savant, sage, commander,
patriarch; —v. learn, triumph, domesticate, tame.
Ant. pupil, apprentice, disciple.

masterful ADJ. dictatorial, authoritative,
commanding, artful, expert.
Ant. subordinate, beginning.

masterly ADJ. skillful, expert, adroit.
Ant. unskilled, learning.

mastermind N. organizer, instigator, genius, brains.

masterpiece N. accomplishment, monument, tour de
force.

mastery N. dominance, skill, power, ascendancy,
grasp.
Ant. downfall, impotence, failure.

match N. equivalent, equal, mate, competitor, contest,
rivalry; —v. equate, balance, liken.
Ant. dissimilarity; separate.

mate N. spouse, friend, companion; —v. match, associate.
Ant. divide, separate, distinguish.

material N. matter, substance, fabric, cloth; —ADJ. substantial, real, tangible.
Ant. intangible, ethereal, spiritual.

materialistic ADJ. earthly, carnal, worldly, mundane.
Ant. spiritual, holy, high.

materialize v. embody, appear, realize.
Ant. vanish, disappear.

maternal ADJ. caring, motherly, kind, protective, gentle.

● **matter** N. substance, material, thing, affair, subject.
We identified the unusual substance.
Ant. spirit, antimatter, nothingness.

mature ADJ. experienced, aged, adult, ripe; —v. grow, develop, ripen, age.
Ant. juvenile, undeveloped, incomplete.

maxim N. precept, proverb, adage, epigram, tenet, teaching.
Ant. hypothesis, conjecture.

maximum ADJ. greatest, largest, supreme, utmost; —N. crest, climax, ultimate, top.
Ant. least, minimum, smallest.

● **maybe** ADV. perhaps, possibly, perchance. *Perhaps it will rain tomorrow.*
Ant. certainly, definitely, unequivocally.

meager ADJ. thin, small, slender, deficit, slight.
Ant. abundant, sufficient, lavish.

mean v. intend, denote, express, state; —ADJ. malevolent, vile, ignoble, despicable.
Ant. noble, honorable, generous.

meander v. wander, ramble, drift, stroll.
Ant. hurry, rush.

● **meaning** N. significance, message, intention, purport.
She explained the significance of the data.
Ant. meaninglessness.

- **meaningful** ADJ. important, pregnant, reasonable, expressive. *They made an important contribution to the project.*
  Ant. unimportant, insignificant.

means N. instrument, medium, channel, agent, method, system, resources, manner.

measure N. volume, dimension, degree, standard, rule; —v. gauge, estimate, rule, weigh.

measured ADJ. rhythmical, deliberate, limited, finite.
  Ant. limitless, unending, infinite, incalculable.

meat N. flesh, animal, food.
  Ant. vegetable, mineral, lean.

meddle V. interfere, intrude, tamper, annoy.
  Ant. oblige, avoid, refrain.

media N. press, radio, television.

median ADJ. average, medium.
  Ant. extreme.

medication N. drug, medicine, prescription, potion.

medicine N. drug, medication, prescription, potion, treatment.

mediocre ADJ. average, ordinary, second-rate, undistinguished.
  Ant. excellent, distinguished, first-rate, prime.

meditate V. think, ponder, contemplate, consider, ruminate.
  Ant. act, disregard, neglect, overlook.

medium N. compromise, average, mean, environment, surrounding, channel, material.
  Ant. extreme, outermost.

meek ADJ. gentle, humble, unassuming, modest, calm, bashful.
  Ant. bold, arrogant, assertive.

meet V. encounter, intersect, converge, rendezvous, greet.
  Ant. shun, avoid, depart.

meeting N. assembly, reunion, convention, conference, junction.

melancholy ADJ. sad, depressed, gloomy, despondent, grim, doleful, joyless, blue.
Ant. gleeful, spritely, happy, joyous, glad.

melodious ADJ. agreeable, harmonious, pleasing, tuneful, musical.
Ant. inharmonious, discordant, dissonant.

melodramatic ADJ. theatric, dramatic, corny, sentimental.
Ant. straightforward, boring, restrained.

melody N. tune, theme, aria, air.

melt V. dissovle, vanish, blend, liquefy.
Ant. condense, thicken, freeze, solidify.

memorial N. commemoration, remembrance, record, monument.

memorize V. learn, retain, remember.
Ant. forget, obliterate.

memory N. recollection, reminiscence, remembrance, retention.
Ant. amnesia, oversight, forgetfulness.

menace N. danger, hazard, threat; —v. threaten, endanger, intimidate.
Ant. reassurance, safety, security; protect, guard.

mend V. fix, restore, collect, improve, recover.
Ant. wound, injure, damage, hurt.

• mental ADJ. intellectual, cerebral, psychological. *His intellectual abilities are particularly admirable.*
Ant. inane, somatic, brainless.

mentality N. psychology, intelligence, state of mind.

mention V. refer, name, note, allude, cite.
Ant. forget, hide, suppress.

mentor N. instructor, advisor, teacher, guide.
Ant. disciple, follower, student, pupil.

merciful ADJ. tolerant, kind, tender, benevolent, gentle, gracious.
Ant. tyrannical, savage, cruel.

merciless ADJ. remorseless, unmerciful, cruel, hard, savage.
Ant. kind, benevolent, humane.

mere ADJ. scant, bare, very.
Ant. substantial, considerable.

merely ADJ. only, barely, hardly, just.
Ant. entirely, completely, definitively, substantially.

merit N. value, quality, worth, virtue, perfection.
Ant. weakness, shame, disgrace.

meritorious ADJ. commendable, praiseworthy, estimable.
Ant. undeserving, unworthy, unfit.

merry ADJ. cheerful, happy, gay, joyous, gleeful, spritely.
Ant. unhappy, pessimistic, mournful.

mess N. disorder, confusion, jumble, melange, combination, mixture.
Ant. order, arrangement, method.

message N. communication, dispatch, letter, signal, report.

metaphor N. allegory, symbol, analogy, comparison, allusion, simile.
Ant. literality, actuality, fact.

metamorphosis N. transformation, change, conversion.
Ant. stability, changelessness.

metaphysical ADJ. abstract, supernatural, immaterial, subjective, psychological.
Ant. concrete, material, realistic.

method N. system, pattern, order, style, way.
Ant. complication, confusion, disorder.

meticulous ADJ. precise, careful, exacting, clean.
Ant. casual, unconcerned, careless.

middle ADJ. central, average, axial, median, intermediate; center, midpoint, core.
Ant. beginning, end; extremity.

midget N. dwarf, little person.
Ant. giant, colossus.

might N. authority, strength, force, power, vigor.
Ant. weakness, feebleness, unimportance.

mighty ADJ. great, forceful, strong, powerful, omnipotent, vigorous, robust.
Ant. placid, puny, delicate, weak.

migrant ADJ. transitory, itinerant, immigrant, nomadic, emigrant, transient.
Ant. stable, permanent, fixed.

migrate V. emigrate, immigrate, move, relocate, resettle.
Ant. stay, remain, endure, continue.

mild ADJ. temperate, gentle, calm, moderate, kind, peaceful.
Ant. rigid, severe, abrupt.

milieu N. setting, environment, surroundings.

military ADJ. martial, warlike, militaristic, bellicose.
Ant. peaceable, tolerant.

mimicry N. imitation, mockery, simulation, parody.
Ant. original.

mind N. intellect, reason, belief, psychology, intention, liking, inclination; —v. care, look, follow, notice.
Ant. body, matter, substance.

mindful ADJ. alert, aware, attentive, careful, observant.
Ant. inattentive, inadvertent, careless, distracted.

mindless ADJ. senseless, foolish, irrational, meaningless, pointless, insane.
Ant. thoughtful, attentive, observant.

mingle V. socialize, mix, combine, blend.
Ant. separate, distinguish, sort.

minimal ADJ. essential, basic, fundamental, smallest.
Ant. greatest, maximal, most important, largest.

• **minimum** ADJ. least, smallest, minimal, margin. *The alternative school required the least amount of discipline.*
Ant. maximum, most.

minor ADJ. inferior, lesser, subordinate, younger, lower, secondary.
Ant. important, first, adult.

minority N. ethnic group, race.
Ant. majority.

minute ADJ. small, detailed, minuscule, tiny; —N. instant, moment, second.
Ant. large, colossal, general.

miracle N. marvel, wonder, prodigy.

miraculous ADJ. wonderful, marvelous, extraordinary, spectacular, fabulous.
Ant. everyday, common, ordinary, trivial.

mirror V. reflect, echo.
Ant. invent, originate.

misadventure N. mishap, accident, catastrophe, disaster; victory, good fortune, triumph.

misapprehension N. misunderstanding, mistake, misinterpretation.
Ant. perception, comprehension, understanding.

misbehave V. malfunction, cut up, act up, carry on.
Ant. obey, behave.

miscalculate V. misfigure, misjudge.
Ant. discover, solve.

miscellaneous ADJ. combined, various, motley, confused, mixed, mingled.
Ant. elemental, homogeneous, similar.

mischief N. injury, detriment, harm, grievance, roguishness.
Ant. improvement, kindness, reparation.

• **misconception** N. misunderstanding, misinterpretation, misapprehension. *Their actions were unfortunately based on a misunderstanding.*

misconstrue V. misunderstand, misconceive, mistake, misinterpret, misjudge, misread.
Ant. solve, construe, unravel.

miscue N. error, mistake, blunder.
Ant. cue, certainty, key.

miser N. scrooge, tightwad, hoarder, skimper, cheapskate.
Ant. spendthrift, big spender, philanthropist.

miserable ADJ. woeful, wretched, pained, sorrowful, unhappy, sick, depressed.
Ant. joyous, lighthearted, happy.

misery N. unhappiness, pain, sorrow, affliction, anguish, grief, despondency.
Ant. rapture, ecstasy, joy.

misfortune N. bad luck, adversity, accident, injury, calamity.
Ant. success, prosperity, good fortune.

mishandle V. botch, abuse, mistreat.
Ant. assist, aid.

mishap N. accident, disaster, calamity.

misjudge V. miscalculate, err, misconstrue, overshoot.
Ant. judge, evaluate.

mismanage V. botch, mishandle, misbehave.
Ant. manage, administrate.

misplace V. lose, displace.
Ant. discover, find.

misrepresent V. exaggerate, misstate, feign, pervert, falsify, distort.
Ant. depict, delineate, represent.

miss V. desire, crave, want, need, yearn for, drop, fumble.
Ant. catch, get, have, obtain.

mission N. affair, purpose, errand, activity.

misstate V. give misinformation, say in error.
Ant. state, declare, pronounce, express, say.

misstep N. error, mistake.

mist N. haze, fog, cloud.

• **mistake** N. error, oversight, failure, flaw. *One error is certainly forgivable.*
Ant. accuracy, fact, authenticity.

mistrust V. suspect, fear, distrust; —N. doubt, suspicion.
Ant. trust, believe, accept; assurance, confidence.

misunderstand V. disagree, misinterpret, misapprehend, misconstrue.
Ant. understand, agree, comprehend.

misuse V. abuse, exploit, manipulate, take advantage of.
Ant. use, employ.

mix V. blend, combine, fuse, merge, stir, mingle.
Ant. separate, sort, remove.

mixture N. blend, amalgam, fusion, compound.
Ant. purification, element.

mob N. crowd, gang, swarm, horde.

mobile ADJ. transportable, movable, free.
Ant. stationary, fixed, immovable, permanent.

mobilize V. organize, drive, rally, marshal.
Ant. disperse, separate, end.

mock V. imitate, ridicule, scorn, jeer.
Ant. praise, honor, applaud.

mode N. fashion, style, method, manner, condition.

model N. pattern, example, miniature, imitation,
copy, style, version, shape, form, design, mold.

moderate ADJ. reasonable, temperate, fair, judicious,
calm, modest.
Ant. unreasonable, unfair, radical, excessive.

moderation N. temperance, measure, calm.
Ant. outrage, extravagance.

modern ADJ. new, recent, current, contemporary.
Ant. obsolete, ancient, primitive.

modest ADJ. retiring, shy, bashful, reserved, diffident.
Ant. excessive, imposing, extravagant.

modesty N. humility, diffidence, humbleness,
simplicity, chastity.
Ant. ego, pomp, arrogance.

modify V. change, alter, convert, transform.
Ant. fix.

moist ADJ. damp, humid, watery, soaked, wet, dank.
Ant. arid, dry, desertlike.

mold V. make, shape, form, cast, model.

molten ADJ. melted, heated to a semiliquid form.
Ant. solid, concrete, frozen.

moment N. minute, flash, second, instant.

momentary ADJ. impending, imminent, transitory.
Ant. permanent, unchanging.

momentous ADJ. serious, important, consequential, critical, eventful, memorable.
Ant. insignificant, trivial, unimportant.

- **money** N. wealth, gold, riches, notes, coins, greenbacks, bills, treasure. *Happiness does not depend primarily upon wealth.*

monitor V. check, watch, observe, supervise.
Ant. ignore, disregard, overlook, neglect.

monopoly N. restriction, limitation, syndicate, corner, cartel, combination.
Ant. free market.

monotony N. tediousness, tedium, boredom, uniformity, monotone, ennui.
Ant. versatility, variance, interest.

monster N. freak, fiend, beast, demon, brute.

monstrous ADJ. huge, enormous, immense, incredible, shocking, outrageous, horrible, awful.
Ant. small, customary, expected.

mood N. temper, spirit, disposition, emotion.

moody ADJ. temperamental, excitable, whimsical, mercurial, fickle.
Ant. constant, levelheaded.

moor V. attach, anchor, fasten.
Ant. loosen, detach, let go.

moral ADJ. honest, ethical, honorable, upright, elevated.
Ant. evil, unethical, amoral, immoral.

morale N. confidence, esprit, assurance.
Ant. apprehension, uncertainty, despondence, fear.

morality N. good, ethic.
Ant. dishonest, indecency.

morals N. values, ethics,

morbid ADJ. sick, morose, melancholic, unwholesome, macabre.
Ant. normal, healthy, wholesome.

more ADJ. additional, extra; —ADV. better, additionally.
Ant. fewer, less.

morose ADJ. sad, gloomy, pessimistic.
Ant. happy, sanguine, optimistic, joyful.

morsel N. piece, bit, bite.
Ant. whole, entirety.

mortal ADJ. human, earthly, temporary, fatal, deadly.
Ant. everlasting, eternal, immortal.

• **mostly** ADV. mainly, generally, principally, largely, chiefly. *The participants were mainly from California.*
Ant. specifically.

motion N. change, movement, gesture, action.
Ant. stillness, repose, inaction.

• **motivate** V. stimulate, encourage, provoke, prompt. *This incentive should stimulate interest among the sales force.*
Ant. discourage, repress, halt.

motive N. purpose, reason, cause.

mount V. climb, ascend, read, prepare.
Ant. descend, fall, decline.

mountain N. ridge, peak, mount.
Ant. valley, depression.

mourn V. lament, bewail, bemoan, grieve.

move V. shift, transfer, advance, relocated, stir, provoke; —N. motion, tactic, procedure, maneuver.
Ant. remain, stand, cease.

moving ADJ. emotional, affecting, touching.
Ant. fixed, stopped, resting.

muddle N. dilemma, confusion, disorder, turmoil, difficulty; —V. confuse, perturb, mix, shuffle.
Ant. order, regulation; adjust, explain.

muffle V. conceal, deaden, soften, mute, stifle.
Ant. reveal, disclose, state.

mundane ADJ. terrestrial, everyday, earthly.
Ant. infinite, heavenly, celestial.

murder V. kill, slay, execute, assassinate.
Ant. vivify, revive, reanimate, save, rescue.

murmur V. whisper, sigh, mumble, mutter.
Ant. shout, scream, cry.

muscular ADJ. sturdy, robust, strong, powerful, brawny.
Ant. weak, feeble, slight.

musical ADJ. melodious, lyrical, euphonic, melodic, harmonious.
Ant. discordant, cacophonous, inharmonious.

must V. need to, have to, obligated to.

mute ADJ. speechless, silent, dumb, soundless, still.
Ant. talkative, vocal, eloquent.

mutilate V. deface, disfigure, maim, injure.
Ant. heal, mend, make well, repair.

mutter V. whisper, murmur, mumble, grumble.
Ant. articulate, speak, clarify.

mutual ADJ. joint, reciprocal, common, shared, identical.
Ant. dissociated, individual, particular.

mysterious ADJ. enigmatic, obscure, mystic, dark, unexplainable, ambiguous, strange.
Ant. precise, unmistakable, distinct.

mystery N. puzzle, enigma, conundrum.
Ant. solution, knowledge, proof.

myth N. fable, vision, allegory, fantasy, creation.
Ant. actuality, history, fact.

N

nab v. catch, trap, arrest, grab, snag.
Ant. lose, miss, release.

naive ADJ. inexperienced, unsophisticated, youthful.
Ant. experienced, sophisticated, worldly.

naked ADJ. bare, nude, exposed, uncovered.
Ant. dressed, covered, clothed.

name N. title, appellation, designation, character,
reputation; —v. call, designate, term, entitle,
mention, cite, appoint.

nap N. doze, siesta, catnap, snooze, rest; —v. doze,
slumber.
Ant. awake, alert.

narrate v. relate, recount, recite, tell.

narrow ADJ. thin, cramped, restricted, confined,
limited, small.
Ant. wide, broad, expansive.

narrow-minded ADJ. bigoted, close-minded,
intolerant, prejudiced.
Ant. tolerant, unprejudiced, liberal, open-minded.

nasty ADJ. offensive, disagreeable, mean, obscene,
foul, dirty.
Ant. kind, attractive, delightful.

nation N. republic, commonwealth, society, people,
country.

native ADJ. indigenous, original, natural, innate,
hereditary, inherent.
Ant. foreign, alien, imported, extrinsic.

- **natural** ADJ. customary, characteristic, usual, normal,
hereditary, innate, organic, pure. *It was customary
that the guest should be given a place at the table.*
Ant. artificial, mechanistic, man-made, awkward,
unusual.

- **nature** N. character, disposition, variety, kind,
universe, world, essence. *We relied upon her character
as an assertive personality in electing her president.*

naughty ADJ. disobedient, contrary, bad, mischievous, rowdy.
Ant. good, docile, obedient.

near ADJ. adjoining, close, adjacent, bordering, neighboring.
Ant. remote, distant, far.

nearby ADJ. convenient, close, neighboring, adjacent, proximal.
Ant. faraway, distant, gone.

neat ADJ. trim, orderly, tidy, well-organized, clean.
Ant. disorderly, unkempt, untidy.

nebulous ADJ. vague, tenuous, hazy, unformed.
Ant. clear, pointed, well-defined, unambiguous.

• **necessary** ADJ. required, needed, essential, indispensable. *Attendance is required.*
Ant. needless, redundant, exorbitant, unnecessary.

• **necessity** N. condition, need, requirement, prerequisite. *Proof of your college education is a condition of your employment.*
Ant. elective, matter of choice.

need V. want, require, lack; —N. necessity, requirement, poverty, want.
Ant. comfort, competence, property, supply.

nefarious ADJ. evil, wicked, corrupt, sinister, vile, depraved.
Ant. right, virtuous, noble.

negate V. abolish, revoke, nullify, deny.
Ant. approve, allow, accept.

negative ADJ. disapproving, unhelpful, pessimistic, unconstructive.
Ant. positive, optimistic, constructive, helpful.

neglect V. ignore, disregard, overlook, omit; —N. omission, oversight, negligence, disregard.
Ant. watch, oversee, survey; prudence, concern.

negligent ADJ. derelict, neglectful, remiss, lax.
Ant. careful, alert, watchful, precise.

negligible ADJ. trivial, remote, petty, insignificant, unimportant.
Ant. significant, important, considerable.

negotiate V. confer, bargain, arrange, contract.
Ant. disagree, refuse.

neighborhood N. quarter, area, environs, vicinity, community.

nervous ADJ. anxious, edgy, timid, restless, excitable, afraid.
Ant. calm, confident, fearless, serene.

neutral ADJ. unbiased, nonpartisan, impartial, unprejudiced, colorless, bland, impersonal, detached.
Ant. positive, involved, biased.

new ADJ. fresh, original, recent, modern, novel.
Ant. ancient, old, antique, outdated.

- **nice** ADJ. pleasing, attractive, agreeable, pleasant, friendly, kind, thoughtful. *The innkeeper had a pleasing face.*
Ant. unpleasant, revolting, disagreeable, ugly.

night N. evening, darkness, dusk, nighttime.
Ant. day, morning, dawn, light, daytime.

noble ADJ. honorable, virtuous, dignified, aristocratic, elevated.
Ant. servile, abject, ignoble, subservient.

nocturnal ADJ. night, nighttime.
Ant. daytime, day.

noise N. uproar, racket, clamor, outcry.
Ant. quiet, calm, silence.

nomadic ADJ. vagabond, roaming, migrant, wandering, vagrant.
Ant. stable.

nonchalant ADJ. indifferent, careless, relaxed, cool, casual, composed.
Ant. attentive, careful, enthusiastic.

- **nonsense** N. absurdity, insanity, pretense, senselessness, folly. *We have no time for such absurdity.*
Ant. exactitude, wisdom, veracity.

normal ADJ. usual, common, ordinary, standard.
Ant. abnormal, unusual, unexpected, extraordinary.

nosy ADJ. curious, prying, intrusive, inquisitive.
Ant. uninterested, restrained, polite.

notable ADJ. remarkable, unusual, renowned, eminent, distinguished.
Ant. trivial, unimportant, insignificant.

note V. observe, view, remark, notice, perceive; —N. comment, letter, acknowledgment, memorandum, message.

• **nothing** N. nil, nonentity, zero, obscurity, nothingness.
Our influence over their actions was nil.
Ant. everything, something, infinity.

notice V. perceive, detect, note, observe; —N. bulletin, notification, announcement, note.
Ant. neglect, overlook, ignore.

noticeable ADJ. outstanding, prominent, obvious, evident, noteworthy, apparent.

notoriety N. fame, infamy.

notorious ADJ. infamous, disreputable, arrant, shameful.
Ant. normal, uninteresting, common.

nourish V. feed, encourage, nurture.
Ant. deprive, take away, deny.

novelty N. innovation, originality, freshness.
Ant. commonality, familiarity, antiquity.

novice N. beginner, newcomer, amateur, student, learner.
Ant. professional, master, expert.

now ADV. today, currently, actually, directly, periodically.
Ant. later, tomorrow, then.

nude ADJ. unclothed, naked, bare, stripped, uncovered.
Ant. clothed, robed, dressed.

numb ADJ. dull, dead, paralyzed, insensitive, unfeeling.
Ant. aware, responsive, alert.

numerate V. count, enumerate, add, compute, calculate.
Ant. guess, estimate.

nurse V. nurture, nourish, foster, tend, suckle.
Ant. slight, neglect, deprive.

nutritious ADJ. healthful, alimentary.
Ant. unhealthful, insufficient.

O

obedience N. compliance, submission, respect, acquiescence.
Ant. insurgence, mutiny, rebelliousness.

obedient ADJ. loyal, compliant, submissive, faithful, respectful.
Ant. mischievous, unwilling, defiant.

obese ADJ. fat, stout, portly, plump, chubby, corpulent.
Ant. slender, thin, lean.

object N. item, article, thing, goal; —V. protest, disapprove.
Ant. accept, acquiesce, consent.

● **objection** N. protest, challenge, disapproval. *The coach lodged a formal protest against the umpire.*
Ant. approval, concurrence, affirmation.

objective N. goal, intention, aim, destination, aspiration; —ADJ. realistic, impartial, unbiased, fair, just.
Ant. subjective, personal, introspective.

obligation N. duty, responsibility, debt, requirement, contract.

oblige V. force, compel, insist, benefit, help, favor.
Ant. release, acquit, absolve.

obliged ADJ. forced, required, bound, grateful, pleased, thankful.
Ant. spared, unbound, excused.

oblique ADJ. indirect, biased, crooked, devious, diagonal, slanting.
Ant. parallel, straightforward, forthright.

obliterate V. delete, cancel, erase.
Ant. build, reconstruct.

obnoxious ADJ. offensive, loathsome, reprehensible, displeasing, filthy.
Ant. attractive, pleasant, delightful.

obscene ADJ. lewd, vulgar, crude, pornographic.
Ant. immaculate, pure, honorable.

obscenity N. filth, dirt, smut, indecency, lewdness, profanity.
Ant. decency, innocence, respectability.

obscure ADJ. mysterious, dark, complex, ambiguous.
Ant. clear, evident, obvious.

observance N. ceremony, celebration, obedience, watch.
Ant. negligence, carelessness, indifference.

observation N. remark, comment, notice, opinion.
Ant. neglect, indifference.

observe V. regard, watch, witness, look, celebrate, honor, obey.
Ant. neglect, overlook, ignore.

obsess V. possess, haunt.

obsolete ADJ. archaic, outdated, superseded, old-fashioned, antique.
Ant. modern, current, new.

obstacle N. barricade, hindrance, bar, difficulty, impediment.
Ant. clearance, aid, help.

obstinate ADJ. resolute, stubborn, opinionated, willful, determined.
Ant. courteous, compliant, obedient.

obstruct V. hinder, block, impede, prevent, stop.
Ant. assist, encourage, aid.

obtain V. acquire, get, attain, achieve.
Ant. sacrifice, forfeit, lose.

● **obvious** ADJ. apparent, unmistakable, plain, visible, clear. *Typographical errors were apparent throughout the term paper.*
Ant. ambiguous, unclear, complex.

occasion N. occurrence, event, happening, opportunity.

occasional ADJ. random, intermittent, infrequent, sporadic.
Ant. frequent, often, regular.

occupant N. inhabitant, dweller, tenant, resident.

occupation N. profession, business, employment, work, vocation, job.

occupy v. inhabit, fill, seize, possess.
Ant. surrender, vacate, leave.

- occur v. happen, befall, take place. *Something may happen at any moment.*

odd ADJ. curious, strange, bizarre, extraordinary.
Ant. habitual, normal, natural.

oddity N. strangeness, eccentricity, characteristic, exception, mystery, peculiarity.
Ant. uniformity, standard.

odds N. chance, luck, advantage.

odious ADJ. foul, abhorrent, hateful, filthy, disgusting.
Ant. wonderful, pleasant, inviting, attractive.

odor N. scent, aroma, smell, essence.

off ADJ. wrong, erroneous; remote, removed from.
Ant. on, right, illuminated.

offend v. anger, provoke, annoy, irritate, insult.
Ant. praise, compliment, placate.

offense N. crime, transgression, attack; wrong, insult.
Ant. defense, retreat.

offensive ADJ. insulting, discourteous, revolting, loathsome, repulsive, disgusting.
Ant. pleasing, decent, agreeable.

offer v. propose, suggest, volunteer, present.
Ant. withhold, deny, refuse.

office N. bureau, study, post, position, occupation.

official ADJ. authentic, reliable, authoritative, genuine.
Ant. informal, unofficial, dubious, questionable, doubtful.

offset v. compensate, counteract, balance, neutralize.

OK ADV. all right, yes; —ADJ. all right, acceptable; —v. permit, give permission.
Ant. impermissible, unacceptable.

old-fashioned ADJ. archaic, vintage, old, dated, antique.
Ant. modern, current, stylish, new.

omen N. sign, mark, forewarning, auspice.

ominous ADJ. fateful, imminent, threatening,
  foreboding.
  Ant. encouraging.

omit V. exclude, drop, forget, disregard, overlook.
  Ant. introduce, include, insert.

omnipotent ADJ. all-powerful, supreme, unstoppable.
  Ant. powerless, weak, frail, feeble.

one ADJ. lone, single, solitary.
  Ant. several, many.

oneness N. unity, sameness, completeness, wholeness.

onerous ADJ. burdensome, tedious, time-consuming,
  arduous.
  Ant. easy, effortless, undemanding, uncomplicated.

only ADV. merely, simply, solely, exclusively, just.

onset N. opening, commencement, beginning, attack.
  Ant. end, retreat.

open ADJ. public, accessible, unclosed, frank, clear,
  straightforward, indefinite, ambiguous; —v.
  unlock, begin, expand.
  Ant. obstructed, closed, insincere, cunning; hinder,
  disallow.

opening N. hole, gap, door, start, beginning,
  opportunity, vacancy.
  Ant. blockage, obstruction, barrier.

operate V. run, perform, handle, conduct, work, use.

operation N. execution, action, process, maneuver.
  Ant. inaction, uselessness, ineffectiveness.

operator N. driver, pilot, aviator, designer, schemer.

opponent N. enemy, adversary, rival, challenger.
  Ant. ally, supporter, comrade, friend, companion.

opportune ADJ. timely, proper, suitable, appropriate,
  favorable.
  Ant. inopportune, untimely, inappropriate,
  unsuitable.

● **opportunity** N. chance, freedom, latitude, occasion.
  The emigrants were given the chance to begin new careers.

oppose V. counteract, resist, combat, contest.
  Ant. approve, support, concur.

opposite ADJ. reverse, contrary, contradictory, converse.
Ant. corresponding, identical, like.

opposition N. resistance, antagonism, defiance, adversary, contestant.
Ant. support, backing, endorsement.

oppress V. persecute, depress, burden, crush, afflict.
Ant. aid, relieve, support.

optimism N. hope, confidence, assuredness, cheer, enthusiasm.
Ant. doubt, dejection, pessimism.

optimistic ADJ. hopeful, confident, assured, enthusiastic, positive.
Ant. hopeless, despairing, pessimistic.

● option N. recourse, choice, remedy, alternative.
We have little recourse but to sue.

optional ADJ. elective, discretionary, alternative.
Ant. required, mandatory, forced, obligatory.

opulent ADJ. wealthy, luxurious, profuse, rich, plentiful.
Ant. poor, destitute, deprived, humble.

oral ADJ. vocal, verbal, spoken, voiced.
Ant. printed, written.

oratorical ADJ. rhetorical, declamatory, elocutionary.
Ant. plain, straightforward.

orb N. globe, sphere, circle, eye.

order N. instruction, command, direction, requirement, regulation, union, hierarchy, class;
—v. instruct, command, arrange.
Ant. confusion, chaos, disorder; permit, allow.

orderly ADJ. regular, neat, methodical, tidy.
Ant. confused, chaotic, untidy.

● ordinary ADJ. common, plain, average, typical, regular. *The movie will appeal most to common tastes.*
Ant. amazing, uncommon, strange.

organ N. means, branch.

organic ADJ. natural, pure, essential, inherent, fundamental.
Ant. inorganic, nonessential, extraneous, mechanical.

- **organize** V. plan, establish, arrange, institute. *She spent more than a week trying to plan the district meeting.*
Ant. disorganize, divide, disperse, disband.

origin N. commencement, source, beginning, route, derivation, ancestry.
Ant. outcome, consequence, determination.

- **original** ADJ. first, primary, fresh, new, inventive, creative, unique. *I liked the first version of your essay.*
Ant. derivative, unoriginal.

originate V. begin, arise, invent, create.
Ant. evolve, derive, follow, emanate from.

ornament N. adornment, decoration, embellishment, beautification.
Ant. austerity, simplicity.

orthodox ADJ. standard, strict, conforming, sanctioned, received.
Ant. heretical, unconventional, secular, agnostic.

oust V. expel, eject, overthrow, get rid of, throw out.
Ant. install, inaugurate, bring in.

outburst N. explosion, eruption, outbreak, blowup.
Ant. quiet, peace.

outcry N. scream, exclamation, shout, protest, uproar.
Ant. acceptance, assent.

outfit V. supply, equip, clothe; —N. gear, equipment, clothing, material.
Ant. disrobe, strip.

outline V. plan, delineate, draft, sketch; —N. profile, draft, plan, delineation.

outlook N. point of view, view, opinion, chance, opportunity, future.

outrage N. crime, indignity, abuse, injury, insult.
Ant. courtesy, pleasure.

outrageous ADJ. flagrant, enormous, unreasonable, preposterous.
Ant. calm, submissive, cool.

outspoken ADJ. forthright, candid, vocal, direct, unreserved.
Ant. timid, subtle, reserved.

• **outstanding** ADJ. magnificent, exceptional, eminent, notable, prominent. *We visited a magnificent cathedral.*
Ant. average, ordinary, common, usual.

outward ADJ. external, obvious, apparent, noticeable, surface.
Ant. inward, internal, interior.

outwit V. trick, outsmart, outmaneuver, hoax.

ovation N. applause, approval, clapping, acclaim.

overbearing ADJ. oppressive, domineering, arrogant, proud, dictatorial.
Ant. bashful, retiring, meek, humble.

overblown ADJ. inflated, exaggerated, fat.
Ant. underestimated, undervalued.

overcast ADJ. clouded, dark, obscure, cloudy.
Ant. clear, bright.

overcome V. defeat, conquer, triumph, overwhelm.
Ant. surrender, yield, fail.

overhaul V. fix, rebuild, revamp, recondition.

overjoyed ADJ. elated, happy, gleeful, delighted.
Ant. melancholy, sorrowful, depressed, distraught.

overlook V. neglect, ignore, disregard, supervise, dominate.
Ant. watch, observe, note.

oversize ADJ. bulky, big, enormous.
Ant. petite, small, thin, manageable.

overthrow V. topple, remove, destroy, overturn.
Ant. restore, maintain, preserve.

overturn V. topple, overthrow, upset, conquer.
Ant. aid, support, restore.

overweight ADJ. plump, flabby, obese, heavy, stout.
Ant. slender, slim, trim, fit.

overwhelm V. inundate, overpower, crush, defeat.
Ant. weaken, befriend, rescue.

own V. hold, have, control, possess.
Ant. lose, lack, reject.

owner N. proprietor, possessor, holder.
Ant. renter, tenant.

ownership N. possession, title, dominion.

P

pace N. velocity, rate, speed, stride.

pacifist ADJ. peaceable, nonviolent; —N. conscientious objector.
Ant. militant, warmonger.

pacify V. quiet, calm, appease, tranquilize, placate.
Ant. anger, stir, antagonize.

pack V. fill, stuff, cram, crowd, press.
Ant. loosen, disperse, scatter.

package V. box, box up, wrap up, enclose.

pact N. treaty, agreement, covenant.

pagan ADJ. heathen, irreligious.
Ant. believer, follower.

pageant N. parade, procession, display.

pain N. discomfort, suffering, affliction, distress.
Ant. pleasure, comfort, enjoyment.

painful ADJ. torturous, agonizing, sharp, piercing, excruciating.
Ant. pleasurable, comfortable, enjoyable.

pair N. couple, duo, twosome, team, match.
Ant. solo, single, alone.

palace N. castle, fortress, mansion.
Ant. hovel, shack, shed, bungalow.

pale ADJ. colorless, white, pallid, faint, dim.
Ant. flushed, glowing, rosy.

palpitate V. beat, flutter, vibrate, pulsate, throb.
Ant. regulate.

panic N. terror, fright, harm, fear, horror.
Ant. calm, tranquility, peace.

pant V. gasp, wheeze, heave, huff.

parade N. procession, march, festival, display.

paradigm N. model, pattern, ideal.

paradise N. heaven, utopia, nirvana.
Ant. hell, netherworld.

parallel ADJ. congruent, collateral, alike, analogous.
Ant. oblique, perpendicular, skewed.

paralyze V. shock, astound, stun, numb, stupefy,
disable, immobilize.
Ant. excite, stimulate, revive.

paraphrase V. explain, restate, reword, translate.

parasite N. sponge, leech, sycophant, dependent,
bloodsucker.
Ant. host.

pardon V. forgive, absolve.

pardonable ADJ. forgivable, excusable, reprievable,
condonable.
Ant. incorrect, unpardonable, inexcusable.

parent N. father, mother, close relative, blood
relation.

parody N. mockery, caricature, imitation, mimicry,
satire, takeoff.

part N. section, fragment, component, division, piece.
Ant. total, whole, entirety, sum.

partake V. participate, contribute, join, eat.
Ant. ignore, shun, reject.

partial ADJ. biased, prejudiced, unfair, fragmentary,
imperfect.
Ant. fair, unbiased, complete, whole.

partiality N. bias, preference, prejudice, leaning,
favoritism.
Ant. equality, fairness, justice.

participant N. partner, actor, player.

• **participate** V. partake, join, indulge, engage. *Everyone
is invited to partake in the Thanksgiving meal.*
Ant. ignore, shun, reject, refuse.

particular ADJ. definite, precise, specific, exact,
meticulous, discriminating.
Ant. indefinite, general, imprudent, neglectful.

partition N. separation, barrier, division, wall.
Ant. connection, conjunction, union.

partner N. associate, colleague, spouse, companion.

party N. troop, company, league, band, gala, festivity.

pass V. convey, hand, approve, accept, adopt, transcend, surpass, overcome.
Ant. stop, hesitate, wait.

passage N. rate, entrance, confirmation, proof, verse, stanza.

passion N. ecstasy, zeal, dedication, devotion, infatuation, desire.
Ant. impassiveness, frigidity, apathy.

passionate ADJ. vehement, earnest, intense, ardent, erotic.
Ant. cool, stolid, dull, phlegmatic.

passive ADJ. submissive, yielding, resigned, acquiescent, compliant.
Ant. active, operative, dynamic.

past ADJ. previous, former, precedent, late.
Ant. future, futurity, later, present, now.

pastoral ADJ. rustic, rural, countrified, idyllic.
Ant. urban, metropolitan.

patch V. repair, fix, mend, restore.
Ant. crack, break, damage.

pathetic ADJ. wretched, dismal, sad, deplorable.
Ant. strong, well-off.

patience N. composure, perseverance, endurance, forbearance, resignation.
Ant. restlessness, impetuosity, impatience.

patron N. advocate, supporter, benefactor, contributor, customer, client, buyer.
Ant. competitor, adversary, rival, foe.

patronage N. business, trade, traffic, sponsorship, backing, clientele.

patronize V. support, sponsor, condescend, mock.
Ant. exult, elevate, praise.

pattern N. guide, example, model, method, habit, form, figure.

pause V. hesitate, linger, rest, wait, discontinue.
Ant. continue, repeat, prolong.

pawn N. tool, puppet, stooge, instrument.
Ant. leader, director, tyrant.

pay V. recompense, compensate, settle, reward.
Ant. seize, forfeit.

peaceable ADJ. tranquil, calm, nonviolent, friendly, pacifist.
Ant. violent, riotous, warlike.

peak N. height, summit, top, climax, crest.
Ant. base, bottom, nadir.

pedagogy N. learning, education, scholarship, teaching, instruction.

pedestrian N. ambler, hiker, walker, strider.

pedigree N. lineage, bloodline.

pejorative ADJ. degrading, disparaging, deprecatory.
Ant. complimentary, flattering, elevating.

penalty N. sanction, fine, punishment.
Ant. benefit, prize, reward.

penetrate V. perforate, puncture, enter, pierce.
Ant. recede, emerge, withdraw.

penitence N. atonement, remorse, attrition, distress, angst, grief, sorrow.
Ant. rejoicing, impenitence, obduracy.

penniless ADJ. impoverished, broke, destitute, bankrupt.
Ant. wealthy, rich, well-off.

pensive ADJ. speculative, thoughtful, reflective, solemn, meditative.
Ant. happy, carefree, unconcerned.

• people N. community, population, humanity, persons, public. *The proposed zoning changes should be approved by the community.*

perceive V. observe, discern, note, distinguish, feel, sense.
Ant. misjudge, misunderstand, ignore.

perceptible ADJ. tangible, visible, noticeable, detectable, discernible, appreciable.
Ant. invisible, imperceptible, unnoticeable.

perception N. awareness, insight, recognition, cognizance, acumen.
Ant. ignorance, blindness.

perfect ADJ. flawless, impeccable, absolute, ideal.
Ant. damaged, flawed, incomplete.

perfection N. precision, excellence, aptness,
flawlessness.
Ant. imperfection, imprecision, mediocrity.

perforate V. puncture, penetrate, breach, pierce.

perform V. execute, do, complete, achieve, fulfill.
Ant. neglect, fail, refrain.

performance N. interpretation, execution, fulfillment,
show, entertainment.
Ant. failure, defeat.

peril N. danger, risk, hazard, threat.
Ant. security, safety.

period N. stage, phase, interval, duration, span,
season.

periphery N. cirumference, border, boundary, edge.
Ant. center, interior, middle, heart.

permissible ADJ. allowable, admissible, legal,
permitted.
Ant. impermissible, prohibited, taboo, inadmissible,
illegal.

permission N. freedom, consent, license, authority,
permit.
Ant. restraint, opposition, refusal, denial.

permit V. consent, allow, authorize, let, approve.
Ant. oppose, prevent, restrict.

perpetual ADJ. incessant, continual, constant, endless.
Ant. short, brief, momentary.

perplex V. confound, complicate, mystify, confuse,
bewilder, puzzle.
Ant. assure, convince, clarify.

persevere V. endure, continue, insist, carry on,
survive.
Ant. stop, cease, suspend.

persist V. persevere, endure, stay, try.
Ant. quit, give up, abandon, cease, stop.

persistent ADJ. constant, determined, relentless.
Ant. inconstant, inconsistent.

- **personal** ADJ. private, secret, intimate, individual.
  Some matters were too private to discuss.
  Ant. universal, public, impersonal.

personify V. represent, embody.

perspective N. view, viewpoint, opinion, point of view.

persuade V. convince, convert, influence, prompt, urge.
  Ant. admonish, discourage, dissuade.

persuasion N. faith, religion, belief, influence.

persuasive ADJ. influential, convincing, suave, agreeable.
  Ant. disheartening, discouraging, restrictive.

pertain V. belong, apply.

pertinent ADJ. relevant, fitting, applicable, apropos.
  Ant. improper, irrelevant, unsuited.

pervade V. penetrate, fill, permeate, saturate, infiltrate.
  Ant. evacuate, withdraw.

pervert V. corrupt, distort, abuse.
  Ant. protect, preserve, defend.

pessimism N. distrust, cynicism, gloominess, negativity.
  Ant. optimism, hopefulness, cheerfulness, sanguinity.

pessimist N. cynic, misanthrope, foreboder, defeatist.
  Ant. optimist, enthusiast.

petite ADJ. little, tiny, small, diminutive.
  Ant. large, heavy, gross.

petty ADJ. trivial, insignificant, small, inconsequential, insignificant, irrelevant.
  Ant. essential, important, significant.

petulant ADJ. grouchy, ill-tempered, snappish.
  Ant. content, happy, cheerful.

phase N. period, side, facet, stage, view.

phenomenal ADJ. wonderful, fabulous, marvelous, miraculous.
  Ant. ordinary, usual, dull, noumenal.

phenomenon N. event, marvel, occurrence, happening, incident.

phony ADJ. fake, counterfeit, insincere.
Ant. genuine, authentic, sincere.

phrase N. wording, sentence, expression; —v. word, formulate, express.

• **physical** ADJ. tangible, corporeal, material, sensual, bodily, carnal. *He was booked on tangible evidence, not supposition.*
Ant. intellectual, mental, emotional, spiritual.

pick V. select, choose, gather, cull, harvest.
Ant. refuse, reject, decline.

picture N. photograph, representation, illustration, drawing; —v. imagine, envision, depict.

picturesque ADJ. scenic, colorful, beautiful, pictorial, pleasing.
Ant. repulsive, ugly, grim.

piece N. part, section, segment, bit, fraction.
Ant. entirety, whole, all, total.

pierce V. perforate, cut, puncture, penetrate.
Ant. withdraw, retract.

piety N. devoutness, holiness, piousness.
Ant. irreverence, sinfulness, unholiness, impiousness.

pile N. collection, stack, heap.

pillage V. rob, spoil, plunder, sack, destroy, loot.
Ant. save, restore, rescue, repair, return.

pillar N. support, column, post.

pilot N. captain, aviator, guide; —v. guide, steer, drive.

pinch N. difficulty, predicament, strain, squeeze.
Ant. prosperity, ease.

pinnacle N. summit, apex, climax, culmination, peak.
Ant. base, bottom, depths, nadir.

pinpoint V. locate, fix, place, find.
Ant. lose, misplace.

pioneer N. adventurer, colonist, builder, settler, founder.

pitch V. throw, toss, incline, grade, angle.
Ant. plane.

pitfall N. peril, hazard, risk, snare, danger, trap.
Ant. safety, security.

pitiful ADJ. pathetic, disgraceful, sorry.
Ant. praiseworthy, estimable, impressive.

pity N. sympathy, compassion, empathy, mercy, kindness.
Ant. severity, mirthlessness, cruelty.

pivotal ADJ. critical, crucial, focal, key, essential.
Ant. unimportant, minor, insignificant.

- **place** N. area, spot, region, location; —v. set, put, position. *We visited an area known for frequent earthquakes.*
Ant. dislodge, unload, misplace.

placid ADJ. calm, quiet, undisturbed, gentle, serene.
Ant. excited, agitated, disturbed.

plague V. curse, annoy, trouble, irritate.
Ant. bless.

plain ADJ. obvious, clear, simple, apparent, modest, unattractive.
Ant. obscure, cryptic, difficult, beautiful, attractive.

plan V. plot, scheme, conspire, devise; —N., v. design, sketch, diagram, chart; —N. method, approach, device.

planet N. orb, earth, globe.

plant V. sew, seed, put, place.
Ant. harvest, uproot, dig up.

plastic ADJ. synthetic, artificial, flexible, ductile, pliant.
Ant. rigid, hard, stiff.

plausible ADJ. acceptable, believable, likely, justifiable, probable, credible.
Ant. unbelievable, incredible, implausible.

play V. frolic, romp, perform, show.
Ant. work, toil, labor.

player N. actor, performer, musician.

plea N. excuse, request, appeal, supplication.

pleasant ADJ. enjoyable, agreeable, pleasing, amusing, comforting.
Ant. disagreeable, irritating, annoying.

please V. satisfy, delight, suit, gratify.
Ant. displease, repel, offend, dissatisfy, torment.

- **pleasing** ADJ. pleasant, agreeable, enjoyable, pleasurable. *The weather remained pleasant throughout June.*
Ant. unpleasant, exasperating, bothersome.

pleasurable ADJ. satisfying, enjoyable, pleasing, delightful, agreeable.
Ant. unenjoyable, disagreeable, unpleasant.

pleasure N. joy, delight, satisfaction, happiness, ecstasy, rapture.
Ant. misery, suffering, grief.

pledge V. commit, promise; —N. contract, vow, guarantee.
Ant. disavow, retract.

plentiful ADJ. profuse, ample, full, generous, rich, sufficient, abundant.
Ant. inadequate, scarce, exhausted.

plenty N. abundance, plenitude, fullness; —ADJ. ample, plentiful.
Ant. poor, deficient, scarce.

pliable ADJ. malleable, flexible, lithe, supple, ductile.
Ant. rigid, intractable, unyielding.

plod N. trudge, wade, grind, stomp, toil.
Ant. dance, skip.

plot N. story, intrigue, theme, design, plan.

plunge V. fall, dive, immerse, submerge, jump.
Ant. clime, rise.

poem N. verse, poetry, rhyme, lyric.

poet N. muse, bard, writer, author.

poignant ADJ. affecting, intense, sharp, piercing.
Ant. insipid, dull, obtuse.

- **point** N. tip, apex, end, location, position, place; —V. direct, aim, indicate, show. *He touched the tip of the needle carefully to his finger.*

- **point of view** N. perspective, outlook, opinion, viewpoint, angle. *We all want to hear your perspective on the issue.*

poise N. assurance, balance, composure, control, dignity.
Ant. awkwardness, vulgarity.

poison N. toxin, venom, virus, contagion.
Ant. curative, tonic, antidote.

poisonous ADJ. venomous, toxic, fatal, deadly, noxious.
Ant. wholesome, healthful, nourishing.

poke V. shove, push, jab, thrust.

police N. law enforcement, officer, cop.

polish V. rub, shine, brighten, gloss.
Ant. spoil, roughen, neglect.

polite ADJ. courteous, refined, civil, tactful, thoughtful.
Ant. uncivil, discourteous, abusive, rude.

pollute V. taint, contaminate, dirty, poison, defile.
Ant. purify, sanitize, clean.

pollution N. impurity, contamination, smog, dirt.
Ant. cleanliness, purity.

pompous ADJ. vain, arrogant, pretentious, inflated, egotistical.
Ant. retiring, timid, meek, bashful.

ponder V. reflect, think, mediate, contemplate.
Ant. forget, overlook, ignore.

ponderous ADJ. boring, dreary, dull, cumbersome, massive, weighty.
Ant. volatile, light, ethereal.

poor ADJ. impoverished, destitute, broke, needy, meager, pitiful.
Ant. affluent, rich, wealthy.

- **popular** ADJ. admired, liked, prevalent, current, favorite, public. *Kennedy was one of our most admired leaders.*
Ant. disreputable, disliked, unpopular.

portion N. share, allotment, part, division, serving.
Ant. entirety, whole, total.

portray V. show, represent, depict, impersonate, describe.

pose V. sit, model, impersonate, masquerade, feign, pretend, put forth, ask.

● position N. location, site, posture, attitude, status, bearing. *Tell us your location on the mountain so we can send help.*

positive ADJ. decided, sure, definite, affirmative, certain, absolute.
Ant. negative, vague, doubtful.

positively ADV. absolutely, certainly, really, surely.
Ant. unlikely, doubtfully, improbably.

● possess V. own, bear, have, hold, control. *Few faculty members own an automobile.*
Ant. sell, disown, lose.

possession N. title, ownership, custody, property.

possessive ADJ. jealous, dominating, controlling.
Ant. giving, sharing, generous.

● possible ADJ. feasible, practical, achievable, likely, potential. *The plan may prove feasible.*
Ant. unattainable, impossible, insurmountable.

post N. position, job; pole, column.

postpone V. put off, reschedule, defer, rearrange.
Ant. take on, engage, confront, schedule.

posture N. carriage, attitude, stance, condition.

potent ADJ. strong, effective, forceful, powerful, intense.
Ant. weak, ineffective, incompetent, fragile, impotent.

pour V. flow, swarm, flood, drench, decant.
Ant. withdraw, suck out.

poverty N. distress, destitution, dearth, want, starvation.
Ant. wealth, plenty, riches.

power N. strength, might, capacity, force, energy, efficacy.
Ant. impotence, inability, weakness.

powerful ADJ. mighty, strong, forceful, potent, dynamic, effective.
Ant. infirm, inept, ineffective, inefficient.

- **practical** ADJ. useful, handy, pragmatic, realistic, implicit. *We need useful ideas, not vague theories.*
Ant. idealistic, unworkable, senseless, unreal.

practice N. rehearsal, repetition, exercise, tradition, custom.

pragmatic ADJ. realistic, practical, down-to-earth.
Ant. theoretical, hypothetical, speculative, ethereal, impractical.

praise N. commendation, esteem, tribute, appreciation, homage; —v. glorify, exalt, honor, compliment.
Ant. contempt, hatred, disapproval, blame, decry, admonish.

prank N. trick, joke, caper, antic.

prate N., V. chatter, babble.

pray V. appeal, entreat, supplicate, beg.
Ant. deny, rebuff.

prayer N. supplication, appeal, invocation, request.

preacher N. cleric, clergyman, reverend (with *the*), minister, parson, priest.

precept N. teaching, rule, guideline, rubric.

precis N. summary, outline, abstract.

precise ADJ. exact, meticulous, rigid, accurate, definite.
Ant. erroneous, faulty, inexact.

- **precisely** ADV. exactly, directly, specifically. *He will join us in exactly one hour.*
Ant. approximately, inexactly, generally.

predicament N. dilemma, trouble, bind, emergency, pinch.
Ant. solution, good fortune.

predict V. forecast, declare, foresee, anticipate, prophecy.

prediction N. forecast, projection, outlook, prophecy, warning.

predisposition N. taste, preference, bent, attitude.
Ant. impartiality.

predominant ADJ. main, chief, most important,
leading, prime.
Ant. minor, secondary, insignificant,
inconsequential.

preference N. favorite, choice, selection.
Ant. least favorite.

pregnant ADJ. expecting, with child, suggestive,
meaningful, significant.

prejudice N. bias, intolerance, bigotry, antipathy,
partiality.
Ant. tolerance, respect, benevolence.

preliminary ADJ. introductory, basic, primary,
elemental, elementary.
Ant. final, concluding, ending.

prelude N. introduction, preface.
Ant. conclusion, ending, epilogue.

premonition N. feeling, intuition, hint, omen,
portent.

preoccupied ADJ. engrossed, absentminded,
distracted, absorbed, oblivious, inattentive.

preparation N. arrangement, planning, readiness,
preparedness.
Ant. neglect.

prepare V. plan, arrange, ready, make, fix.
Ant. overlook, ignore, neglect.

preponderance N. weight, dominance, abundance.
Ant. dirth, absence.

preposterous ADJ. extravagant, ridiculous,
unreasonable, foolish, absurd.
Ant. realistic, sensible, practical.

prerogative N. privilege, right, authority, liberty,
claim.
Ant. duty, obligation, limitation.

presence N. occurrence, attendance, vicinity,
nearness.
Ant. absence, lack.

present ADJ. current, existing, attending, here; —v. donate, give, introduce, exhibit, offer.
Ant. future, past; receive, accept, take.

presentation N. introduction, gift, exhibition, speech.

preserve V. maintain, keep, save, protect, conserve.
Ant. spend, destroy, abolish, lose.

press V. push, compress, finish; iron; insist, urge.
Ant. retract, pull.

pressure N. tension, stress, force.
Ant. relaxation.

presume V. assume, suppose, guess, believe.
Ant. know, prove, discover.

presumption N. assumption, supposition, arrogance, guess.
Ant. discovery, knowledge, proof.

• **pretend** V. imagine, feign, simulate, fake, falsify. *The children liked to imagine they lived in a magic forest.*
Ant. live, exist.

pretense N. fraud, sham, charade, deception, air, facade.
Ant. honesty, truthfulness, simplicity.

pretext N. facade, excuse, guise, pretense.
Ant. honor, reality, truth.

prevailing ADJ. widespread, current, popular, general, predominant, common.
Ant. individual, isolated, sporadic.

prevalent ADJ. general, widespread, comprehensive, prevailing, rife.
Ant. exclusive, private, peculiar.

prevent V. deter, avert, interrupt, block, hinder, stop.
Ant. support, allow, encourage.

prevention N. deterrence, forestalling, circumvention, preclusion, hindrance.
Ant. aid, permission, assistance.

• **previous** ADJ. former, prior, aforementioned, earlier, past. *Her former teacher plays in the symphony orchestra.*
Ant. subsequent, latter, following.

prick V. stab, puncture, perforate, sting.

pride N. ego, confidence, assuredness, arrogance, self-esteem, vanity, conceit, satisfaction, fulfillment. *Ant.* humility, bashfulness, modesty.

• **primary** ADJ. main, first, paramount, capital, key, initial. *Our main interest is in the welfare of our elders.* *Ant.* secondary, subordinate, subsequent.

primitive ADJ. early, primeval, uncivilized, simple, rough. *Ant.* advanced, civilized, complicated.

principal ADJ. foremost, primary, chief, first, leading, essential. *Ant.* subsidiary, auxiliary, trivial.

print V. publish, issue, letter.

printing N. publication, lettering, impression.

prior ADJ. previous, earlier, preceding, past. *Ant.* after, later, subsequent.

private ADJ. confidential, personal, secret, concealed. *Ant.* public, social.

prize N. award, reward, trophy, treasure. *Ant.* punishment, penalty.

• **probable** ADJ. likely, possible, conceivable, presumable. *Two developments seem likely.* *Ant.* unlikely, incredible, improbable.

probe V. explore, investigate, feel, inquire.

problem N. dilemma, predicament, riddle, difficulty. *Ant.* solution, explanation, resolution, certainty.

proceed V. continue, go, progress, come. *Ant.* stop, halt, return, end, terminate.

proclamation N. declaration, announcement, broadcast, revelation.

prod V. encourage, push, urge. *Ant.* allow, leave alone.

prodigal ADJ. profuse, extravagant, wasteful. *Ant.* saving, avaricious.

prodigious ADJ. giant, fabulous, marvelous, talented. *Ant.* ordinary, common, insignificant.

produce v. make, spawn, bear, create, originate, manufacture.
Ant. destroy, destruct.

product N. outcome, result, goods, merchandise, yield.

production N. manufacturing, creation, composition.
Ant. destruction.

productive ADJ. efficient, creative, effective, fertile.
Ant. lazy, lethargic, unproductive.

profane ADJ. obscene, temporal, secular, worldly, vulgar.
Ant. spiritual, sacred, holy.

proficient ADJ. skilled, adept, competent, efficient, able.
Ant. unskilled, incompetent, incapable.

profit N. benefit, improvement, earnings, advantage.
Ant. ruin, loss, failure, bankruptcy.

profitable ADJ. gainful, desirable, moneymaking, lucrative.
Ant. ruinous, unprofitable.

profound ADJ. abysmal, deep, learned, great, philosophical, serious, fathomless.
Ant. simple, shallow, superficial.

profuse ADJ. excessive, abundant, plentiful, opulent, thick.
Ant. meager, scarce, deficient.

program N. schedule, calendar, agenda, syllabus.

progress N. development, growth, advancement, progression, movement, increase.
Ant. regression, stagnation, retrogression, relapse.

progressive ADJ. broad, liberal, open-minded, advanced.
Ant. reactionary, retrogressive, stagnant, immobile.

• **project** N. venture, enterprise, undertaking, design.
Broad public support will be required for the success of the venture.

projection N. extension, outline, design, bulge, prominence, protuberance.
Ant. indentation, concavity.

prolific ADJ. fertile, productive, teeming, propagating.
Ant. unfruitful, barren, sterile.

prolonged ADJ. sustained, continued, lengthened, stretched, chronic.
Ant. curtailed, shortened.

promise V. pledge, vow, guarantee, assure, swear.
Ant. disavow, deny, reject.

promote V. encourage, publicize, advertise, elevate, advance, upgrade.
Ant. obstruct, impair, impede.

pronounce V. utter, speak, vocalize, proclaim, announce.
Ant. silence, hide.

proof N. testimony, evidence, reason, confirmation.
Ant. uncertainty, hypothesis.

propel V. move, thrust, urge, shoot, drive.
Ant. delay, hold, hinder.

prophecy V. forecast, foretell, predict, portend.

prophet N. clairvoyant, oracle, seer, fortune-teller.

prophetic ADJ. oracular, sybilline.
Ant. exaggerated, untruthful.

proportion N. share, piece, section, balance, comparison, symmetry.

proposal N. suggestion, proposition, offer, plan.
Ant. refusal, denial, denunciation.

propose V. suggest, offer, pose, state.
Ant. negate, reject, refuse.

prosaic ADJ. ordinary, common, dull, everyday.
Ant. special, beautiful, extraordinary.

prosecute V. sue, wage, perform, try.
Ant. release, acquit.

prosper V. thrive, flourish, succeed.
Ant. suffer, fail, lose.

prosperity N. success, welfare, comfort, ease, opulence, affluence.
Ant. adversity, destitution, poverty.

protective ADJ. preventive, careful, preservative.
Ant. forgetful, careless, neglectful.

prototype N. original, model, ancestor.
Ant. successor, product.

proud ADJ. confident, arrogant, vain, egotistical, conceited, self-assured, dignified, honorable, high-minded.
Ant. meek, humble, modest.

prove V. demonstrate, show, verify, justify, corroborate.
Ant. deny, refute, disprove.

proverb N. maxim, adage, saying, aphorism, byword.

• provide V. supply, offer, give, bestow. *The company will supply materials for the display.*
Ant. deprive, withhold, remove.

province N. area, department, domain, district.

provision N. condition, arrangement, stipulation, specification.

provocative ADJ. challenging, stimulating; insulting, confrontational.

provoke V. incite, anger, taunt, annoy, irritate.
Ant. soothe, lull, placate.

prudence N. discretion, restraint, caution, economy, foresight.
Ant. negligence, indiscretion, carelessness.

prudent ADJ. cautious, sane, wary, economical, wise, sensible.
Ant. careless, thoughtless, reckless.

psychology N. mind, psyche, mentality, ethos.

public ADJ. civil, popular, open, national, civic; —N. people, society, community.
Ant. private, individual, personal.

publish V. print, issue, reveal, publicize, announce.
Ant. conceal, hide, censor, cover.

pull V. tug, draw, pluck, drag, haul, tow.
Ant. push, drive, propel.

punch V. kick, hit, drive, pound.
Ant. caress, soothe.

punctual ADJ. exact, timely, prompt, on time.
Ant. tardy, irregular, late.

pungent ADJ. acid, biting, sharp, strong.
Ant. pleasant, mild, vapid.

punish V. correct, discipline, scold, imprison, chastise.
Ant. comfort, pardon, reward, exonerate.

punishment N. discipline, correction, punition.
Ant. encouragement, praise, reward.

puny, ADJ. weak, stunted, small.
Ant. strong, mighty, powerful.

purchase V. obtain, buy, acquire.
Ant. sell.

pure ADJ. genuine, authentic, unadulterated, absolute, perfect.
Ant. foul, polluted, unclean, spoiled.

purge V. purify, cleanse, clear, eliminate.
Ant. retain, keep, hold.

purification N. disinfection, cleansing, catharsis, purgation.
Ant. contamination, corruption, putrification.

purify V. clear, wash, cleanse, refine, clarify.
Ant. debauch, pollute, stain, dirty.

purity N. chastity, cleanliness, clarity, virginity.
Ant. filth, dirtiness, obscenity, indecency.

purport N. significance, meaning, idea, tendency, trend.

• **purpose** N. function, objective, intention, aim, goal.
The function of this gear is to drive the flywheel.

pursue V. chase, follow, seek, hunt.
Ant. ignore, stop, abandon.

pursuit N. chase, search, quest, vocation, occupation, business.

push V. shove, force, propel, elbow, encourage, drive.
Ant. pull, drag, discourage.

put V. deposit, set, place, lay, install, position.
Ant. remove, transfer, misplace.

putrid ADJ. rotten, moldy, bad, decayed.
Ant. sanitary, pure, clean.

puzzle N. question, mystery, problem, riddle.
Ant. explanation, interpretation, solution.

Q

quaint ADJ. unusual, strange, curious, funny.
Ant. ordinary, modern.

quake V. tremble, shake, shudder, vibrate.
Ant. rest, remain.

qualification N. eligibility, fitness, provision.
Ant. incompetence, incapability.

qualified ADJ. capable, adequate, experienced, able.
Ant. unsuitable, ineffectual, unskilled.

• qualify V. limit, suit, fit, restrict, distinguish. *Let me limit my comments by confining them to recent legislation.*
Ant. disqualify, eliminate.

• quality N. grade, class, caliber, condition, characteristic, feature, attribute. *We tried to purchase the best grade of lumber.*

qualm N. doubt, foreboding, misgiving.

quantity N. amount, measure, bulk, total, whole.
Ant. part, portion.

quantum N. quantity, allotment, amount.

quarrelsome ADJ. irritable, argumentative, belligerent, unruly, petulant.
Ant. tolerant, temperate, easygoing.

quarter N. neighborhood, area, section.

quash V. nullify, invalidate, cancel, repeal.
Ant. validate, authorize, endorse, certify.

queer ADJ. unique, extraordinary, eccentric, unusual, curious, fantastic.
Ant. normal, ordinary, orthodox.

quench V. repress, extinguish, crush, destroy.
Ant. fuel, ignite, start.

query N. question, inquiry.

quest N. pursuit, journey, search, inquiry, expedition.

• question N. inquiry, problem, doubt, uncertainty;
—V. ask, interrogate, doubt. *Send your inquiry to the appropriate office.*
Ant. answer, response, reply, certainty, assurance.

questionable ADJ. debatable, uncertain, doubtful, enigmatic, ambiguous.
Ant. believable, reliable, certain.

questioning ADJ. incredulous, curious, doubtful, uncertain.
Ant. sure, certain.

quick ADJ. fast, hurried, brief, speedy, rapid, instantaneous.
Ant. slow, indolent, apathetic.

quicken V. enliven, animate, speed up, energize.
Ant. hinder, slow, block.

quickness N. speed, facility, sharpness, agility.
Ant. sloth, listlessness, indolence.

quiet ADJ. serene, still, calm, peaceful, silent, tranquil.
Ant. loud, deafening, noisy.

quintessence N. basis, nature, essence, heart.
Ant. inessentials.

quintessential ADJ. essential, basic, typical.
Ant. insignificant, unusual, unimportant.

quit V. leave, abandon, resign, retire, relinquish.
Ant. stay, begin, remain.

quite ADV. somewhat, completely, rather, entirely, considerably.

quiz N. examination, puzzle, test, riddle.

quotidian ADJ. daily, regular, everyday.
Ant. irregular, uncommon.

R

race N. competition, contest, match, breed, nation, people, tribe; —v. compete, run, hurry, dash.

radiate V. shed, gleam, diffuse, spread.
Ant. absorb, concentrate, gather.

radical ADJ. primary, original, intrinsic, basic, extreme, violent.
Ant. stable, conservative, extrinsic.

rage N. fury, anger, enthusiasm, wrath.
Ant. calm, humor, tranquility.

raid V. assault, invade, attack, steal.
Ant. repair, replenish.

rain N. precipitation, rainfall, drizzle, downpour.
Ant. drought.

raise V. increase, boost, lift, produce, cultivate.
Ant. reduce, lower, curtail.

rally V. assemble, meet, concentrate, mobilize.
Ant. retreat, disperse, surrender.

ram V. push, drive, stab, cram, crowd.
Ant. expand, loosen, release.

rancor N. resentment, acrimony, bitterness, animosity.
Ant. serenity, affability, friendliness.

random ADJ. irregular, haphazard, indiscriminate, accidental, purposeless.
Ant. specific, definite, planned.

range N. scope, area, extent, limit, territory; —v. roam, wander, change, arrange, go.
Ant. stay, rest, remain.

rank N. order, class, degree, level.

ransack V. search, go through, rummage, scour.

rant V. fume, rave.
Ant. whisper, speak.

rape V. assault, violate, force.

rapport N. relationship, bond, connection.
Ant. alienation, isolation, estrangement, unfriendliness.

rapture N. ecstasy, delight, bliss.

rare ADJ. scarce, uncommon, infrequent, unique, extraordinary.
Ant. common, typical, recurring.

rascal N. scoundrel, rogue.

rash ADJ. foolhardy, thoughtless, precipitate, hasty, impulsive.
Ant. observant, thoughtful, prudent.

rate N. velocity, speed, ratio, proportion; —v. estimate, class.

rational ADJ. sane, reasonable, logical, sensible, normal.
Ant. erratic, senseless, unreasonable.

rationalize V. justify, account for.
Ant. admit.

rattle V. shake, clatter, clack; embarrass, confuse, fluster.
Ant. settle, clarify, calm.

rave V. rant, fume, rage, storm.

ravenous ADJ. ferocious, insatiable, greedy, voracious.
Ant. gentle, temperate, forbearing.

raw ADJ. green, crude, uncooked, rude, obscene.
Ant. cooked, adult, mature.

raze V. burn down, destroy, demolish.
Ant. build, construct, establish, erect.

reach V. attain, achieve, get, accomplish.
Ant. fail, leave, miss.

reactionary ADJ. royalist, unprogressive, ultraconservative, fanatic.
Ant. liberal, open-minded, progressive.

read V. browse, study, understand, perceive, foresee, indicate.
Ant. misinterpret, misread.

readiness N. preparation, ease, dexterity.
Ant. difficulty, unsuitability, deficiency.

• **ready** ADJ. prepared, equipped, willing, suitable, disposed. *They were prepared for a long siege.*
Ant. undeveloped, slow, unprepared.

real ADJ. authentic, tangible, actual, genuine.
Ant. false, erroneous, untrue.

realistic ADJ. natural, lifelike, objective, pragmatic.
Ant. fake, false, unnatural.

● **reality** N. actuality, verity, truth, existence. *In actuality, few miners fell ill from the gas leak.*
Ant. imagination, fantasy, illusion.

realize V. accomplish, actualize, carry out, recognize, understand.
Ant. misunderstood, misinterpret, overlook.

● **really** ADV. actually, positively, indeed, absolutely, honestly. *The clown is actually a famous actress in disguise.*
Ant. doubtfully, improbably.

rear N. bottom, back, rump, tail.
Ant. forefront, front.

reason N. motive, ground, purpose, argument, understanding, intelligence, sanity; —V. justify, conclude, argue.
Ant. emotion, illogic, feeling.

reasonable ADJ. rational, sensible, logical, sane.
Ant. extreme, exorbitant, excessive.

rebel V. overthrow, revolt, rise up.
Ant. follow, tolerate, submit.

rebellion N. revolution, mutiny, insurrection, upheaval, riot.
Ant. patience, tranquility, order.

rebirth N. revival, conversion, renaissance.
Ant. stagnation, death.

recall V. remember, recollect, reminisce, annul, revoke.
Ant. reestablish, forget, restore.

recede V. retreat, withdraw, wane, regress, ebb.
Ant. near, approach, advance.

● **receive** V. get, acquire, obtain. *They frequently get compliments on their ability to work together as a team.*
Ant. expend, return, give.

receptive ADJ. open-minded, accepting, responsive, sensory, open.
Ant. unresponsive, close-minded, blocked.

reciprocate V. return, give back, retaliate, requite.
Ant. forgive, take.

reckless ADJ. foolhardy, rash, careless, wild, irresponsible.
Ant. prudent, circumspect, careful.

reckon V. estimate, suppose, regard, count.

reckoning N. calculation, estimation, count, account.

reclaim V. save, redeem, restore, renovate.
Ant. neglect, abandon, forget.

recline V. rest, lie, relax.
Ant. stand up.

recognition N. credit, acknowledgment, recollection.

• **recognize** V. know, recall, acknowledge, perceive, accept. *Do you know all of the guests by first name?*
Ant. forget, overlook, ignore.

recoil V. reflect, bounce, rebound, react, echo.

recollection N. remembrance, memory.
Ant. amnesia, forgetfulness, oblivion.

recommendation N. reference, advice, praise, approval, suggestion.
Ant. condemnation, disapproval.

recompense V. pay, compensate.
Ant. rob, loot, neglect.

reconcile V. reunite, conciliate, settle, harmonize, mediate.
Ant. aggravate, incite.

reconciliation N. rectification, conciliation, rapprochement.
Ant. disunification, split.

recondition V. restore, rebuild, renew, overhaul.
Ant. damage, destroy, abuse.

reconsider V. review, rethink, reevaluate.
Ant. refuse, deny, reject.

reconstruct v. remold, repair, rejuvenate, put together again.
Ant. destroy, deconstruct, ruin.

record N. document, schedule, history, chronicle, report; —v. transcribe, register, enter, log.
Ant. erase, destroy.

recover v. redeem, retrieve, reclaim, mend, improve, recuperate.
Ant. decline, lose, deteriorate.

recovery N. recuperation, comeback, retrieval.
Ant. forfeiture, loss, death.

recreation N. amusement, relaxation, play, pastime, game.
Ant. work, labor, toil.

rectify v. correct, fix, remedy, improve, adjust.
Ant. damage, destroy, falsify.

recur v. reappear, return, revive.
Ant. cease, stop, disappear.

recurrent ADJ. chronic, seasonable, periodic, cyclic.
Ant. singular.

redeem v. liberate, free, rescue, compensate, atone.
Ant. neglect, abandon, disregard.

redress v. remedy, amend, restore, repair, compensate.
Ant. wreck, destroy, ruin, damage.

reduce v. curtail, lower, lessen, decrease.
Ant. augment, increase, magnify.

reduction N. decrease, cutback, demotion.
Ant. enlargement, inflation, expansion.

redundant ADJ. wordy, verbose, repetitious, superfluous.
Ant. concise, succinct.

refer v. mention, allude, specify, attribute, cite.

referee N. arbitrator, judge, moderator, umpire.

reference N. recommendation, testimonial, allusion, citation.
Ant. condemnation, detraction.

refine v. purify, perfect, clean, clarify.
Ant. debase, sully, mix.

refined ADJ. cultured, delicate, elegant, purified.
Ant. crude, barbaric, rude.

reflect V. contemplate, think, reason, consider.

reflection N. thought, study, echo, image.

refrain V. withhold, keep, abstain, inhibit, restrain.
Ant. allow, continue, liberate.

refresh V. restore, renew, energize, awaken, animate.
Ant. exhaust, fatigue, tire.

refusal N. rejection, denial, decline, turndown.
Ant. assent, acceptance, approval.

refute V. counter, disprove, rebut.
Ant. propose, assert, offer, claim, state.

regal ADJ. royal, imperial, noble.
Ant. common, humble.

register V. catalog, record, list, enter, enroll.

regret V. lament, sorrow, rue, repent, deplore; —N.
rue, repentance, grievance.
Ant. satisfaction, contentment, serenity.

• **regular** ADJ. ordinary, steady, uniform, customary. *The military will follow ordinary procedures in acquiring new weaponry.*
Ant. extraordinary, unusual, uncommon, strange.

regulate V. control, standardize, legalize.
Ant. deregulate, give up control.

rehearse V. practice, prepare, go through.

reiterate V. repeat, restate, reinforce.
Ant. overlook, omit.

rejection N. refusal, denial, exclusion, dismissal, elimination.
Ant. selection, admission, acceptance.

rejoice V. celebrate, delight, exalt, revel.
Ant. lament, mourn, rue.

rejuvenate V. refresh, restore, modernize, renew.
Ant. tire, bore.

relapse V. regress, backslide, retrogress, revert, lapse.
Ant. improve, progress.

relate V. narrate, recount, describe, report, tell.
Ant. suppress, hide.

related ADJ. kindred, akin, associated, allied.
Ant. foreign, dissimilar, dissociated.

relation N. association, connection, link, similarity.
Ant. dissimilarity, disassociation.

- **relative** N. relation, family, kin; —ADJ. conditional, dependent, relevant, pertinent. *He willed the property to a relation.*
Ant. independent, unrelated, unconditional.

relax V. rest, recline, ease, unwind, loosen.

release V. liberate, free, emancipate, discharge, announce, emit.
Ant. halt, arrest, incarcerate, bind.

relent V. weaken, soften, subside, relax, abate.
Ant. toughen, harden, persevere.

relentless ADJ. rigorous, hard, strict, unyielding, stubborn, continual.
Ant. compassionate, merciful, lenient.

relevant ADJ. pertinent, applicable, appropriate, germane.
Ant. unrelated, separate, inconsistent.

reliable ADJ. dependable, trustworthy.
Ant. irresponsible, unreliable.

relic N. trace, fossil, ruin.

relief N. assistance, help, support, comfort, deliverance.
Ant. burden, impediment, restriction.

relieve V. comfort, aid, help, console, appease.
Ant. aggravate, worsen, intensify.

religious ADJ. devout, holy, spiritual, pious, reverent.
Ant. heretical, profane, impious.

relinquish V. forego, abandon, renounce, reject, abdicate.
Ant. keep, hold, retain.

relish V. appreciate, enjoy, prefer, admire.
Ant. disfavor, dislike, rebuff.

rely V. depend on, count on.

remain V. wait, continue, endure.
Ant. depart, vanish, leave.

remainder N. surplus, balance, remains, rest.
Ant. whole, entirety.

remark N. comment, observation, statement; —V.
mention, comment, observe.

• **remarkable** ADJ. extraordinary, unusual, rare,
striking. *We witnessed an extraordinary feat of strength.*
Ant. normal, common, inconspicuous.

remedial ADJ. curative, corrective.
Ant. advanced.

remedy N. medicine, cure, antidote, counteraction.
Ant. disease, germ, illness.

remember V. recall, reminisce, retrace, recollect,
think of.
Ant. repress, forget, disregard.

remit V. forgive, pardon, release, absolve, alleviate.
Ant. withhold, retain, keep.

remnant N. residue, surplus, remainder, relic, ruin.
Ant. entire, whole, all.

remorseful ADJ. repentant, penitential, contrite,
sorry, regretful.
Ant. complacent, shameless, callous.

remote ADJ. separate, distant, obscure, isolated,
slender, negligible.
Ant. related, near, adjoining.

remove V. eliminate, withdraw, take out, annihilate,
transport, dislodge, move.
Ant. imbed, place, establish.

render V. return, abdicate, give, pay, express,
communicate.
Ant. abstract, withdraw, seize.

rendezvous N. meeting, engagement, date,
appointment.

renew V. restore, refresh, renovate, recondition,
continue, extend.
Ant. deplete, exhaust, diminish.

renovate V. remodel, renew, modernize, repair.
Ant. ruin, ignore, destroy.

renown N. fame, eminence, distinction, reputation.
Ant. disrepute, notoriety, isolation.

repair V. fix, mend, restore, refurbish.
Ant. destroy, demolish, wreck.

repast N. meal, banquet, feast.

repay V. compensate, return, avenge.
Ant. default, swindle, cheat.

repeal V. lift, abolish, cancel, end, reverse.
Ant. maintain, validate, continue.

repeat V. restate, reiterate, echo, recapitulate, recite.
Ant. cease, stop.

repel V. rebuff, parry, repulse, reject, disgust.
Ant. attract, draw.

repent V. apologize, atone, ask forgiveness for.
Ant. remain unrepentant, unapologetic.

repetition N. reiteration, echo, restatement.
Ant. singularity.

repetitive ADJ. reiterative, repetitious.
Ant. concise, direct, succinct.

replace V. substitute, restore, reconstruct, reinstate, supplant, supersede.
Ant. exchange, modify, alter.

reply V. respond, answer, react.
Ant. speak, assert, say, claim, aver.

report N. record, account, story, description, news, announcement.
Ant. cancellation, concealment, secrecy.

repose N. relaxation, rest, ease.
Ant. commotion, activity, agitation.

represent V. describe, delineate, depict, illustrate, epitomize, personify, embody.

repress V. silence, suppress, quell, subdue.
Ant. allow, permit, approve.

reproduce V. multiply, breed, proliferate, copy.

repudiate V. disclaim, deny, forsake, abandon, banish, expel.
Ant. accept, profess, acknowledge.

repugnant ADJ. disgusting, repulsive, hideous.
Ant. pleasing, pleasant, attractive, enjoyable.

repulse v. disgust, offend, nauseate, repel.
Ant. entice, lure, please.

reputation N. name, character, honor, repute.

repute v. think, suppose, believe, report.

request v. appeal, entreat, ask, solicit.
Ant. answer, help, aid.

require v. demand, expect, mandate, suppose.

requirement N. demand, mandate, exigency, claim,
need, necessity, condition.

requite v. compensate, reciprocate, reward, pay,
retaliate, avenge.
Ant. neglect, absolve, pardon.

rescind v. revoke, annul, veto, cancel, abolish.
Ant. allow, permit, propose.

rescue v. free, save, liberate, release, recover, salvage.
Ant. hinder, obstruct, incarcerate.

resemble v. agree, correspond, take after, favor.
Ant. vary, differ, contrast.

reserve v. hold, save, keep, maintain.
Ant. give, release.

reside v. exist in, live in, locate in.

resign v. leave, quit, abandon, surrender, renounce,
abdicate.
Ant. stay, remain, assume.

resist v. obstruct, contest, withstand, combat, oppose.
Ant. surrender, comply, submit, yield.

resistance N. insusceptibility, immunity, opposition,
refusal.
Ant. susceptibility.

resistant ADJ. impervious, immune, resistive.
Ant. weak, susceptible.

resolute ADJ. constant, determined, faithful, decisive,
steadfast, firm.
Ant. cautious, afraid, hesitant.

resolution N. decision, resolve, determination,
courage, devotion.
Ant. indecision, instability, hesitation.

resolve V. settle, decide, unravel, solve, determine.
Ant. investigate, question, wonder.

resonant ADJ. sonorous, mellow, resounding, vibrant.
Ant. silent, dead, still.

resort N. refuge, expedient; —V. turn, refer, use.

resourceful ADJ. inventive, creative, ingenious, fertile.
Ant. dull, incompetent, stupid, uninventive,
unresourceful.

respect N. admiration, esteem, reverence, honor; —V.
admire, revere, esteem.
Ant. scorn, contempt, irreverence.

respectable ADJ. honorable, decent, acceptable,
upright, good.
Ant. unworthy, scandalous, dishonorable,
unrespectable.

respite N. pause, break.
Ant. continuation.

respond V. reply, react, acknowledge.
Ant. delay, hesitate, ignore.

response N. answer, reaction, reply, acknowledgment.
Ant. silence.

responsible ADJ. accountable, dependable.
Ant. irresponsible, undependable, unreliable.

responsive ADJ. receptive, sensitive, approachable.
Ant. silent, unapproachable, unreceptive,
insensitive, unresponsive.

restate V. repeat, paraphrase.

restless ADJ. uneasy, nervous, jumpy, anxious,
worried.
Ant. quiet, tranquil, composed.

restore V. renew, reinstate, replace, mend, repair,
revamp, reestablish, reinstall.
Ant. reject, rebuff, discontinue.

restrain V. check, control, inhibit, bridle, hold.
Ant. liberate, loosen, release.

restricted ADJ. limited, fixed, local, confidential.
Ant. expanded, enlarged, free.

result N. conclusion, outcome, consequence, effect, answer.
Ant. origin, source, cause.

resume V. continue, recommence, reoccupy, reclaim.
Ant. forget, quit, stop, halt.

retain V. hold, keep, maintain, preserve, employ.
Ant. dismiss, discard, surrender.

retaliation N. retribution, vengeance, reciprocation, counterattack.
Ant. forgiveness, pardon.

retard V. delay, hinder, hamper, interrupt, slow.
Ant. speed, hasten, expedite.

retinue N. following, entourage, train.

retire V. withdraw, leave, step down, retreat.
Ant. continue, stay.

retirement N. seclusion, retreat, withdrawal.
Ant. work, employment, activity.

retort V. answer, respond, comeback, reply.
Ant. question, ask, demand.

retract V. disavow, withdraw, revoke, abjure, recall.
Ant. declare, assert, affirm.

retreat V. withdraw, pull back, depart, leave, recede.
Ant. advance, progress, attack.

retrieve V. recover, reclaim, regain, get back.
Ant. lose, misplace.

retrograde V. deteriorate, recede, retrogress, backslide, degenerate.
Ant. proceed, improve, develop.

return V. restore, revert, recur, earn, draw, yield.

revamp V. modernize, fix, rebuild, revise.
Ant. use, destroy, maintain.

reveal V. expose, divulge, unveil, uncover, disclose, show.
Ant. hide, cover, conceal.

revelation N. disclosure, unveiling, exposé, apocalypse.
Ant. deception, evasion, concealment.

revenge N. retaliation, vengeance, retribution, vindictiveness.
Ant. acquittal, forgiveness, amnesty.

reverence N. honor, respect, adoration, homage, esteem.
Ant. discourtesy, irreverence, disrespect.

reverie N. dream, daydream, trance.
Ant. soberness, seriousness, lucidity.

reverse V. repeal, annul, retract; invert, turn around, shift, transfer; —ADJ. opposite, transposed.
Ant. institute, apply, continue.

- **review** V. critique, judge, examine, analyze, rehearse, inspect; —N. critique, commentary, examination.
The author disliked the biting critique of her play.

revise V. amend, rework, alter, update, improve.
Ant. disregard, ignore.

revision N. improvement, alteration, amendment, reworking.

revival N. reawakening, resurrection, renewal, rebirth, rejuvenation.
Ant. deterioration, decay, decline.

revive V. reawaken, revitalize, arouse, rejuvenate, restore, remember.
Ant. lessen, weaken, deteriorate.

revoke V. lift, repeal, reverse, overturn, annul.
Ant. validate, renew, keep.

revolution N. upheaval, cataclysm, rebellion, overthrow, uprising.
Ant. peace, tranquility, serenity, stagnation.

revolve V. rotate, turn, spin, circle.

reward N. recompense, award, prize, dividend, bounty.
Ant. confiscation, penalty, fine.

rhetorical ADJ. sonorous, oratorical.
Ant. straightforward, plain, honest.

rhythm N. cadence, beat, meter, pulsation, measure.

rich ADJ. opulent, abundant, wealthy, affluent, luxurious.
Ant. poor, destitute, barren.

riches N. treasure, fortune, wealth, worth.
Ant. impoverishment, depletion, squalor.

rid V. free, eliminate, clear, release, shed,
exterminate.
Ant. keep, maintain, hold.

ride V. drive, journey, go, drift.

ridicule V. mock, satirize, deride, mimic, caricature.
Ant. praise, respect, admire, honor.

right ADJ. correct, appropriate, true, proper, lawful,
honest.
Ant. fallacious, wrong, incorrect, inappropriate.

righteous ADJ. honest, ethical, moral, upstanding.
Ant. dishonest, immoral, unethical.

rigid ADJ. unbending, inflexible, stiff, stubborn,
severe.
Ant. flexible, yielding, elastic.

rigor N. severity, difficulty, oppression, inflexibility.
Ant. leniency, ease.

ring N. loop, circle, band, gang, confederation,
league.

riot N. disturbance, rebellion, uprising, tumult,
insurgence.
Ant. tranquility, order, peace, serenity.

riotous ADJ. violent, disorderly, profuse.
Ant. calm, peaceful, tranquil, controlled.

rise V. scale, climb, ascend, mount, increase,
heighten, escalate, succeed.
Ant. decline, fall, descend.

risk N. chance, danger, hazard, gamble, adventure.
Ant. certainty, safety, security.

ritual N. ceremony, formality, sacrament, observance,
service.
Ant. informality.

rival N. competitor, adversary, opponent, challenger;
—V. challenge, oppose, dispute, confront, contest.
Ant. patron, champion, friend, supporter.

roar V. cry, yell, shout, call, scream.
Ant. whisper, murmur.

rob V. steal, burglarize, plunder, thieve, deprive.
Ant. return, give back.

rock V. shake, toss, disturb, agitate.

roll V. tumble, rotate, turn, revolve.

romantic ADJ. idealistic, sentimental, poetic, fanciful, imaginary, beautiful, amorous.
Ant. practical, realistic, pragmatic.

room N. margin, space, leeway; chamber.

root N. basis, cause, origin, heart, center.
Ant. result, outcome, fruit.

rot V. decompose, decay, putrefy.
Ant. grow, germinate, develop, thrive.

rotate V. revolve, turn, spin, alternate.

rotation N. interchange, alternation, revolution, circulation.

rotten ADJ. filthy, bad, degenerate, spoiled, putrid, decayed.
Ant. fresh, good, clean, ripe.

rough ADJ. coarse, jagged, uneven, harsh, abrasive, impolite, violent, agitated, unfinished, preliminary, tentative.
Ant. smooth, level, courteous.

round ADJ. spherical, circular, orbed, globular.

routine N. method, system, way, habit; —ADJ. customary, habitual.
Ant. uncustomary, extraordinary, unusual.

row N. quarrel, disturbance, argument; file, line, series.
Ant. agreement, harmony.

rubric N. rule, prescript, regulation, law.

rude ADJ. vulgar, insolent, uncouth, disrespectful, impolite.
Ant. polite, courteous, gentle.

rueful ADJ. sorrowful, melancholy, regretful, plaintive, depressed, sad.
Ant. content, cheerful, insensitive.

rugged ADJ. rough, hard, difficult, harsh, arduous.
Ant. level, delicate, courteous.

ruin v. destroy, spoil, wreck, break, demolish; —N. devastation, destruction, downfall, undoing; relic, wreckage, remnant.
Ant. rebuild, restore, create.

rule N. law, regulation, prescript, rubric.
Ant. anarchy, chaos, disorder.

ruler N. sovereign, king, queen, emperor, leader.
Ant. citizen, commoner, peasant.

ruling N. pronouncement, decree, edict; —ADJ. dominant, supreme, prevailing.

rumble v. thunder, roar, growl, boom.

run v. sprint, dash, bolt, hurry, hasten; work, operate, function.
Ant. amble, stroll.

rupture N. breech, breakage, crack.
Ant. seal, patch.

rural ADJ. rustic, countrified, bucolic.
Ant. urban, metropolitan.

rush v. hasten, hurry, speed, hustle, dash.
Ant. loiter, procrastinate, delay.

rustic ADJ. natural, unpolished, pastoral, rural, unadorned.
Ant. elegant, polished, sophisticated.

S

sabotage v. undermine, impair, subvert, disable.
Ant. resuscitate, strengthen, aid.

sack v. loot, rummage through, ransack.
Ant. restore, return, give back.

sacred ADJ. hallowed, blessed, holy, divine, consecrated.
Ant. blasphemous, worldly, temporal.

sacrifice N. offering, libation, abnegation, atonement, cost.
Ant. hoard, keep, profit.

sacrilege N. profanity, irreverence, blasphemy, desecration, impiousness.
Ant. reverence, piousness, piety.

sad ADJ. gloomy, sorrowful, unhappy, depressing, melancholy.
Ant. cheerful, happy, blithe.

saddened ADJ. depressed, sorrowed, dejected, dismayed.
Ant. cheered, gladdened, overjoyed.

sadistic ADJ. cruel, vicious, brutal.
Ant. kind, caring, gentle.

sadness N. gloom, sorrow, unhappiness, dejection, melancholy, woe.
Ant. glee, delight, ecstasy.

safe ADJ. secure, sheltered, protected, guarded, unhurt, unharmed.
Ant. hazardous, dangerous, risky.

safety N. preservation, assurance, security, escape.
Ant. peril, jeopardy, risk.

sag v. droop, sink, wilt, slip.
Ant. lift, elevate, raise.

sage ADJ. rational, wise, logical, experienced; —N. intellectual, savant, scholar.
Ant. dunce, idiot.

sail v. rush, flow, fly.

salutation N. greeting, welcoming, hello.
Ant. farewell.

salvage V. save, recover, rescue.
Ant. dump, trash, eliminate, discard.

salve V. ease, soothe, pacify, heal.
Ant. irritate, abrade, annoy, aggravate.

same ADJ. identical, equal, consistent, equivalent.
Ant. different, inconsistent, unequal.

sample N. specimen, model, example, case, illustration.

sanction N. penalty, approbation, approval, privilege, authorization; —v. support, encourage, authorize.
Ant. denunciation, objection, restraint.

sanctity N. sacredness, holiness, inviolability.
Ant. irreverence, blasphemy, profanity.

sane ADJ. sensible, rational, reasonable, prudent, lucid, levelheaded.
Ant. deranged, irrational, mad.

sanguine ADJ. optimistic, upbeat, positive.
Ant. pessimistic, negative, gloomy.

sanity N. reason, sense, saneness, lucidity, sound mind.
Ant. irrationality, imprudence, lunacy, insanity.

sarcasm N. irony, scorn, bitterness, causticity, hostility.
Ant. civility, courtesy, respect.

sarcastic ADJ. satirical, ironic, bitter, derisive, scornful.
Ant. complimentary, polite, civil, pleasant.

satanic ADJ. evil, sinful.
Ant. godly, heavenly, holy.

satiate V. satisfy, fulfill, gratify, gorge.
Ant. desire, long, want.

satire N. sarcasm, humor, irony, ridicule, lampoon.

• **satisfactory** ADJ. acceptable, sufficient, adequate, convincing. *The changes you recommend are acceptable to the committee.*
Ant. insufficient, inadequate, unacceptable.

satisfy V. fulfill, please, gratify, placate, content.
Ant. taunt, tempt, lure.

saturate V. drench, soak, permeate, wet, charge.
Ant. dehydrate, dry.

savage ADJ. uncivilized, crude, wild, fierce, cruel.
Ant. civilized, gracious, benevolent.

save V. store, collect, conserve, accumulate, redeem.
Ant. waste, destroy, discard.

savor V. enjoy, appreciate, feel.
Ant. dislike, reject.

say V. communicate, tell, express, articulate, assert, claim.
Ant. suppress, conceal.

saying N. proverb, maxim, adage, quotation, byword.

scale V. climb, ascend, mount, grapple; —N. ratio, gradation, balance, proportion.
Ant. descend, fall.

scan V. skim, inspect, examine, browse, glance at.

scandalous ADJ. disreputable, shameful, outrageous, disgraceful, dishonorable.
Ant. virtuous, praiseworthy, honorable, respectable.

scant ADJ. slight, little, scarce.
Ant. plenteous, abundant, bounteous, substantial.

scarce ADJ. rare, insufficient, infrequent, uncommon.
Ant. prevalent, abundant, sufficient.

scare V. shock, frighten, startle, terrify, intimidate.
Ant. calm, encourage, placate.

scary ADJ. frightening, startling, alarming, terrifying, fearful.
Ant. soothing, calming.

scatter V. disperse, sprinkle, spread, dispel.
Ant. collect, gather, assemble.

scene N. setting, locale, site, view, area.

scent N. odor, smell, aroma, fragrance.

- **schedule** N. program, plan, timetable, list. *Be sure to make time in your program for the treasurer's report.*

scheme N., V. plot, design, plan, intrigue.

scholar N. student, intellectual, savant, researcher.
Ant. illiterate, barbarian, ignorant.

scholastic ADJ. pedagogic, learned, pedantic.

scold v. punish, reprimand, berate, reprove.
Ant. compliment, encourage, praise, laud.

scorch v. burn, char, singe.
Ant. soothe, douse.

score N. tally, record, rating; —v. grade, mark, accomplish.

scorn N. belittle, ridicule, disparage.
Ant. praise, extol, eulogize, compliment.

scour v. clean, scrub, scrape, forage, comb, seek, search.
Ant. stain, dirty.

scout v. search, explore, seek; —N. explorer, lookout.

scowl v. frown, glare, glower.
Ant. smile, grin.

scramble v. blend, combine, shuffle, confuse.
Ant. organize, clarify, separate.

scrape v. scrub, grate, scratch.

scratch v. scrape, mark, grate, nick.
Ant. itch.

scream N., v. wail, cry, howl, shriek, yell.
Ant. whisper, silence.

screech N., v. yell, cry, scream, shriek.

screen v. censor, shade, separate, protect, shield.
Ant. show, reveal, expose, uncover.

scrub v. scour, wash, clean, scrape.

scrutiny N. study, examination, inspection, investigation, search.
Ant. discovery.

search v. examine, inspect, scrutinize, investigate, scour.
Ant. find, discover, reveal.

seat N. chair, bottom, center, base.

secluded ADJ. isolated, solitary, private, withdrawn, remote, hidden.
Ant. populated, central, public.

seclusion N. retirement, separation, hiding, isolation, withdrawal.
Ant. involvement.

secondary ADJ. subordinate, minor, derivative.
Ant. primary, first, foremost.

secrecy N. privacy, seclusion, concealment, mystery.
Ant. openness, clarity, obviousness.

secret ADJ. hidden, restricted, classified, confidential,
private, unknown.
Ant. apparent, evident, undisguised.

secretly ADV. covertly, clandestinely, furtively.
Ant. publicly, openly.

sect N. group, faction, religion, faith.
Ant. majority.

section N. division, part, segment, share, slice.
Ant. whole, entirety, total.

secure ADJ. fastened, tight, stable; sure, safe,
confident; —v. tighten, fasten, acquire, obtain,
protect.
Ant. endangered, threatened, jeopardized.

seduce V. entice, tempt, allure, bait, coax.
Ant. rebuff, offend, repel.

seduction N. lure, debauchery.
Ant. repulsion.

seductive ADJ. enticing, alluring, tempting, inviting,
bewitching.
Ant. offensive, repulsive, sickening.

see V. view, observe, regard, perceive, look,
comprehend, understand, ascertain, determine.
Ant. overlook, disregard, misunderstand.

seed N. pit, kernel, germ, spore; children, offspring.
Ant. fruit, adult.

seek V. search, quest, attempt, look for.
Ant. discover, perceive, find.

seem V. look, appear.

segment N. division, part, section, portion, cut.
Ant. whole, total, entirety.

segregate V. isolate, separate, ostracize.
Ant. join, connect, mix.

seize V. confiscate, grab, capture, arrest, catch, take.
Ant. return, leave, relinquish.

seldom ADV. infrequently, rarely, scarcely.
  Ant. often, frequently, commonly.

select V. pick, choose, elect; —ADJ. preferred, elite, best.
  Ant. refuse, eliminate, reject.

selection N. choice, preference, pick.

selective ADJ. discriminating, choosy.
  Ant. relaxed, unaware.

self N. ego, character, personality, person.

self-assured ADJ. confident, proud.
  Ant. timid, weak.

self-confident ADJ. confident, assured, bold.
  Ant. unsure, hesitant, fearful, timid.

self-control N. reserve, restraint, caution, demure.
  Ant. irresponsibility, thoughtlessness.

self-esteem N. pride, self-respect, reserve.
  Ant. self-loathing, self-hatred.

self-important ADJ. pompous, egocentric, conceited.
  Ant. humble, modest.

selfish ADJ. greedy, self-centered, stingy.
  Ant. giving, benevolent, philanthropic.

selfless ADJ. altruistic, kind, generous, unselfish.
  Ant. greedy, conceited, selfish.

self-respect N. pride, self-esteem.
  Ant. self-hatred, self-loathing.

self-restraint N. reserve, self-control.
  Ant. irresponsibility, carelessness.

self-sufficient N. independent, self-supporting.
  Ant. dependent.

sell V. market, trade, retail, peddle.
  Ant. purchase, buy, obtain.

semblance N. shade, facade.
  Ant. reality.

seminar N. meeting, class, conference, grouping.

send V. ship, forward, dispatch, mail.
  Ant. receive, keep, get.

senile ADJ. aged, doddering, weak, feeble, infirm.
  Ant. strong, sharp, alert.

senior ADJ. superior, advanced, higher, older, elder;
—N. elder, superior, chief.
Ant. youth, baby, child, boy, girl.

sensation N. feeling, perception, sense, response,
wonder, marvel.
Ant. numbness.

sensational ADJ. marvelous, dramatic, wonderful,
thrilling, spectacular.
Ant. drab, dull, boring, colorless.

sense V. perceive, feel; —N. sanity, intelligence,
reason, logic.
Ant. ignore, misread.

senseless ADJ. useless, unreasonable, mindless.
Ant. reasonable, thoughtful, responsible.

sensibility N. sensation, feeling, sense, insight.
Ant. apathy, indifference, lethargy.

sensible ADJ. reasonable, logical, rational,
responsible, sane.
Ant. irrational, illogical, irresponsible.

• **sensitive** ADJ. tender, delicate, emotional, susceptible.
The photographs touched our most tender emotions.
Ant. heartless, unfeeling.

sensitivity N. sensitiveness, sensation, tenderness.
Ant. numbness, hardness.

sensual ADJ. carnal, earthy, material, physical,
suggestive, sexual.
Ant. austere, temperate, moderate.

sensuous ADJ. sensual, voluptuous, epicurean.
Ant. plain, unattractive.

sentiment N. feeling, emotion, belief, attitude.
Ant. logic, reason.

sentimental ADJ. emotional, romantic, tender,
maudlin.
Ant. pragmatic, reserved, objective.

separate V. divide, isolate, sever, detach; —ADJ.
divergent, distinct, unique, individual.
Ant. united, joined.

separately ADV. apart, discretely.
Ant. together.

separation N. division, distinction, isolation, segregation.
Ant. unison, attachment, fusion.

sequence N. series, order, arrangement, succession.
Ant. disarray, disorder.

serene ADJ. tranquil, calm, peaceful, quiet.
Ant. stormy, rough, violent.

series N. chain, succession, run, order.
Ant. disorder.

serious ADJ. earnest, solemn, sober, pensive, grave, important.
Ant. insignificant, trivial, flippant.

serve V. wait on, attend, aid, help, do.
Ant. subvert, revolt.

service N. duty, ceremony, favor, observance.
Ant. rejection, omission.

set N. collection, group, series, class; —V. lay, place, settle, establish, appoint, solidify.

setback N. hindrance, obstacle, problem.
Ant. advancement, progress.

settle V. establish, decide, conclude, arrange.
Ant. disarrange, confuse, shift.

• **several** ADJ. some, many, a few, various. *Some autograph seekers waited by the stage door.*
Ant. one, none.

severe ADJ. rigid, firm, hard, powerful, difficult, cruel.
Ant. lenient, merciful, gentle.

severity N. harshness, intensity, rigor, austerity.
Ant. kindness, ease, clemency, tolerance.

sexual ADJ. erotic, sensual, reproductive.
Ant. spiritual, intellectual.

sexy ADJ. erotic, sensual, desirable.
Ant. unattractive, undesirable.

shabby ADJ. scruffy, tattered, threadbare, worn out.
Ant. elegant, tailored, well-kept.

shade N. dusk, shadow, darkness, penumbra, hue, tint, color.
Ant. light, sun, brilliance.

shadow N. shade, darkness, dusk, image.
Ant. light, beam.

shaft N. hole, tunnel, stick, beam.

shake V. shiver, quake, tremble, rock, vibrate.

shaky ADJ. unstable, unsteady, wobbly.
Ant. stable, steady, certain.

shallow ADJ. superficial, weak, shoal.
Ant. deep, cavernous, profound.

shame V. embarrass, dishonor; —N. humiliation, disgrace.
Ant. glorify, honor, respect.

shameful ADJ. disgraceful, humiliating, dishonorable, embarrassing.
Ant. honorable, worthy, respectful, decent, praiseworthy.

shameless ADJ. bold-faced, audacious, immodest, presumptuous, blatant.
Ant. modest, reserved, honest.

shape N. figure, pattern, image, form, mold.

shapeless ADJ. amorphous, formless, unshaped, unformed.
Ant. formed, patterned, shaped.

share V. distribute, allot, contribute.
Ant. hoard, keep, take.

sharp ADJ. clear, acute, distinct, clever, intelligent.
Ant. blunt, dull, flat.

shatter V. destroy, smash, break.
Ant. repair, restore, fix.

shave V. scrape, brush.

shed V. throw, cast, emit, project, molt.
Ant. grow, retract.

shelter N. housing, sanctuary, haven, refuge; —V. hide, house, protect, shield.
Ant. neglect, endanger, expose.

shield V. defend, protect, guard, shelter, cover.
Ant. uncover, expose, imperil.

shift V. disturb, move, turn, change.
Ant. fix, restrain.

shine v. glow, radiate, glimmer, glare, irradiate.
Ant. darken, dim.

shock v. startle, frighten, appall, alarm, horrify; —N.
collision, jolt, impact.
Ant. calm, soothe, allay.

shocking ADJ. outrageous, infamous, appalling,
scandalous, terrible.
Ant. pacifying, calming, pleasant.

short ADJ. abrupt, brief, condensed, curt, sudden,
little.
Ant. long, lengthy, endless.

shortage N. lack, deficit, failure, scarcity,
insufficience.
Ant. abundance, sufficience.

shortcoming N. deficiency, limitation, failing.
Ant. strong point, virtue.

shorten v. edit, reduce, abridge, condense, shrink.
Ant. prolong, perpetuate, lengthen.

shortsighted N. thoughtless, limited, restricted.
Ant. thoughtful, farsighted, considered,
perspicacious.

shout v. yell, cry, call, holler.
Ant. suppress, whisper.

shove v. push, poke, drive, jostle.
Ant. pull, yank.

show v. exhibit, display, demonstrate, divulge, unveil,
indicate, guide.
Ant. hide, cover, conceal.

shrill ADJ. piercing, high, sharp.
Ant. low, bass.

shrink v. contract, dwindle, diminish, wither, deflate.
Ant. enlarge, expand, grow.

shrivel v. shrink, wither, contract.
Ant. expand, inflate, bloat.

shun v. avoid, eschew, reject, turn away from.
Ant. embrace, welcome, befriend, accept.

shy ADJ. withdrawn, timid, diffident.
Ant. extroverted, friendly, garrulous, affable,
personable.

sick ADJ. ill, unhealthy, morbid, impaired, ailing.
Ant. vigorous, healthy, well.

sickening ADJ. unspeakable, offensive, disgusting.
Ant. wonderful, appetizing, delicious.

side N. part, flank, hand.
Ant. top, bottom, front, back.

sign V. signal, gesture, endorse, autograph; —N.
indication, symptom, gesture.

• significance N. importance, meaning, notability,
prominence, weight. *We weighed the relative
importance of the new developments.*
Ant. worthlessness, unimportance, insignificance.

significant ADJ. important, expressive, meaningful,
suggestive, critical, momentous.
Ant. trivial, shallow, worthless.

signify V. emphasize, express; count, show, indicate,
communicate, signal.

silence N. still, quiet, hush, soundlessness.
Ant. noise, clamor, cacophony.

silent ADJ. still, quiet, hushed, tranquil, calm,
speechless, noiseless, mute.
Ant. noisy, talkative, communicative.

simple ADJ. plain, clear, easy, uncomplicated, natural.
Ant. ornate, complicated, intricate.

simpleminded ADJ. slow, dumb, stupid, backward.
Ant. intelligent, wise, educated.

simpleton N. imbecile, moron, idiot.
Ant. genius, mastermind, whiz kid.

simplicity N. naiveté, modesty, informality.
Ant. embellishment, sophistication, complication.

simulate V. act, fake, copy, represent, imitate.

simulated ADJ. imitation, fake, replicated.
Ant. authentic, real, genuine.

sin N. evil, corruption, crime, trespass.
Ant. good, good deed, honor.

sincere ADJ. earnest, honest, frank, candid, truthful,
open.
Ant. insincere, phony, dishonest, untruthful.

sing v. chant, serenade, vocalize, hum.

single ADJ. sole, individual, unique, solitary, unmarried, free.
Ant. married, multiple, plural.

singular ADJ. exceptional, extraordinary, rare, unique, uncommon.
Ant. ordinary, familiar, usual.

sinister ADJ. disturbing, menacing, evil, threatening.
Ant. assuring, nonthreatening.

sink v. fall, drop, descend, submerge; —N. basin.
Ant. rise, climb.

• situation N. circumstances, condition, position, location, place. *Welfare seemed the only alternative in his circumstances.*

size N. dimension, volume, expanse, magnitude, bulk.

skeptic N. doubter, pessimist, misanthrope, cynic, nihilist.
Ant. believer, disciple, devotee.

skeptical ADJ. doubtful, cynical, pessimistic, unbelieving, incredulous.
Ant. devoted, unquestioning, believing.

skill N. ability, proficience, mastery, training, dexterity.
Ant. ineptitude, incompetence, ignorance.

skim v. brush, glance, graze, browse, scan.
Ant. examine, study.

skip v. overlook, disregard, omit, jump, hop, leap.

slam v. smash, bang, crash, wham.

slap v. hit, smack, slam, box.

slay v. kill, murder, exterminate, annihilate.

sleep N., v. slumber, nap, doze, snooze.
Ant. wake, awake.

sleepy ADJ. drowsy, somnolent, slumberous.
Ant. alert, awake, conscious.

slender ADJ. slim, slight, trim, thin.
Ant. fat, overweight, chubby, corpulent, stout.

slide v. drift, glide, slip, coast, slither.
Ant. stick, rest, stay.

slim ADJ. slender, slight, wiry, thin, trim.
Ant. fat, overweight, flabby, hefty.

slip V. glide, err, slide, sag, blunder.

slippery ADJ. slick, shifty, evasive, sharp.
Ant. sticky, dry.

slope N. slant, inclination, incline, ascent.
Ant. plain, plateau.

slot N. position, place.

slothful ADJ. lazy, sluggish, idle, apathetic.
Ant. energetic, vigorous, brisk, active.

slow ADJ. gradual, unhurried, leisurely, delayed, boring, dull.
Ant. fast, quick, hurried, hasty, active, alert.

sluggishness N. laziness, slowness.
Ant. activity, energy, quickness.

slumber N., V. sleep, rest, repose.
Ant. wakefulness, activity.

sly ADJ. shrewd, crafty, wily, cunning.
Ant. simple, candid, open.

small ADJ. miniature, minute, little, minor, petty.
Ant. considerable, large, huge, immense, big.

smart ADJ. intelligent, bright, wise, clever, keen.
Ant. stupid, crass, dense.

smash V. destroy, break, crush, hit, demolish.
Ant. repair, mend.

smear V. spread, cover, coat, wipe.

smell N. scent, aroma, odor, fragrance; —v. sniff, scent.

smile N., V. grin, beam.
Ant. scowl, frown.

smooth ADJ. even, flat, uniform, fluid, easy, effortless.
Ant. rough, corrugated, wrinkled, difficult.

snap V. crack, break, click, clack.

snatch V. seize, catch, snare, grab.
Ant. return, release, give back, free.

sneak V. steal, creep, crawl, skulk.

snob N. elitist, sycophant.

soak V. wet, drench, immerse.
  Ant. dry.

soar V. rise, fly, rocket, shoot.
  Ant. sink, descend, crash.

sober ADJ. temperate, clear-headed, abstemious.
  Ant. drunk, giddy, tipsy.

sociable ADJ. friendly, gracious, social.
  Ant. unfriendly, introverted, discourteous.

social ADJ. friendly, sociable, affable, outgoing,
  communicative.
  Ant. morose, austere, secluded.

socialize V. mingle, talk, nationalize, civilize.
  Ant. reject, isolate.

● **society** N. public, civilization, community, nation.
  *Television programs must appeal to a broad segment of
  the public.*
  Ant. nature, anarchy, isolation.

sodden ADJ. saturated, sopping, drenched.
  Ant. dry, parched, dessicated.

soft ADJ. pliant, flexible, smooth, silky;
  compassionate, sensitive, gentle, quiet.
  Ant. brittle, hard, calloused; strict, insensible.

soften V. pacify, weaken, moderate.
  Ant. stiffen, harden.

soil V. stain, dirty, blacken, taint.
  Ant. clean, cleanse, scrub.

sojourn N. stopover, stay.

solace N. relief, support, comfort, succor.
  Ant. aggravation, irritation, annoyance.

sole ADJ. single, alone, exclusive, only.
  Ant. numerous, many.

solemn ADJ. somber, serious, grave.
  Ant. light-spirited, humorous, cheerful.

solid ADJ. firm, hard, sound, substantial, dense.
  Ant. porous, thin, vulnerable.

solitary ADJ. isolated, alone, lonely, deserted.
  Ant. inhabited, populated.

solitude N. isolation, detachment, removal, loneliness.
   Ant. involvement.

● solution N. answer, explanation, mixture. *The answer
   seemed simple once it was found.*
   Ant. question, investigation, inquisition.

solve V. explain, resolve, decipher, unfold.
   Ant. ask, investigate, work.

somber ADJ. solemn, serious, glum.
   Ant. cheerful, happy, joyful.

some ADJ. several, few.
   Ant. many, numerous.

sonorous ADJ. resonant, bombastic, rhetorical.
   Ant. quiet, silent.

soon ADV. rapidly, quickly, in a short while.
   Ant. later, late, after a while.

soothe V. comfort, calm, lull, quiet, pacify.
   Ant. stimulate, excite, awake, annoy.

sophisticated ADJ. experienced, worldly, wise,
   cosmopolitan.
   Ant. rustic, naive, young, simple.

sordid ADJ. contemptible, ignoble, base, dirty.
   Ant. pure, noble, honorable.

sorrow N. grief, remorse, sadness, heartache, anguish.
   Ant. pleasure, happiness, joy.

sorrowful ADJ. mournful, grievous, sad, remorseful,
   distressed.
   Ant. glad, blissful, pleased.

sorry ADJ. apologetic, regretful, remorseful.
   Ant. unrepentant.

sort V. arrange, separate, order; —N. variety, type,
   kind.
   Ant. mix, confuse.

soul N. spirit, heart, being, essence, core.
   Ant. body.

sound N. noise; —ADJ. secure, stable, whole,
   unharmed, rational, sensible, cogent.
   Ant. quiet, silence; unsound, ailing, irrational.

sour ADJ. tart, acerbic, tangy, sharp.
   Ant. sweet, tasty, agreeable.

source N. origin, beginning, foundation, route, cause.
Ant. result, outcome.

sovereign ADJ. independent, self-ruled.
Ant. dependent, reliant.

space N. room, area, expanse, distance.
Ant. proximity.

spacious ADJ. broad, large, roomy.
Ant. crowded, enclosed, claustrophobic.

span N. period, term, spread, extent.

spare V. save, economize, reserve; forgive, excuse.
Ant. waste, expend, consume.

spark V. flash, blink, light.

sparkle V. glisten, shine, flash, glimmer.

sparse ADJ. meager, spare, slight.
Ant. bountiful, plenteous, copious, abundant.

speak V. say, tell, talk, utter, articulate, communicate,
express, converse.
Ant. conceal, withhold.

speaker N. talker, presenter, spokesperson, orator.
Ant. listener, audience.

special ADJ. distinctive, particular, exceptional,
singular, individual.
Ant. ordinary, unimportant, general.

• specific ADJ. particular, explicit, express, special,
limited. *The panel wanted to examine particular aspects
of the issue.*
Ant. general, vague, uncertain.

specify V. name, designate, stipulate, define.
Ant. generalize.

spectacular ADJ. staggering, amazing, dramatic,
extraordinary.
Ant. uninteresting, dull, usual, unimaginative.

spectator N. viewer, onlooker, watcher, bystander,
witness.
Ant. participant, actor, player.

speculate V. consider, think, surmise, suppose,
gamble.
Ant. act, react.

speech N. oration, lecture, address, talk, discourse.

speechless ADJ. mute, silent, wordless, dumb.
Ant. talkative, wordy.

speed N. pace, velocity, rapidity, tempo, haste.
Ant. slowness.

spend V. pay, give, disburse, consume, use.
Ant. hold, collect, save.

spin V. rotate, turn, revolve, oscillate.

spineless ADJ. cowardly, weak, fearful, gutless.
Ant. brave, bold, daring, valiant, fearless.

spirit N. vitality, enthusiasm, liveliness, animation,
soul, psyche, animus, phantom, ghost.
Ant. body.

spirited ADJ. excited, lively, vibrant, animated, fiery.
Ant. lethargic, dull, uninterested.

spiritless ADJ. dull, boring, languid, unenthusiastic.
Ant. vibrant, lively, excited.

spiritual ADJ. religious, immaterial, ecclesiastical,
unworldly.
Ant. faithless, worldly, material.

spiteful ADJ. mean, malicious, unkind.
Ant. considerate, kind, caring, pleasant.

splash V. soak, douse, splatter, drench.
Ant. dry.

splendid ADJ. marvelous, superb, glorious, excellent,
grand.
Ant. dull, plain, uninteresting.

splendor N. magnificence, grandeur, majesty.
Ant. dullness, poverty.

split V. break, cut, divide, crack.
Ant. mend, repair, fix.

spoil V. ruin, injure, damage, rot, decay.
Ant. remake, remodel.

spontaneous ADJ. distinctive, involuntary, automatic,
compulsive.
Ant. premeditated, deliberate, considered.

sport N. game, recreation, play, athletics.
Ant. work, labor, toil.

spot N. place, position, location; —N., v. stain, mark, blemish; —v. find, sight.

spread v. scatter, disperse, circulate, diffuse, strew.
Ant. collect, focus, assemble, gather.

spring N., v. jump, skip, bounce, leap.

sprinkle v. scatter, speckle, dust, spread.

squabble v. argue, bicker, quarrel.
Ant. harmony, agreement, concurrence.

squalid ADJ. dirty, filthy, neglected, unclean.
Ant. clean, cared for, tidy, neat, well-kept.

squander v. waste, dissipate, misuse.
Ant. save, spend wisely, conserve.

squash v. smash, crush, suppress, crowd.

squeeze v. press, grip, crush, express, crowd.
Ant. let go, release, loosen.

stabilize v. balance, steady, solidify.
Ant. shake, fluctuate.

stagger v. wobble, sway, totter, reel, alternate, vary.

stain v. smear, discolor, tarnish, blot, soil.
Ant. bleach, clean.

stale ADJ. dry, flat, old, trite, old-fashioned.
Ant. fresh, new.

stamp v. engrave, imprint, mark, crush, trample.

stand v. rise, endure, tolerate; —N. opinion, attitude.
Ant. sit, recline, lie.

• standard ADJ. common, accepted; —N. measure, mark, mean, model, average. *The house was built according to common construction practices.*

start v. begin, initiate, commence, launch; —N. commencement, beginning, onset.
Ant. finish, end, terminate, conclude.

startle v. frighten, shock, alarm, surprise, jolt.
Ant. calm, soothe, forewarn.

startling ADJ. astounding, shocking, surprising, astonishing.
Ant. relaxing, soothing.

starve v. waste away, go hungry, go without eating.
Ant. eat, consume, devour.

state N. nation, country, land, condition, situation;
—v. assert, announce, declare, say, express.
Ant. repress, conceal, hide.

statement N. assertion, announcement, declaration,
account.

station N. base, post, depot; —v. put, place, position.
Ant. remove.

status N. condition, state, place, standing, rank.

stay V. continue, remain, rest, stop, hinder.
Ant. leave, depart, go.

steadfast ADJ. fixed, faithful, stable.
Ant. unreliable, unfaithful, unstable.

steady ADJ. regular, even, steadfast, stable, solid, firm.
Ant. erratic, unstable, restless.

steal V. rob, take, burglarize, plunder.
Ant. return, purchase.

steep ADJ. sheer, abrupt, sharp, towering.
Ant. flat, level.

steer V. drive, guide, maneuver, direct.

stem V. come, arrive, originate, hinder, stop.
Ant. allow, further.

step V. walk, come, move; —N. measure, action,
stage.
Ant. inaction.

sterile ADJ. unproductive, barren, infertile, impotent,
boring.
Ant. fertile, productive, prolific.

sterilize V. fix, neuter, geld, castrate, sanitize,
decontaminate, disinfect.
Ant. infect, contaminate.

stick N. staff, cane, branch, twig; —v. puncture, stab,
pierce.

stiff ADJ. firm, rigid, inflexible, hard, unyielding.
Ant. flexible, pliable, soft.

stifle V. muffle, smother, repress, censor.
Ant. state, express, allow.

still ADJ. quiet, motionless, peaceful, calm.
Ant. moving, loud, noisy.

stimulate v. encourage, inspire, arouse, excite, animate.
Ant. deaden, bore, tranquilize.

stimulation N. encouragement, invigoration, arousal, excitement.
Ant. depression, deterrence, tranquilization.

stimulus N. motivation, prod, catalyst, incitement.
Ant. discouragement, repression.

sting v. prick, bite, irritate; —N. scam.

stir v. mix, agitate, arouse, inspire, stimulate.
Ant. calm, settle, placate.

stop v. cease, halt, discontinue, hinder, delay, obstruct.
Ant. begin, start, initiate.

store N. reserve, supply; market, shop; —v. keep, save, stockpile.
Ant. spend, waste, use.

story N. narrative, tale, account, description.

stout ADJ. heavy, bulky, strong, fat, obese.
Ant. slim, thin, slender, spare, lean.

straight ADJ. direct, unswerving, unbent; honest, trustworthy, candid, frank.
Ant. curved, twisting, unreliable, dishonest.

straightforward ADJ. frank, direct, candid, honest, plain.
Ant. ambiguous, indirect, unclear.

strain v. stress, harm, pull, injure, tighten, stretch.

strange ADJ. peculiar, odd, fantastic, bizarre, eccentric.
Ant. typical, average, normal.

strength N. power, might, force, energy, muscle.
Ant. weakness, sterility, impotence.

• strengthen v. reinforce, toughen, confirm, tighten. *It was necessary to reinforce the bridge pilings.*
Ant. weaken, loosen, destruct.

strenuous ADJ. difficult, forceful, energetic, rough.
Ant. easy, painless, effortless.

stress v. emphasize, underline, accentuate; —N.
strain, pressure, importance, emphasis.
Ant. relaxation, ease, underplay, de-emphasize.

strict ADJ. severe, rigorous, harsh, stern,
uncompromising.
Ant. flexible, lenient, easygoing.

stride v. stalk, march, stamp, stomp.
Ant. amble, stroll.

strike v. beat, hit, attack, affect; —N. protest, walkout.
Ant. caress, soothe.

striking ADJ. awesome, noticeable, shocking,
impressive.
Ant. ordinary, uninteresting, drab.

string N. line, series, run.

strive v. endeavor, labor, try, attempt.
Ant. succeed, give up.

stroll v. wander, amble, walk, saunter.
Ant. rush, hurry.

strong ADJ. powerful, mighty, forceful, resistant, solid,
firm.
Ant. fragile, weak, sickly.

struggle v. battle, fight, contend, strive, clash.
Ant. succeed, overcome.

stubborn ADJ. uncompromising, rigid, adamant,
obstinate, relentless.
Ant. reasonable, yielding, compromising, lenient.

study v. consider, investigate, examine; —N.
examination, research.

stumble v. lurch, blunder, trip, err.

stupefy v. perilize, daze, amaze.
Ant. lull, bore.

stupendous ADJ. fabulous, amazing, marvelous, giant.
Ant. dull, foolish, minor.

stupid N. witless, inane, moronic, foolish, crass,
asinine.
Ant. wise, intelligent, bright.

stupor N. daze, apathy, lethargy, torpor, inertness.
Ant. consciousness, feeling, sensibility.

style N. mode, fashion, way, manner, tone.

suave ADJ. gallant, polite, gracious, courteous, tactful.
Ant. awkward, crude, ignorant.

subdue V. restrain, control, check, tame, repress.
Ant. emancipate, free, unbind.

subject N. topic, theme, point, area, matter.

sublime ADJ. glorious, exalted, grand, magnificent.
Ant. insignificant, unimpressive, trivial.

submerge V. sink, submerse, flood, dip.
Ant. raise, retract, rise.

submissive ADJ. passive, obedient, subservient,
compliant.
Ant. assertive, bold, aggressive, self-assured.

submit V. surrender, propose, yield, offer.
Ant. deny, obstruct, resist.

subordinate ADJ. lower, secondary, inferior,
subservient.
Ant. dominant, superior, chief.

subsequent ADJ. consecutive, following, future, later.
Ant. former, prior, preceding.

subservient ADJ. subordinate, servile, inferior,
dependent.
Ant. independent, superior, forceful.

subside V. ebb, abate, wane, moderate, slacken.
Ant. continue, intensify, expand.

substance N. matter, body, import, material.
Ant. nothingness.

• substantial ADJ. large, heavy, considerable, sizable,
important. *The performer balanced a large plate of fruit
on his head.*
Ant. unimportant, insignificant, minuscule.

substantiate V. prove, concern, back.
Ant. refute, disprove, reject.

substitute N. replacement, stand-in, alternate,
surrogate.
Ant. original, initial.

subtle ADJ. indirect, fine, delicate.
Ant. obvious, direct, open.

succeed V. accomplish, triumph, prevail, achieve, surmount.
Ant. lose, fail, miss.

success N. prosperity, achievement, triumph, accomplishment.
Ant. loss, failure.

succinct ADJ. concise, terse, to the point.
Ant. long, wordy, verbose, long-winded, rambling.

succumb V. capitulate, bow, yield, fold, surrender.
Ant. resist, fight off.

suffer V. grieve, bear, endure, allow, tolerate.
Ant. enjoy, celebrate.

suffering N. misery, agony, grief.
Ant. joy, exultation, celebration.

sufficient ADJ. adequate, plenty, enough, acceptable.
Ant. deficient, inadequate, lacking.

suggest V. imply, recommend, indicate, propose, hint.
Ant. declare, express, state.

● **suggestion** N. recommendation, hint, allusion, proposal, implication. *All of us are in favor of accepting your recommendation.*
Ant. assertion, revelation, declaration.

suggestive ADJ. evocative, allusive, pregnant, insinuating, sensual.
Ant. straightforward, frank.

suit V. become, satisfy, gratify, fit, conform, adapt; —N. litigation, prosecution.
Ant. disagree with, displease.

suitable ADJ. becoming, fitting, eligible, appropriate.
Ant. unsuitable, inappropriate, unfit, incongruous.

sully V. pollute, contaminate, foul.
Ant. clean up, purify, praise.

summarize V. review, outline.
Ant. expand.

summary N. synopsis, résumé, recapitulation, abstract, outline; —ADJ. concise.

summation N. summary, total, addition.

summit N. peak, height, climax, top.
Ant. bottom, base.

summon V. call, assemble, invoke.
Ant. reject, revoke.

super ADJ. marvelous, excellent, great.
Ant. negligible, inferior, unimpressive.

superb ADJ. marvelous, extraordinary, magnificent,
excellent, wonderful.
Ant. dull, drab, uninteresting.

superficial ADJ. shallow, one-dimensional, surface,
cursory, flimsy.
Ant. profound, deep, thorough.

superfluous ADJ. excessive, unnecessary, useless,
redundant, gratuitous.
Ant. useful, helpful, necessary.

• superior ADJ. greater, higher, better, excellent,
supreme, sovereign. *Her daughter's achievement is
certainly greater than her own.*
Ant. minor, inferior, lower.

superiority N. arrogance, excellence, advantage.
Ant. inferiority, minority.

supernatural ADJ. miraculous, transcendental,
metaphysical, superhuman, divine, celestial.
Ant. mortal, human, earthly.

supersede V. replace, take the place of, stand in for.

supervise V. overlook, administer, run, guide,
conduct.
Ant. follow, work for.

supple ADJ. limber, flexible, malleable, lithe.
Ant. hard, stiff, inflexible.

supplement N. complement, addition, attachment,
extension.
Ant. original, intended.

supply V. substitute, provide, give, furnish.
Ant. take, receive.

support V. maintain, keep, uphold, advocate,
corroborate.
Ant. block, hinder, counteract.

• suppose V. guess, presume, postulate, assume. *I guess
his age to be well over fifty.*
Ant. know, discover.

suppress V. overpower, crush, censor, quell, repress.
Ant. liberate, free.

sure ADJ. certain, positive, strong, solid, definite.
Ant. uncertain, unsure.

surmise V. guess, gather, assume, conjecture.
Ant. prove, determine, authenticate, substantiate.

surpass V. outdo, exceed, overcome, go beyond.
Ant. fall short, fail, go amiss.

surplus N. overage, excess, profusion, overabundance.
Ant. lack, need, dearth.

surprise V. astonish, shock, startle, amaze, stun.
Ant. bore, placate.

surrender V. relinquish, succumb, abdicate, submit, collapse.
Ant. fight, resist, win.

surround V. encompass, circle, confine, besiege, enclose.
Ant. retract, retreat.

survey V. overlook, examine, watch, scan.

survive V. persist, outlast, weather.
Ant. die, perish, succumb, give in.

suspend V. discontinue, terminate, cease, interrupt.
Ant. reinstate, continue, renew.

suspicion N. doubt, distrust, feeling.
Ant. trustworthiness, faith.

suspicious ADJ. doubtful, mistrustful, shady, distrustful.
Ant. unquestioning, trusting.

sustain V. carry, support, bear, uphold, maintain.
Ant. discontinue, stop, end.

sway V. wobble, teeter, bend; persuade, influence, affect.

swear V. curse, damn, blaspheme; declare, assert, vow.

sweet ADJ. adorable, attractive, sugary, pleasant, agreeable, nice, charming.
Ant. sour, disagreeable, unpleasant.

swift ADJ. fast, quick, speedy, rapid.
Ant. lethargic, slow.

swing v. sway, pivot, oscillate, waver.

symbol N. emblem, character, representation, attribute.

symbolic ADJ. indicative, emblematic, representational.
Ant. realistic, actual, straightforward.

symbolize v. represent, stand for.

symmetrical ADJ. regular, balanced, proportional, accordant, congruous.
Ant. imbalanced, disproportionate, different.

sympathize v. empathize, understand, identify, feel.
Ant. injure, rebuff.

sympathy N. pity, empathy, compassion, feeling, sentiment.
Ant. indifference, intolerance.

synopsis N. summary, abstract, brief, condensation.

synthetic ADJ. plastic, man-made, artificial, chemical.
Ant. natural.

system N. arrangement, plan, way, method, totality, whole, entity.
Ant. confusion, disorder, chaos.

T

table N. inventory, chart, catalog; counter, desk.

taboo ADJ. forbidden, prohibited.
Ant. acceptable, normal, orthodox.

tacit ADJ. silent, implicit, implied, presupposed, accepted.
Ant. direct, overt, open.

taciturn ADJ. reticent, reserved, silent, uncommunicative, laconic.
Ant. communicative, talkative, verbose.

tack N. turn, approach.
Ant. retreat.

tact N. diplomacy, savoir faire, judgment, subtlety, poise, acumen.
Ant. thoughtlessness, imprudence, incompetence.

tactic N. move, maneuver, strategy, approach.

tactless ADJ. impolite, brash, rude, indelicate.
Ant. diplomatic, acute, insightful.

tail N. end, rear; —V. follow, watch, shadow.
Ant. avoid, evade.

taint V. corrupt, pollute, dirty, contaminate.
Ant. clean, purify.

take V. seize, hold, capture, select, choose, bring, lead, buy, purchase, steal, remove.
Ant. give, return, donate.

tale N. anecdote, lie, story.
Ant. truth.

talent N. faculty, aptitude, gift, skill.
Ant. inability.

talented ADJ. gifted, endowed, clever, capable.
Ant. incapable, untalented, ungifted, average.

talk V. converse, speak, communicate, address, verbalize, articulate.

talkative ADJ. conversational, chatty, garrulous, glib.
Ant. silent, quiet, reserved.

tall ADJ. high, elevated, towering, big.
Ant. short, low, small.

tally V. add, score, count.

tame ADJ. docile, domesticated, gentle, broken, boring, unexciting.
Ant. fierce, wild, interesting.

tamper V. meddle, fool, interfere, trouble, intervene.

tangible ADJ. tactile, palpable, physical, real.
Ant. intangible, metaphysical, unreal, abstract.

tangle V. snarl, confuse, jumble, complicate; —N. maze, jungle, puzzle, quandary.
Ant. clarify, order, simplify.

tantalize V. tease, bait, provoke, tempt, lure.
Ant. soothe, appease.

tap V. strike, pat, hit.

tardy ADJ. slow, late, overdue.
Ant. punctual, early, prompt.

target N. aim, goal, mark, intention.

tarnish V. blacken, dirty, taint, stain, discolor.
Ant. brighten, clean, restore, polish.

tarry V. loiter, linger, remain, pause.
Ant. depart, hurry, leave.

task N. duty, job, chore, effort.
Ant. play, enjoyment.

taste V. savor, try, feel, experience.

tasteful ADJ. pleasing, aesthetic, delicious.
Ant. tasteless, crude, uncouth, tacky.

tasteless ADJ. flavorless, flat, insipid, bland.
Ant. flavorful, delicious, pleasing.

tasty ADJ. tasteful, delicious, flavorful.
Ant. unsavory, flavorless, bland.

tattle V. blab, gossip, inform, reveal.
Ant. conceal, cover.

taunt V. bother, ridicule, tease, pester.
Ant. respect, honor, praise.

taut V. tight, close, snug, neat.
Ant. loose, untied, relaxed.

tawdry ADJ. tasteless, cheap, crude.
Ant. refined, sophisticated, elegant, expensive.

tax N. duty, tariff, levy, assessment.

teach V. educate, instruct, school, tutor, train.
Ant. follow, learn, understand.

teaching N. education, instruction, guidance, doctrine.

team N. group, crew, band, assembly.

tear V. rip, rupture, split, cleave.
Ant. mend, sew, repair.

tearful ADJ. weeping, crying, mournful, sobbing, lamenting.
Ant. calm, serious, coldhearted.

tease V. tantalize, annoy, irritate, pester, bother.
Ant. praise, compliment, applaud.

technicality N. detail, specific.

• **technique** N. approach, method, system, way. *Your approach obviously requires great skill.*

tedious ADJ. boring, wearisome, monotonous, drowsy.
Ant. amusing, refreshing, lively.

tedium N. monotony, boredom, fatigue.
Ant. excitement, inspiration, fascination.

teem V. bustle, overflow, swarm, abound.

teeter V. sway, wobble, lurch, totter.

telephone V. call, dial, buzz, ring, phone.

tell V. inform, explain, advise, relate, say.
Ant. conceal, withhold, suppress.

temerity N. blodness, rashness, nerve, audacity, indiscretion, daring.
Ant. care, prudence, caution.

temper N. fury, anger, passion, rage; mood, spirit, disposition.
Ant. calm, coolheadedness.

temperament N. disposition, mood, humor, personality, character, nature.

temperamental ADJ. moody, capricious, irritable, sensitive.
Ant. relaxed, calm, easygoing.

temperate ADJ. moderate, mild, frugal, reasonable, abstinent.
Ant. stormy, passionate, immoderate.

tempestuous ADJ. stormy, turbulent, rough.
Ant. mild, reasonable, moderate.

temporal ADJ. earthly, terrestrial, impermanent, transitory.
Ant. perpetual, everlasting, eternal.

• temporary ADJ. provisional, passing, momentary, acting, interim, transitory. *The committee can give only provisional approval to the request.*
Ant. permanent, fixed, endless.

tempt V. seduce, entice, allure, attract, invite.
Ant. disenchant, repel, discourage.

tenable ADJ. justifiable, defensible, defendable.
Ant. indefensible, unjustifiable.

tenacious ADJ. obstinate, tough, stubborn, persistent, sticky, resolute.
Ant. delicate, fragile, irresolute.

tend V. incline, lean, dispose; watch, guard, protect.
Ant. neglect, ignore.

• tendency N. propensity, bent, thrust, predisposition, inclination. *She has a propensity for saying just the right thing at the right time.*
Ant. aversion, antipathy, opposition.

tender ADJ. loving, gentle, kind, compassionate, warm.
Ant. callous, harsh, severe.

tense ADJ. stiff, rigid, taut, edgy, uptight.
Ant. calm, relaxed, tranquil, loose.

• tension N. stress, pressure, strain, apprehension, fear. *Most of the engineers admitted to feeling stress during the strike.*
Ant. relaxation, calm, tranquility.

tentative ADJ. anticipated, indecisive, untested, temporary.
Ant. permanent, conclusive, definitive.

tenuous ADJ. insignificant, weak, insubstantial, implausible, feeble.
Ant. important, essential, significant.

tenure N. occupancy, incumbency, occupation.
Ant. apprenticeship, inexperience.

tepid ADJ. unenthusiastic, dull, lukewarm, halfhearted.
Ant. enthusiastic, hot.

term N. interval, period, duration, span, expression, phrase, word.

terminal ADJ. concluding, last, final, ending; deadly, fatal.
Ant. opening, initial, beginning.

terminate V. end, close, suspend, cease, dismiss.
Ant. start, begin, open.

terrain N. land, topography, territory.

• **terrific** ADJ. marvelous, excellent, extraordinary, horrible, ghastly. *The art exhibit was marvelous in its range and variety of paintings.*
Ant. dull, uninteresting, tedious.

terrify V. frighten, shock, panic.
Ant. reassure, pacify, calm, appease. `

territory N. terrain, area, country, region, section.

terror N. fear, panic, horror, dread, alarm.
Ant. calm, security, peacefulness.

terrorize V. frighten, abuse, bother.
Ant. placate, soothe.

test N. examination, proof, essay; —V. examine, inspect, try, assess, verify, experiment.

testify V. witness, attest, confirm, certify, state.
Ant. disavow, reject, deny.

testimony N. confirmation, proof, affirmation, declaration, witness.
Ant. rejection, denial.

testy ADJ. irritable, ill-tempered, petulant, touchy.
Ant. easygoing, calm, relaxed.

text N. subject, passage, verse; manual, book.

texture N. grain, fiber, essence, feel, character, constitution.

thank V. oblige, bless.

thankful ADJ. obliged, grateful, appreciative.
Ant. careless, ungrateful, critical.

thankless ADJ. ungrateful, critical, unappreciative, insensible.
Ant. grateful, appreciative.

thaw V. melt, dissolve, liquefy.
Ant. congeal, freeze, chill.

theatrical ADJ. dramatic, spectacular, showy, affected.
Ant. modest, unaffected, humble.

theft N. robbery, larceny, embezzlement, burglary, misappropriation.
Ant. return, indemnity, restoration.

thematic ADJ. topical.

theme N. topic, subject, composition, thesis.

theoretical ADJ. speculative, hypothetical, abstract.
Ant. proven, certain.

theory N. hypothesis, premise, supposition, speculation, conjecture.
Ant. proof, certainty.

therapy N. treatment.

thesis N. dissertation, essay, theme, doctrine.

thick ADJ. solid, crowded, compact, heavy, dense, stupid.
Ant. thin, slender, slim.

thicken V. condense, solidify, compact.
Ant. reduce, weaken, dilute.

thief N. robber, criminal, burglar, larcener.
Ant. crime-fighter.

thin ADJ. gaunt, slender, bony, lean, skinny.
Ant. thick, massive, obese, fat.

thing N. object, being, entity, obsession, mania.

think V. contemplate, ponder, consider, meditate, feel, believe.
Ant. act.

thirst N. craving, desire, appetite, longing.
Ant. satisfaction.

thirsty ADJ. parched, dry, eager.
Ant. satiated, satisfied.

thorny ADJ. spiny, prickly, perplexing, complicated, difficult.

- thorough ADJ. careful, complete, accurate, entire, absolute. *The task was accomplished in a careful way.* *Ant.* incomplete, shallow, inefficient.

thoroughly ADV. completely, scrupulously, meticulously, painstakingly.
Ant. partially, incompletely, in part.

thought N. reflection, consideration, idea, meditation.
Ant. vacancy, emptiness, vacuity.

thoughtful ADJ. attentive, kind, pensive, museful, speculative.
Ant. reckless, indifferent, careless.

thoughtless ADJ. careless, impulsive, inconsiderate, foolish.
Ant. pensive, deliberative, thinking.

thrash V. whip, beat, punish, defeat, flail.
Ant. soothe, caress.

thread N. filament, strand, fiber.

threat N. menace, warning, intimidation, danger.
Ant. reassurance, protection, defense, conservation.

threaten V. intimidate, menace, forewarn, impend.
Ant. protect, conserve, preserve.

thrift N. prudence, economy, frugality.
Ant. extravagance, waste.

thrill N. excitement, shock, sensation.
Ant. boredom, numbness.

thrive V. prosper, flourish, succeed, increase.
Ant. decline, fall, lose.

throb V. pulsate, palpitate, beat.

throe N. convulsion, pain, spasm, grip.

throttle V. repress, choke.
Ant. proclaim, breathe.

through ADJ. over, finished, completed, done; —ADV. completely, out; —PREP. past.

throw V. cast, toss, project, fling, pitch.
Ant. catch, receive.

thrust V. push, shove, penetrate, pierce; —N. essence, substance, core.
Ant. pull, retract.

thug N. hooligan, bully, gangster, punk, ruffian.

ticket N. marker, tag, label.

tickle V. delight, please, amuse.
Ant. irritate, bother, annoy.

ticklish ADJ. fragile, capricious, delicate.

tidy ADJ. neat, clean, orderly, trim.
Ant. confused, messy, disorganized.

tie V. bind, fasten, secure, attach, link.
Ant. divide, separate, loosen.

tight ADJ. secure, taut, firm, sealed, locked, tense, arduous, difficult.
Ant. slack, loose, comfortable.

tight-lipped ADJ. taciturn, speechless.
Ant. talkative, verbose.

till V. labor, work, plow, cultivate, sow.

tilt V. slant, lean, incline.

time N. interval, period, season, occasion, tempo, rhythm.

timeless ADJ. eternal, continual, everlasting, ageless.
Ant. earthly, mortal, temporary.

timely ADJ. appropriate, opportune, convenient, proper, suitable.
Ant. immature, early, late.

timid ADJ. shy, fearful, cowardly, weak, modest.
Ant. bold, courageous, brave.

tinge N.,V. shade, tint, color.

tinker V. fiddle, putter, tamper.

tint N. color, tinge, hue, shade, tone.

tiny ADJ. small, miniature, diminutive, little.
Ant. immense, large, gigantic, giant, vast.

tip N. end, peak, point; hint, clue.
Ant. body, base.

tirade N. condemnation, abuse, denunciation, sermon, lecture.
Ant. praise, approval.

tire V. exhaust, weaken, fatigue, bore.
Ant. awaken, arouse.

tireless ADJ. active, enthusiastic, inexhaustible, energetic.
Ant. weak, unenthusiastic, exhausted.

tiresome ADJ. tedious, wearisome, annoying, irritating.
Ant. interesting, fascinating, exciting, motivating.

tiring ADJ. exhausting, boring, wearying, taxing, fatiguing.
Ant. interesting, enthralling.

title N. possession, ownership, claim, heading, name.

titter V. chuckle, laugh, snicker.

toast N. pledge, congratulations.

together ADV. simultaneously, concurrently, in unison.
Ant. alone, separately, individually.

toil V. labor, work, slave, drudge; —N. labor, grind, struggle.
Ant. play, enjoyment, leisure.

token N. symbol, mark, sign, memorial, keepsake.

tolerable ADJ. bearable, allowable, acceptable.
Ant. unbearable, intolerable, reprehensible.

tolerance N. leniency, charity, forbearance, consideration.
Ant. prohibition, intolerance, restraint.

tolerant ADJ. patient, charitable, soft, lenient, merciful.
Ant. strict, stubborn, inflexible.

tolerate V. stand, permit, endure, suffer, allow, bear.
Ant. obstruct, disallow, forbid.

tone N. tint, color, intonation, accent, inflection.

tonic ADJ. refreshing, stimulating, energizing, invigorating.

tool N. instrument, utensil, implement, apparatus.

top N. summit, peak, pinnacle; —ADJ. maximum, excellent, uppermost, highest.
Ant. base, foot, bottom, nadir.

topple V. overturn, fall, surrender, overthrow.
Ant. raise, build, construct.

torment V. annoy, provoke, torture, harass, bother.
Ant. help, relieve, comfort.

torpor N. lethargy, inaction, sluggishness, apathy, indolence.
Ant. energy, agility, activity.

torrid ADJ. passionate, hot, sweltering, sultry.
Ant. cool, passionless.

tortuous ADJ. winding, indirect, curving.
Ant. straight, unbending, direct.

torture N. anguish, torment, cruelty, persecution.
Ant. relief, comfort, ease.

toss V. throw, fling, pitch, hurl, tumble, writhe.

total N. summation, aggregate, whole, sum, all; —ADJ. complete, absolute, entire.
Ant. part, section, division, portion.

totally ADV. completely, thoroughly, entirely, absolutely.
Ant. partially, incompletely.

tote V. carry, bear.
Ant. put down.

touch V. handle, feel, move, affect, contact; talent, ability.

touching ADJ. effective, moving, affecting, tender, emotional.
Ant. unemotional, unsentimental.

tough ADJ. difficult, hard, rough, severe, strong.
Ant. submissive, mild, obedient.

tour V. visit, travel; —N. voyage, trip, excursion, turn, circle.

tourist N. sightseer, visitor.
Ant. local, inhabitant.

towering ADJ. overwhelming, outstanding, awesome, lofty.
Ant. short, small, diminutive, miniature.

toxic ADJ. lethal, poisonous, deadly, fatal.
Ant. healthy, clean, pure.

toy N. plaything, game.

trace N. remnant, hint, suggestion, mark, sign.
Ant. deletion, obliteration, extinction.

track N. trace, print, trail; —v. follow.
Ant. evade, escape.

tract N. area, lot, region, territory.

tractable ADJ. obedient, loyal, submissive, compliant.
Ant. intractable, stubborn, obstinate, unruly.

trade N. business, dealings, commerce, exchange.

tradition N. lore, convention, heritage.

traffic N. business, commerce, patronage, trade.

tragedy N. misery, disaster, misfortune, accident.
Ant. comedy, recovery, boon, prosperity.

tragic ADJ. sad, heartbreaking, dreadful, appalling.
Ant. comic, happy, humorous, joyous.

trail V. draw, drag, track, follow, pursue.
Ant. evade, escape.

train V. educate, prepare, teach, tutor.

traitor N. conspirator, spy, counteragent, turncoat, defector.
Ant. comrade, compatriot, companion, ally, supporter.

trample V. stomp, tramp, squash, crush.

tranquil ADJ. calm, peaceful, undisturbed, quiet, still.
Ant. disturbing, noisy, agitated.

transcend V. surpass, go beyond.
Ant. stay, regress.

transcendent ADJ. theoretical, ultimate, original, idealistic, visionary.
Ant. plain, transparent, simple.

transfer V. give, seed, change, assign, move, shift.
Ant. keep, hold.

transform V. revolutionize, change, convert, modify, remodel.
Ant. guard, fix.

transgress v. breach, infringe, violate, offend, trespass.
Ant. obey, follow.

transient ADJ. fleeting, changing, short-lived, ephemeral.
Ant. permanent, immutable, changeless.

transition N. passage, change, transformation, development.
Ant. permanence, endurance.

transitory ADJ. temporary, momentary, fleeting, transient.
Ant. everlasting, unending, permanent.

translate v. decipher, interpret, transform, convert.

transmit v. conduct, send, pass, communicate.
Ant. receive.

transparent ADJ. obvious, clear, evident, explicit, translucent, limpid.
Ant. opaque, dark, obscure.

transpire v. ooze, come, happen, come about.
Ant. delay, hinder.

transport v. carry, move, transfer, shift.
Ant. leave, store.

transportation N. transport, transit, carriage, conveyance.

trap N. ambush, snare, pitfall, ruse, lure.

trash N. garbage, waste, refuse, rubble, junk.
Ant. valuables, treasures, goods.

trauma N. shock, wound.
Ant. cure, healing.

travel v. journey, roam, wander, go.
Ant. stay, reside, remain.

traverse v. cross, pass, cover, span.

travesty N. parody, caricature, ridicule, mockery.
Ant. admiration, praise, respect.

treacherous ADJ. dangerous, unreliable, malevolent, evil, vile, base.
Ant. honest, reliable, easy.

treachery N. treason, betrayal, disloyalty, perfidy.
Ant. fidelity, loyalty, allegiance.

tread V. step, walk, track.

treason N. betrayal, treachery, deception, subversion, sedition.
Ant. devotion, support, fidelity.

treasure N. prize, riches, gem, wealth, value.
Ant. trash, trivia.

treasury N. vault, bank, treasurehouse.

treat V. manage, handle, arrange; heal, attend; explain, interpret; host, indulge.
Ant. deny, neglect, mismanage.

treatment N. regimen, therapy, care, attention.
Ant. neglect, denial.

treaty N. agreement, pact, alliance, charter, accord.
Ant. disagreement, disaccord.

tremble V. vibrate, shake, pulsate, shudder, quiver.

• **tremendous** ADJ. enormous, giant, huge, amazing, marvelous. *An enormous cloud approached from the west.*
Ant. trivial, insignificant, small.

tremor N. earthquake, temblor, shudder, quiver, quake.

trespass V. intrude, encroach, invade, offend, breach.
Ant. obey, respect, follow.

trial N. test, examination, ordeal, crucible, hardship, difficulty.

tribute N. testimonial, compliment.
Ant. admonishment, mockery.

trick N. swindle, illusion, deception, fraud, artifice; —v. deceive, delude, cheat.

tricky ADJ. deceiving, delicate, tight, difficult, artful.
Ant. easy, straightforward, apparent.

trim ADJ. compact, tidy, neat, clean, shapely.
Ant. disorderly, unclean, overweight.

trip N. journey, voyage, excursion; —v. stumble, slip, blunder.

trite ADJ. ordinary, dull, unimaginative, stupid, wearisome.
Ant. expedient, original, interesting.

triumph N. achievement, defeat, conquest; —V. win, succeed, prevail, conquer.
Ant. defeat, catastrophe, misfortune.

triumphant ADJ. victorious, exultant, prevailing.
Ant. vanquished, ruined, repulsed.

trivia N. minutiae, froth, triviality, trifles.

• trivial ADJ. unimportant, frivolous, insignificant, petty, small. *We have little time to debate unimportant details.*
Ant. consequential, important, serious.

troop N. company, assembly, party, group, army, soldiers; —V. assemble, throng.

trophy N. prize, award, plaque, token, memento.

trot V. lope, jog.
Ant. sprint, run.

trouble N. distress, hardship, difficulty, inconvenience; —V. distress, disturb, worry, bother.
Ant. calm, assist, soothe.

troublesome ADJ. disturbing, bothersome, annoying, upsetting, vexing.
Ant. easy, soothing, calming.

truce N. ceasefire, peace, pause, armistice.
Ant. battle, war, fight.

trudge V. shuffle, slog, drag, walk.

true ADJ. authentic, real, legitimate, genuine, factual, valid, correct.
Ant. erroneous, wrong, false, inaccurate.

truncate V. shorten, prune, abbreviate, cut.
Ant. extend, amplify, develop.

trust N. faith, belief, confidence, certainty.
Ant. skepticism, doubt, suspicion.

trustworthy ADJ. reliable, faithful, loyal, honest, reputable, dependable, authentic.
Ant. dishonorable, ignominious.

truth N. honesty, sincerity, fact, precision, veracity.
Ant. hypocrisy, deception, lying.

truthful ADJ. honest, frank, candid, veracious.
Ant. evasive, deceptive, exaggerated.

try V. test, use, tackle, experiment, undertake.

tug V. hold, draw, drag, tow, yank.
Ant. push, shove, throw.

tumble V. roll, fall, trip, toss, stumble.

tumult N. disturbance, confusion, disorder, agitation, noise.
Ant. peace, quiet, tranquility.

tune N. melody, harmony, air, song.

turbid ADJ. muddy, dense, thick, dark, opaque.
Ant. pure, limpid, clear.

turbulent ADJ. tempestuous, stormy, tumultuous, rough.
Ant. orderly, quiet, peaceful.

turmoil N. uproar, pandemonium, disorder, unrest, agitation.
Ant. order, tranquility, peace.

turn V. revolve, rotate, spin, sprain, deviate, avert;
—N. bend, twist, shift, movement, circle.

tutor N. teacher, instructor, mentor, coach.
Ant. student, pupil, trainee, mentee, tutee.

twin ADJ. indentical, double, similar, matched.
Ant. dissimilar, unlike.

twinkle V. blink, flash, shine, sparkle.

twist V. distort, warp, bend, turn, wrinkle.
Ant. straighten.

type N. kind, sort, category, variety, genre.

• **typical** ADJ. characteristic, classic, symbolic, usual, common. *A gruff manner is characteristic of the manager.*
Ant. peculiar, abnormal, deviant.

tyrannize V. oppress, dictate, boss.
Ant. liberate, free.

tyranny N. fascism, oppression, despotism, autocracy, dictatorship.
Ant. democracy, freedom.

U

ugly ADJ. plain, unattractive, homely, rough; hideous.
   Ant. appealing, beautiful, splendid.

ulterior ADJ. concealed, shrouded, obscured, covert, enigmatic, hidden.
   Ant. obvious, clear, open.

ultimate ADJ. absolute, final, extreme, maximum, supreme.
   Ant. preliminary, first, beginning.

unaccountable ADJ. mysterious, inexplicable, unexplained.
   Ant. explainable, normal, observed.

unadorned ADJ. rustic, plain, bare.
   Ant. opulent, baroque, gorgeous.

unadulterated ADJ. pure, original, natural.
   Ant. impure, unnatural, corrupted.

unanimity N. consensus, accord, agreement.
   Ant. dissonance, disagreement, variance.

unanimous ADJ. concurrent, in agreement, unified, solid.
   Ant. discordant, divided.

unapproachable ADJ. intolerant, impossible, aloof.
   Ant. forward, tolerant, exposed.

unavoidable V. inescapable, inevitable, obvious.
   Ant. avoidable, preventable, needless.

unaware ADJ. uninformed, ignorant, blind.
   Ant. knowledgeable, informed.

unbearable ADJ. painful, distressing, agonizing.
   Ant. bearable, tolerable, easy.

unbecoming ADJ. improper, indecent, unfit, inappropriate.
   Ant. suitable, appropriate, decent, proper.

unbelievable ADJ. implausible, fabulous, amazing, incredible.
   Ant. plausible, credible, believable.

unbending ADJ. rigid, firm, stubborn, determined, obstinate.
Ant. flexible, lenient.

unblemished ADJ. good, clean, innocent, clear.
Ant. stained, marred, dirty.

uncertain ADJ. doubtful, debatable, ambiguous, indefinite, irresolute.
Ant. sure, certain, clear, definite.

uncivilized ADJ. crude, barbarous, savage, wild, primitive, rude.
Ant. refined, cultured, courteous.

unclear ADJ. indefinite, faint, vague, ambiguous, obscure.
Ant. obvious, straightforward, simple.

uncomfortable ADJ. uneasy, awkward, harsh, distressing, comfortless.
Ant. comfortable, easy, relaxed.

unconditional ADJ. implicit, absolute, complete.
Ant. limited, conditional.

● **unconscious** ADJ. senseless, ignorant, cold. *After he fell, he lay senseless on the ground for more than an hour.*
Ant. awake, alert, conscious.

uncover V. reveal, expose, unearth, betray.
Ant. hide, conceal, cover.

undecided ADJ. indefinite, doubtful, ambiguous, unclear.
Ant. sure, definite, decided.

● **undeniable** ADJ. certain, sure, actual, *The facts in the case are certain.*
Ant. refutable, questionable, disputable.

undependable ADJ. trustless, unreliable.
Ant. reliable, dependable, trustworthy.

underground ADJ. subterranean, underneath; —N. resistance.
Ant. open, above ground.

underhand ADJ. sneaky, devious, guileful, indirect.
Ant. artless, straightforward, honest.

underprivileged ADJ. poor, denied, depressed, suppressed.
Ant. rich, wealthy, plentiful

underscore V. highlight, accentuate, emphasize, call attention to.
Ant. ignore, disregard, overlook, pass over.

● **understand** V. grasp, realize, conceive, know, comprehend. *The student found it difficult to grasp the unusual concept.*
Ant. misinterpret, mistake, misunderstand, confuse.

understanding N. sympathy, empathy, knowledge, comprehension.
Ant. incapacity, stupidity, confusion.

undertake V. try, attempt, assume, begin, start.
Ant. release, quit, terminate.

● **undesirable** ADJ. unwelcome, objectionable, unwanted. *Horseflies and other pests were unwelcome guests at the campsite.*
Ant. welcome, wanted, desirable.

undo V. loosen, disengage, unbind, cancel.
Ant. tie, tighten, bind.

undulate V. wave, rock, slither.

uneasy ADJ. nervous, anxious, edgy, restless.
Ant. calm, relaxed, steady.

unemotional ADJ. impassive, composed, dispassionate.
Ant. emotional, passionate, expressive.

unequivocal ADJ. sharp, definite, sure, utter.
Ant. unclear indefinite, ambiguous.

unethical ADJ. wrong, corrupt, unscrupulous.
Ant. right, honest, ethical, scrupulous.

uneven ADJ. rough, unsteady, irregular, inconsistent.
Ant. consistent, regular, level.

unexplainable ADJ. mysterious, inexplicable.
Ant. obvious, explainable, clear.

unfair ADJ. unjust, wrong, unethical, biased, prejudiced, partial.
Ant. just, honest, impartial.

unfaithful ADJ. disloyal, treacherous, traitorous, undependable.
Ant. faithful, loyal, trustworthy.

• **unfavorable** ADJ. disadvantageous, adverse, unsatisfactory, bad, negative. *The candidate excluded disadvantageous information from his résumé.*
Ant. satisfactory, positive, advantageous.

unfit ADJ. inappropriate, unsuitable, improper, unqualified, unhealthy.
Ant. suitable, competent, skilled.

unforgivable ADJ. inexcusable, outrageous, extreme.
Ant. excusable, forgivable.

unfortunate ADJ. calamitous, unlucky, disastrous, untimely, ill-fated.
Ant. opportune, advantageous, prosperous.

unhappy ADJ. sad, melancholy, miserable, depressed.
Ant. gay, joyous, gleeful.

unify V. integrate, unite, organize, consolidate, connect.
Ant. separate, split, segregate.

uninspired ADJ. dull, laconic, apathetic, lethargic, lazy.
Ant. energetic, inspired, enthusiastic.

unintelligible ADJ. unclear, meaningless, garbled, jumbled.
Ant. intelligible, clear, meaningful, lucid, cogent.

unintentional ADJ. unintended, inadvertent, unthinking, unplanned.
Ant. intended, planned, intentional.

uninterested ADJ. detached, cold, distant, apathetic.
Ant. interested, involved, attached.

union N. association, confederation, league.
Ant. divergence, opposition, difference.

unique ADJ. unparalleled, matchless, only, original, single.
Ant. customary, normal, ordinary.

unite V. consolidate, combine, unify.
Ant. separate, segregate, split.

universal ADJ. total, comprehensive, cosmic, worldwide, global, general, broad.
Ant. individual, singular, restricted, narrow.

universe N. cosmos, world, earth, heavens, galaxy.

unjust ADJ. unfair, unreasonable, undeserved.
Ant. just, deserved, fair, reasonable.

unkempt ADJ. messy, disheveled, rumpled.
Ant. tidy, neat, well kept, cared for.

unlawful ADJ. illegal, criminal, illicit, wrongful, lawless.
Ant. legal, permissible, right.

unlearned ADJ. ignorant, unscholarly, simple.
Ant. educated, learned, schooled.

● unlimited ADJ. unrestricted, endless, limitless, boundless. *The bank offered unrestricted access to one's account.*
Ant. confined, restricted, constricted, bounded, limited.

unload V. discharge, dump, remove.
Ant. charge, load, fill.

unlucky ADJ. fateful, unfortunate, ill-fated, disappointing.
Ant. fortunate, lucky, blessed.

unmistakable ADJ. noticeable, observable.
Ant. mistakable, unclear.

unnatural ADJ. abnormal, bizarre, taboo, preternatural.
Ant. common, normal, natural.

● unnecessary ADJ. needless, uncalled for, superfluous, pointless. *Some provisions of the contract were needless.*
Ant. needed, necessary, called for.

unobtrusive ADJ. quiet, inconspicuous, subdued.
Ant. conspicuous, forward, blatant.

unorganized ADJ. disorderly, chaotic, messy.
Ant. organized, orderly, planned, systematic.

unpleasant ADJ. disagreeable, offensive, repulsive, bad.
Ant. pleasant, nice, agreeable.

unpretentious ADJ. informal, modest, humble.
Ant. brazen, proud, ostentatious, bold.

unprincipled ADJ. unscrupulous, corrupt, immoral, lawless.
Ant. conscientious, principled, careful, just.

unprotected ADJ. insecure, helpless, open.
Ant. guarded, protected, secure.

● **unreasonable** ADJ. outrageous, irrational, illogical.
The visitor's outrageous conduct led to his expulsion from the meeting.
Ant. rational, logical, reasonable.

unreserved ADJ. open, free, unoccupied, implicit, plain.
Ant. conditional, occupied, closed.

unruly ADJ. disobedient, ungovernable, defiant, disorderly.
Ant. obedient, docile, manageable.

unsafe ADJ. dangerous, hazardous, risky.
Ant. safe, secure, protected.

unsatisfactory ADJ. unfavorable, poor, bad.
Ant. good, favorable, sufficient.

unsettled ADJ. indefinite, restless, disturbed, anxious.
Ant. certain, stable, calm.

unsound ADJ. insane, mad, false, erroneous.
Ant. solid, true, sane.

unsure ADJ. indefinite, ambiguous, insecure.
Ant. positive, definite, sure, certain.

unsympathetic ADJ. removed, cold, untouched, uncaring.
Ant. passionate, caring, sympathetic.

unusual ADJ. abnormal, extraordinary, infrequent, atypical, eccentric, novel.
Ant. ordinary, prevalent, commonplace.

unwelcome ADJ. unwanted, undesirable, objectionable, uninvited.
Ant. invited, desirable, welcome.

unwholesome ADJ. dangerous, unhealthy, demoralizing, offensive, corrupting.
Ant. healthy, wholesome, natural.

unyielding ADJ. rigid, stubborn, severe, inflexible.
Ant. flexible, tolerant, yielding.

upgrade V. promote, improve, better.
Ant. decrease, demote, lessen.

uplift V. elevate, inspire, exalt, elate.
Ant. depress, lower, berate.

uproar N. disturbance, commotion, noise, disorder.
Ant. calm, quiet, peace, tranquility.

upset V. topple, overturn, disorder, agitate, disrupt;
disturb, bother, pain; —N. agitation, disruption,
disordering.
Ant. calm, placate, pacify.

urge V. push, press, insist, implore, persuade,
recommend.
Ant. allow, permit.

use V. implement, utilize, employ, apply; consume,
expend, abuse.

• **usually** ADV. typically, consistently, generally,
normally, regularly, frequently, commonly. *Bulbs are
typically planted in the early fall.*
Ant. seldom, infrequently, rarely.

usurp V. seize, appropriate, assume, take, claim.
Ant. relinquish, abdicate.

utter ADJ. complete, extreme, absolute, entire, sheer;
—V. speak, announce, declare, assert, talk.
Ant. partial, diminutive, small.

V

vacant ADJ. empty, unoccupied, uninhabited, vapid, thoughtless.
Ant. occupied, full, complete.

vacation N. break, holiday, respite, rest.
Ant. job, labor, occupation.

vacillate V. change, sway, hesitate, alter, fluctuate.
Ant. act, advance.

• **vague** ADJ. indefinite, unclear, ambiguous, uncertain, obscure. *I could make out only the indefinite outline of the large building in the distance.*
Ant. positive, clear, evident.

vain ADJ. trivial, frivolous, narcissistic, proud, conceited, egotistic, futile, empty.
Ant. advantageous, adequate, unassuming.

valid ADJ. authentic, real, sound, genuine.
Ant. erroneous, fallacious, insufficient.

valor N. heroism, courage, bravery.
Ant. cowardice, fright, fear.

• **valuable** ADJ. expensive, costly, treasured, prized, priceless. *Expensive jewelry should be kept in the hotel safe.*
Ant. worthless, undesirable, useless.

value N. price, worth, importance, usefulness, utility; —v. appraise, treasure, revere.
Ant. worthlessness, uselessness; discard, relinquish.

vanish V. disappear, fade, evaporate, dissolve.
Ant. appear, emerge.

variation N. fluctuation, deviation, change, variance, diversity.

• **variety** N. mixture, difference, diversity, assortment, heterogeneity. *The pet's ancestry included a mixture of breeds.*
Ant. homogeneity, commonality, similarity.

various ADJ. diverse, mixed, assorted, miscellaneous, varied.
Ant. singular.

vary V. alter, change, differ.
Ant. steady, fix.

vast ADJ. huge, enormous, infinite, beyond measurement.
Ant. small, limited, diminutive, minute, minuscule.

vein N. streak, mood, style.

vend V. sell, peddle, market.
Ant. purchase, buy.

vent N. hole, opening; —v. emit, air, discharge, release, expel.
Ant. guard, hold.

venture N. peril, risk, hazard, attempt, experiment.
Ant. certainty.

veracity N. truthfulness, truth, reality, sincerity, fidelity, honesty.
Ant. lying, dishonesty, untruthfulness, deception.

verbal ADJ. oral, spoken, literal, lingual, vocal.

verbatim ADJ. literal, word-for-word.
Ant. varied, summarized.

verbose ADJ. wordy, garrulous, long-winded.
Ant. succinct, brief, curt, to the point, terse.

verge N. point, brink, edge, border, margin.
Ant. center, whole, inside.

verify V. affirm, corroborate, prove, confirm.
Ant. disprove, revoke.

versatile ADJ. multifaceted, adaptable, skillful, flexible, ready.
Ant. unchanging, unadaptable.

very ADV. greatly, extremely, exceedingly, thoroughly, highly.

veteran N. old-timer, campaigner; —ADJ. practical, experienced.
Ant. apprentice, newcomer, beginner.

veto V. refuse, deny, negate, reject, prohibit.
Ant. approve, pass.

vicious ADJ. fierce, evil, cruel, malevolent.
Ant. decent, righteous, admirable.

victim N. scapegoat, puppet, prey, sacrifice.
Ant. criminal, culprit.

victor N. winner, champion, conqueror.
Ant. loser, vanquished.

victory N. conquest, success, win, triumph.
Ant. defeat, failure, downfall, rout.

view N. perspective, outlook, belief, sight, scene.

vigil N. wake, lookout, watch, observance.

vigilant ADJ. alert, attentive, watchful, observant.
Ant. indiscreet, careless, negligent.

vigor N. vitality, energy, drive, spirit, strength.
Ant. weakness, lethargy, inactivity.

vile ADJ. evil, despicable, wicked, immoral.
Ant. good, upright, virtuous, praiseworthy.

vindicate V. avenge, defend, clear, assert.
Ant. accuse, charge, blame.

vindictive ADJ. vengeful, spiteful, malicious, relentless.
Ant. placable, excusing, forgiving.

vintage N. classic, year; —ADJ. classical.
Ant. new, modern, current.

violent ADJ. intense, forceable, strong, savage, rough.
Ant. mild, gentle, tame.

virtue N. merit, distinction, excellence, good, chastity.
Ant. evil, vice, depravity.

virulent ADJ. malignant, deadly, poisonous, baneful,
resentful.
Ant. weak, conquerable.

visible ADJ. perceptible, apparent, visual.
Ant. imperceptible, invisible.

vision N. dream, foresight, prophecy, sight, seeing.
Ant. substantiality, fact, reality.

visit V. attend, call on, see, drop in.

vital ADJ. critical, essential, necessary, important,
alive, existing.
Ant. unnecessary, trivial, dispensable.

vivacious ADJ. exuberant, animated, spirited, lively.
Ant. dull, inactive, lethargic.

vocabulary N. language, lexicon, dictionary.

vocal ADJ. oral, spoken, uttered, articulate, voiced.
Ant. quiet, silent, inarticulate.

vociferous ADJ. loud, clamorous, vehement, blatant, unruly.
Ant. peaceful, calm, silent.

voice N. intonation, speech, expression; —v. declare, express, utter, speak.

void ADJ. unoccupied, hollow, empty, destitute.
Ant. full, complete, occupied, useful.

voluntary ADJ. deliberate, intentional, spontaneous.
Ant. obligatory, compelled, forced.

vow V. swear, promise, declare, give one's word.

vulgar ADJ. lowly, rude, coarse, ignorant, uncouth.
Ant. elegant, refined, cultured.

W

wage V. pursue, conduct, engage in, carry out.
Ant. cease, desist, call off.

wager N., V. bet, gamble, stake, risk.

wail V. scream, howl, bawl, cry.
Ant. whisper, murmur.

wait V. linger, remain, pause, delay, serve, attend.
Ant. depart, proceed, leave.

waive V. defer, abdicate, relinquish.
Ant. accuse, prosecute, implicate.

wake V. arouse, stir, waken; —N. vigil.

wakeful ADJ. awake, alert, sleepless, unsleeping.
Ant. sleepy, tired.

walk V. stroll, promenade, amble, hike, step.
Ant. sprint, run, stop, stand.

wall N. partition, barrier, bar.

wander V. roam, stroll, drift, stray, meander.
Ant. pause, stop, stay.

wane V. diminish, fade, decrease, get smaller.
Ant. wax, grow, develop, increase, get larger.

want V. desire, need, lack; —N. insufficiency, desire,
necessity, need.
Ant. have; abundance, enough.

wanton ADJ. gratuitous, unnecessary, easy, immoral.
Ant. righteous, moral, ethical.

warfare N. combat, battle, conflict, fighting, struggle.
Ant. peace, armistice, truce.

warm ADJ. sympathetic, compassionate,
approachable, kind, tepid, feverish.
Ant. cool, unsympathetic, insensitive, unfriendly.

warmth N. heat, warmness.
Ant. cold, chill, frozen.

warn V. admonish, caution, alert, appraise.
Ant. surprise, ambush.

warp V. bend, twist, distort.
Ant. straighten, clarify.

warrant V. guarantee, pledge; —N. assurance, license.

wary ADJ. careful, cautious, prudent, alert.
Ant. reckless, careless, impulsive.

wash V. clean, scrub, drift, bathe.
Ant. dirty, sully.

waste N. trash, garbage, loss, consumption; —v.
consume, squander, abuse, exhaust, devastate.
Ant. save, guard, preserve, conserve.

wasteful ADJ. extravagant, lavish, careless, reckless,
destructive, prodigal.
Ant. careful, saving, conserving.

watch V. observe, look, scrutinize.
Ant. ignore, neglect.

watchful ADJ. prudent, careful, wary, alert, cautious.
Ant. oblivious, careless, negligent.

water V. irrigate, wet, soak, wash.
Ant. dehydrate, dry.

watery ADJ. diluted, pale, insipid.
Ant. rich, thick, undiluted.

way N. system, method, fashion, mode, behavior;
avenue, path, street, road.

● **weak** ADJ. feeble, helpless, exhausted, languid, faint.
The flu left the patient exhausted and feeble.
Ant. vigorous, strong, powerful, forceful.

weaken V. exhaust, reduce, impair, debilitate,
diminish, dilute.
Ant. invigorate, revitalize, strengthen.

weakness N. infirmity, fault, failing, shortcoming.
Ant. strength, power, potency.

wealth N. riches, money, opulence, means, prosperity.
Ant. poverty, dearth, need, want.

wear V. carry, use, dress in, attire, bear, diminish,
erode, waste.
Ant. discard, take off.

wearisome ADJ. tiresome, boring, trying, irritating.
Ant. interesting, fascinating, involving, motivating,
inspiriting.

weary ADJ. tired, exhausted, discouraged, bored.
Ant. refreshed, animated, encouraged, interested.

weave V. braid, twist, crochet, intertwine, knit.

web N. net, network, mesh.

wed V. marry, espouse.
Ant. separate, divorce.

weep V. cry, lament, sob.
Ant. grin, smile.

weigh V. ponder, consider, steady.

weight N. mass, heaviness, authority, significance, importance.
Ant. lightness.

weighty ADJ. burdensome, heavy, significant, important.
Ant. light, insignificant, unimportant.

● weird ADJ. strange, odd, bizarre, eerie, peculiar, *They observed a strange array of moving lights in the midnight sky.*
Ant. normal, common, usual.

welcome N. reception, greeting, salutation.

welfare N. good, prosperity, fortune, advantage.
Ant. disadvantage, misfortune, bad luck.

well ADV. satisfactorily, completely, favorably, considerably; healthy, certainly, surely.
Ant. ill, sick, incompletely, poorly.

well-off ADJ. wealthy, rich, prosperous.
Ant. poor, impoverished, deprived, unfortunate.

wet ADJ. drenched, soaked, damp, moist, saturated.
Ant. parched, dry, arid.

wheel N. disk, circle, roller, revolution.

whim N. impulse, caprice, notion, craze.
Ant. plan, program, strategy.

whimsical ADJ. capricious, fanciful, wondrous, arbitrary.
Ant. sober, serious, deliberate.

whine V. cry, whimper, complain.

whip V. beat, lash, defeat.

whirl V. spin, rush, swirl.

whisper V. murmur, confide, mutter.
Ant. shout, cry, exclaim, yell.

whole ADJ. entire, complete, total, undivided, absolute.
Ant. partial, fractional, divided.

wholesome ADJ. nourishing, healthy, clean, good.
Ant. unnatural, unhealthy, bad.

wholly ADV. completely, purely, entirely, totally.
Ant. insufficiently, partially.

wicked ADJ. evil, vicious, wrong, vile, malevolent.
Ant. good, noble, decent.

wide ADJ. broad, full, extensive.
Ant. thin, narrow.

widen V. extend, broaden, stretch.
Ant. shrink, contract.

width N. wideness, breadth, broadness.

wiggle V. twist, squirm, worm, writhe.

wild ADJ., ADV. natural, untamed, native, savage, rough, frantic, unruly.
Ant. tame, calm, domesticated.

wile N. trick, dodge, subterfuge, deception.

will N. desire, wish, determination, decision, resolve.

willful ADJ. deliberate, strong, stubborn, obstinate.
Ant. weak, flexible, reasonable.

wilt V. slouch, droop, sag.
Ant. grow, rise, lift.

win V. earn, succeed, obtain, attain, capture, gain.
Ant. lose.

wind N. gust, draft, breeze, air; —V. curl, weave, twist, coil.
Ant. stagnation.

winding ADJ. meandering, twisting, curving.
Ant. direct, straight, unbending.

window N. portal, casement, pane, glass.

windy ADJ. breezy, blustering, stormy.
Ant. temperate, calm.

winner N. conqueror, victor, champion.
Ant. loser.

wipe out V. cancel, annihilate, eliminate.
Ant. reinstate, continue, replace.

wisdom N. insight, intelligence, acumen, commonsense, sagacity, good sense.
Ant. stupidity, imprudence, irrationality.

wise ADJ. shrewd, insightful, rational, enlightened, sensible, profound, sage.
Ant. ignorant, foolish, stupid.

wish V. desire, choose, crave, want.

wit N. humor, intelligence, understanding, wisdom.
Ant. flatness, sobriety, dullness.

witch N. magician, sorceress, warlock, enchanter.

withdraw V. retract, detach, recall, remove.
Ant. introduce, return, insert.

wither V. dry up, shrivel, fade, languish.
Ant. grow.

withhold V. repress, hold back, refuse, refrain.
Ant. concede, give, yield.

witness N. attester, observer, spectator; —V. observe, perceive, notice, see.
Ant. ignore, overlook.

witty ADJ. clever, humorous, funny.
Ant. dry, dull, flat, unamusing.

wobbly ADJ. insecure, hesitant, unstable.
Ant. stable, secure.

woe N. distress, grief, sorrow.
Ant. joy, gladness, mirth.

womanly ADJ. feminine, effeminate.
Ant. masculine, manly.

wonder N. awe, admiration, marvel, amazement, dread.
Ant. answer, calmness, anticipation.

word N. remark, comment, vocable, statement, assurance, term, guarantee, expression.

wording N. phrase, wordage, diction.

wordy ADJ. long-winded, verbose, talkative, garrulous.
Ant. brief, succinct, concise.

work N. labor, effort, employment, job; —V. perform, operate, run.
Ant. play, relax, enjoy.

worldly ADJ. materialistic, earthly, profane, secular.
Ant. spiritual, immaterial, holy.

worn ADJ. tired, exhausted, weary, used, threadbare.
Ant. unused, new.

worry V. annoy, irritate, disturb, fret, trouble; —N. anxiety, doubt, concern.
Ant. soothe, placate, calm.

worship V. adulate, venerate, respect, give devotion to.

worth N. value, merit, estimation, importance, price.

• **worthless** ADJ. inferior, useless, valueless, insignificant, unimportant. *The inspector rejected the inferior products.*
Ant. useful, beneficial, valuable.

worthy ADJ. reliable, dependable, good, honorable, valuable.
Ant. vicious, reprehensible, corrupt.

wrap V. clothe, envelop, shroud, veil, package.
Ant. open, unwrap.

wrath N. fury, anger, rage.
Ant. praise, congratulations.

wreck V. destroy, damage, ruin, trash.
Ant. save, preserve, rebuild, repair.

wrench V. jerk, twist, ring, distort, turn.

wrinkle N., V., fold, crease, crumple, crimp.
Ant. smooth, iron, straighten.

write V. compose, record, inscribe, draft.
Ant. erase.

writhe V. squirm, wiggle, agonize, toss, twist.

wrong ADJ. false, erroneous, evil; —N. sin, cruelty, malevolence.
Ant. correct, just, good, right.

wrongdoing N. crime, misbehavior, injury, sin.
Ant. virtue, righteousness, charity.

wrongful ADJ. criminal, unlawful, evil, spiteful, illegal.
Ant. legal, lawful, moral, ethical.

X Y Z

x out V. cancel, omit, cross out, erase.
Ant. fill in, add.

yank V. jerk, pull, tug.

yarn N. fable, tale, story, anecdote, legend.
Ant. truth, history.

yawn V. nap, doze, snooze.

yearn V. wish for, desire, crave.
Ant. avoid, reject, shun.

yell V. shout, cry, roar, scream, howl.
Ant. whisper, murmur.

yes ADV. agreed, absolutely, certainly, gladly, willingly.
Ant. no, never.

yet ADV. still, however, furthermore, although; —
CONJ. but, nevertheless.

yield V. defer, relinquish, succumb, return, surrender.
Ant. forbid, deny, refuse.

• **young** ADJ. juvenile, immature, infantile, new. *The
theater offered special prices for juvenile customers.*
Ant. old, ancient, senior.

youth N. immaturity, adolescence, springtime.
Ant. aged, elderly, decrepit, senior citizen, elder.

zany ADJ. foolish, amusing, wacky, comical, madcap.
Ant. calm, stolid, sober.

zeal N. enthusiasm, fervor, passion, eagerness.
Ant. reluctance, indifference, apathy.

zealot N. supporter, enthusiast, fanatic, devotee.

zenith N. peak, summit, acme, apex, high point.
Ant. nadir, depth, low point.

zephyr N. breeze, wind, air, draft.

zero N. nothing, naught, nobody, void, nil, nonentity.
Ant. something, anything, substantiality.

zest N. desire, pleasure, relish, enjoyment,
exhilaration, enthusiasm, gusto, vigor.
Ant. disgust, apathy, distaste.